Kevin Peter Pietersen, MBE, was born in Pietermaritzburg, Natal, South Africa in June 1980. He made his debut for Natal in 1997 before moving to England in 2000 to further his opportunities to play at international level. KP made his debut for the English national team in 2005, and has scored over 13,000 international runs across all forms of the game.

@KP24

KP

THE AUTOBIOGRAPHY

Kevin Pietersen

SPHERE

First published in Great Britain in 2014 by Sphere
This paperback edition published in 2015 by Sphere

1 3 5 7 9 10 8 6 4 2

A CIP catalogue record for this book
is available from the British Library.

ISBN 978-0-7515-5757-2

Typeset in Bembo by M Rules
Printed and bound in Great Britain by
Clays Ltd, St Ives plc

Papers used by Sphere are from well-managed forests
and other responsible sources.

MIX
Paper from
responsible sources
FSC
www.fsc.org   FSC® C104740

Sphere
An imprint of
Little, Brown Book Group
Carmelite House
50 Victoria Embankment
London EC4Y 0DZ

An Hachette UK Company
www.hachette.co.uk

www.littlebrown.co.uk

For Jess, and the family and friends
who've supported me throughout
my incredible journey

Contents

1

Fred

There's an old joke about a mother watching a column of soldiers pass by. Her son is in the ranks. All those men out of step, she says, except our Fred.

I don't know if my mum ever thinks something similar, but I do know that if I was in the trenches I'd want Fred at my side.

I don't march in step. I don't ask people to trample all over me just because it might make them feel better. That's not who I am.

Those qualities (or flaws, if that's your view) have brought me many good things in life. And lots of trouble.

Fred doesn't try to march out of step. He just follows a different drummer. I don't set out to go against the flow. I don't enjoy trouble. Like most people, I want to be happy. If I don't understand you, though, and I don't see the logic of what you tell me to do, then I am going to ask you questions.

I won't sit down and be told to bat this way or train that way without asking why. I have one career. One shot. I have to make the most of whatever talent I have. If I do that, it's good for your team. Our team. If all the guys around me do that, it's great for your team. Our team.

But if all you want is to see your team marching in step, if you are just trying to impress the generals above you, I will call you on that.

A Monday in February 2014, and I am walking into the Danubius Hotel right by Lord's, to meet with the three wise men. Alastair Cook will be there. James Whitaker, the chairman of selectors, will be there. And Paul Downton will be there. He is the brand-new managing director of the England and Wales Cricket Board (ECB). He's hardly been a wet day in the job.

The three wise men have decided that the disastrous Ashes tour was all my fault. Take me out of the picture and all will be good again.

I know what's coming.

I only met Paul Downton properly a few days ago.

I had previously discussed the tour with Angus Porter, chief executive of the Professional Cricketers' Association, and we had decided that Downton would be the next stop. I had to Google him to discover his background: international, but not world class. I hoped that as an administrator he would be better.

I called Downton up and said that I thought we should meet. There would have to be debriefings after all that had happened in Australia, and as a senior player I felt the need to be in that loop.

He said okay, so I arranged to see him in the ECB offices. On the morning of the meeting he texted me to say that James Whitaker would be sitting in. I had a little history with Whitaker but I said, okay, no worries.

But I did have worries about Whitaker.

In August 2013, during the Old Trafford Test against the Australians, my family and Jonathan Trott's parents were sitting together at a table in the players' family enclosure. There was one other person at the table. An older man.

Leading up to that Test I had torn my calf, but the rehab had gone well and the day before I'd pronounced myself fit. It had been between me and James Taylor. I was fully recovered, though. I was fine. I got picked and scored a hundred. All good.

Mum, Dad and the Trotts were sitting there, chatting away with their strong South African accents, and this older man was just hammering me. My century – which had saved the match – hadn't gone down well.

They all just nodded. They sat and they listened. Exchanged glances. Let's not get defensive, don't make a scene. But the man didn't stop after one or two stabs in my back; he didn't seem to notice how uncomfortable his audience were.

After a while they asked the man what brought him to Old Trafford.

James Whitaker had given him the tickets.

Aha. So it was reasonable to suggest that Whitaker might agree with what he was spouting. My parents told me all this the next day. We wondered about the arrogance – or stupidity – of somebody sitting in the players' family enclosure with four middle-aged people with strong South African accents and feeling free to run down a player who was most likely the son of one or other of the couples.

A few days later, James Whitaker was behind my net while I was training. I asked for a quick word, and told him that my parents had had an awkward and embarrassing experience with somebody he had given tickets to. I said that I would really appreciate it if he could apologise to them, or if the man he gave the ticket to would apologise.

Whitaker mumbled something about the man, how he'd done this and that.

Very interesting, I said, because a lot of the views he was expressing at the table sounded like they might have come from you. Was it really right for him to come out with that sort of thing when he was sitting at a table with the parents of two players?

Things have been frosty between us ever since. And now James Whitaker would be sitting in on my meeting with Paul Downton.

I went anyway. Turned up on time. Downton asked me to tell him about the tour to Australia. We had brought the Ashes with us, having won them in the summer of 2013, and we left them behind. Whitewashed. Five–nil. I gave Downton my views on how that happened.

How honest was I? Really honest. Brutally honest. I didn't

want to tell him a story that might help or protect me. I wanted to tell him the truth. I knew there were stories being told against me, so I had said to myself when I asked for the meeting that I would tell the guy everything. Whatever happened afterwards, I would be able to look him in the eye.

I wanted to speak to Downton about my relationship with Andy Flower, the team director, which had been a huge issue. It had been played out in the media and refreshed day after day with a steady stream of leaks.

With that in mind, I said to Downton, let's make sure that the discussion we are having here doesn't leave these four walls.

He seemed offended by the very thought. How dare I even suggest such a thing?

Aw, none of that, I said. I've been in meetings and the next day I'll read a version in the media.

Then we talked about the tour.

Look, I said, I didn't bat as well as I could. I did okay.

I had averaged 29 in the Test series. I'd got past fifty just twice in ten innings. I'd carried a knee injury and lived through various problems off the field, but I was disappointed with the numbers. Still, I was the team's leading run-scorer on 294.

Downton said he had seen the way I had played – I hadn't batted well. Careless.

Really? I looked at him, my mouth hanging open. I didn't mind that Paul Downton, according to Google, was a lower-middle-order batsman with a Test average of under 20. But I did mind that as an administrative employee of the ECB he felt free to critique the performances of players, indeed that he had a right to do so.

Sorry? Are you my batting coach?

I have scored over thirteen thousand runs for England, I said. Do you think I am proud of the way I got out sometimes? No, of course not. But I must have been doing something right to score all those runs. Did you see me bat in Melbourne?

No, he was flying. He was 'in the air'.

Interesting.

No, he went on, but he saw the way I got out. Reckless.

I just said, wow.

Two thoughts entered my head. One, Downton was possibly trying to wind me up so that we would have a bad meeting in front of Whitaker and he could use that later. So I stayed polite, careful in what I said. Second possibility: I am interviewing for my own job here. I have played 104 Tests and now I am interviewing for my job.

Next question from Downton: where do you see yourself in the future?

I would love to get ten thousand Test runs, and I still think I can offer that. I want to pursue that dream.

Hmm, he said, I would have preferred you to have said, I would like to help England win matches.

If I score ten thousand runs the way I am batting, England will win matches.

Well, he said, I still would have preferred you to have said the other thing.

I left, and phoned my wife.

'All these years, Jess, and I think I've just interviewed for my own job.'

*

So for this second meeting I am to go to the Danubius Hotel, just across the road from the ECB.

I am glad that we are doing this in a hotel. As I walked past all the desks in the ECB offices for my first meeting with Downton a few days ago, I felt like the school troublemaker on his way to the headmaster's office.

The media was already full of speculation. Who would go, Flower or Pietersen? Just one person tweeting 'Pietersen at ECB #SkySports' would start the media cavalry charge.

They have taken a suite here in the Danubius, where they are waiting for me. The Grace Suite.

I'm not sure how it will go. When I left Sydney my relationship with all but one of the players (Matt Prior – you'll find out why) was absolutely fine, and I'd chatted with many of them since then. They had spoken very favourably about me in the media. I knew that I didn't want to burn any bridges between myself and future England teams. Why would I? But while I was getting on fine with individuals, there were problems in the dressing room that needed to be addressed. I'd not mentioned these in my first meeting with Downton, but I wasn't going to be the first to air them.

There were major issues. Prior, for instance, was a massive negative influence on the dressing room, and when I said that to Andy the night before the Sydney Test, the head coach didn't disagree.

Downton has told me that, as well as having Whitaker present at the meeting, he has also asked Alastair Cook to join us. I'm not optimistic about how it's all going to go down.

Alastair Cook knows that on the Ashes tour there were

absolutely no problems with me in the dressing room. Alastair Cook knows that I scored the most runs for England on that tour. Alastair Cook knows that I had his back 100 per cent. Any advice I could give, I did. I opened the door and said to him, listen, I am here to help you. I want you to be successful. I told him that again and again. If he needed me at any time, I would be there.

I know, though, that while Cooky is a nice man, he is also a company man. A safe pair of hands; he won't rock the boat.

A woman meets me in reception and takes me up to the Grace Suite.

Cook shakes my hand, but he doesn't want to look at me. He looks at the floor. I feel sorry for him; it must be one of the most uncomfortable experiences of his career.

Whitaker shakes my hand. Downton shakes my hand.

I say, what's up?

Well, says Downton, we have come to the decision that we are at a bit of a crossroads. We believe you are not going to be part of the process going forward so we would just like to tell you that now.

Right. So you are sacking me?

Oh no. The squad that was selected for the World T20 won't have you in it.

That means I'm done?

No. We haven't convened for the summer but you are not part of our plans going forward now.

Silence. Whitaker nodding, Cook still looking at something really fascinating on his shoe.

So that's it. Basically, I am being sacked: you guys have finished

8

with me. I'm putting two and two together and I'm getting four every time.

No, no, no, no.

I just sat there.

Then Downton spoke: You can go speak to your people and then we can discuss things.

Okay. Is that it?

Yes. Thank you very much.

My agent, Adam Wheatley, had arranged for a driver to take us to the hotel. I'd told them that I'd be gone for an hour or so, and Adam and the driver were still in the lobby, wondering how to kill the time, when I came back down.

Adam, I said, I am gone, buddy.

Those words exactly.

What? he said. So quick?

Yeah? How long was I in there? Five minutes?

From getting out of the car to getting back into it now, five minutes at most.

I had hoped to go home, but instead we told the driver to go across town to my lawyer's.

I said to Bob Mitchell, my lawyer, when he greeted us, okay this is what has happened. We need to get moving sharpish.

We began making arrangements for severance. It was over. That was all that I could think. Over.

Paul Downton has since repeated his criticisms of my performance in the Sydney Test. He's been forced to admit that there was no smoking gun. The only charge seems to be that Paul Downton, watching his very first Test in his brand-new job, opted to study me exclusively and concluded that I looked 'disengaged'.

Downton said he 'watched every ball of the Sydney Test live and I've never seen anyone as disinterested or distracted as Kevin'. I would love to know how any cricketer facing Aussie bowlers on their home turf could look 'disinterested'. Or does it have nothing to do with my batting? Is Downton claiming that he was watching me when I was in the outfield? Why would he do that, if not in order to gather evidence to strengthen a case that somebody must have already made to him?

'I was quite frustrated watching him as a fan, and there was a feeling he wasn't engaged as he should be as a senior player.' If there really were signs of a lack of engagement from a player who walked through a minefield of stress just to play for England, a player competing in his 104th Test for England, a player known to be still troubled by a knee injury, shouldn't Paul Downton have been asking Andy Flower what the hell was going on? Why does England's highest run-scorer in history seem disengaged? What have you been doing?

Following the decision to exclude me, Paul Downton said 'the time is right to look to the future and start to rebuild not only the team but also a team ethic and philosophy'. He later said, 'The team had to grow and be rebuilt and we couldn't do that with Kevin in the side . . . We couldn't trust him as a senior player to build the side around.' I was going to impede this rebuilding of team ethic and philosophy, was I?

They know the truth. They know why we 'fell apart in

Australia under immense pressure'. They know the pressure we were under.

They know that a clique choked our team, and that Andy Flower let that clique grow like a bad weed.

Flower could never stop its growth, so he focused instead on managing upwards. He did this well.

In the end, when we didn't have success as a distraction, they needed a scapegoat. Preferably somebody big, boisterous and annoying. Somebody with a little history. Somebody who left colourful footprints on the pristine white carpets.

I didn't always tread wisely. I was often naive and sometimes stupid. I was no villain, though.

And I'm not prepared to accept I will never play for England again. Cricket is politics. Bad politics. Things change overnight. I believe that the governing body of English cricket could change; I believe it should change. I am happy for now, but I would be happy to come back. Anything can happen in cricket.

English cricket provided me with an amazing opportunity to fulfil my dreams. I wouldn't be where I am today if it wasn't for the ECB. And I love this country, I really do. It's a special place, and I will be forever grateful for what English cricket has given me.

The stories you've been told over the last few years, especially over the last few months, have left a lot of gaps. I want to tell my side of the story now, and I believe that in trying to fill the gaps we might be able to face up to some of the problems facing the game and the team I love. I care about cricket. I care about youngsters coming into the game.

I don't remember every word of every exchange, so I won't be quoting conversations word for word. I'm just going to state them as I remember them. But it all happened.

All I ask is that you read it. Then you can judge.

2

Last Batsman Standing

Where is the rap sheet? Nobody has handed me a rap sheet. I've had to put it together myself from all the rumours and innuendo. It's like swatting flies in the dark: you think you have killed one off and another one starts buzzing near your ear.

I've read that there is a 'dossier', a four-page document that lists my crimes in Australia. Fifty crimes. A nice round number. Fifty of them spread over four pages. I would love to see a copy of this dossier. The problem is, it doesn't actually exist.

I know this for two reasons. First, people from the ECB have told me so. And second, there would be nothing to fill a dossier with.

If a dossier did exist the ECB would have reason to sack me, simple as that.

News of the crimes I am supposed to have committed comes to me drip by drip. Even the small stuff gets twisted and lied about.

Here's one. After the Ashes finished I left Australia a day earlier than the rest of the team. The tabloids claimed that I had organised my exit from Australia while the Test match was still on. I'd told the team in the middle of the Sydney Test that I was heading off as soon as possible. Just like that.

A fabrication. A total lie.

When the cricket is done I never hang around in Australia. Once the job is finished I am out of there like a bat out of hell – there's just too much abuse. I contacted the ECB on the night we lost the fifth Test and asked them to get me back to London as soon as possible.

There was no request or message to that effect before the last Test had ended. The ECB couldn't get me out the next day but they booked flights for the day after that. The rest of the team left the day after I left. I was one day ahead of everybody else: shoot me. I had checked with Andy Flower, and he'd no problem with me going as long as I saw the team physiologists for my skinfold tests before I went.

My wife, my child, my mother-in-law and my parents were all in Australia. We needed to get out. I'd had enough abuse.

Is abuse too strong a word? Maybe. The Aussies think it is all good fun, but when you are at the end of a long and disastrous tour, when you have people you love around you and you're being called a wanker ten times a day, the joke wears thin. I was in a bad place and it was time to go.

So we had one great day on Bondi as a family and then we were on our way.

We had a layover in Dubai, where the English papers were available. My name was on the back page of every one of them: Pietersen or Flower. Flower or Pietersen. Showdown. Gunfight at the OK Corral.

Interesting timing. When the journalists had been writing their copy, I was, as Paul Downton might say, in the air.

I rang Rhian Evans, the ECB media manager. Rhian said that she didn't know where it had all come from, but she did know that some people had been out with certain journalists at the end of the tour. It might have come from there.

I could name names here, but I won't. That was what I heard then. That is what I have heard ever since.

Rhian said she would try to get to the bottom of it.

I laughed and told her, well, we have been down this route before with the ECB. Him or me? It doesn't work like that.

When I had the England captaincy the papers wrote up the ending of that business as a him-or-me showdown as well.

It was never like that. And in the end, it wasn't him or me. Both of us went. Having the captaincy was a short, sharp lesson about the way things work in the rooms and corridors far away from the crease. I got sucked in to those places. I was a cricketer stuck in a world of small-time politicians and bluff merchants, where nothing ever turned out to be what it looked like.

I bang my head against a brick wall sometimes and ask myself why I ever accepted the England captaincy.

I came to England in 2000 as a wide-eyed little off-spinner from Pietermaritzburg.

Five years later I made my Test debut in the first Ashes Test at Lord's. I'd got the call from David Graveney: one of the best phone calls I ever had from the authorities at the ECB in my career. I became the 626th man to play for England, and hit half-centuries in my first two Test innings. It was such an overwhelming, exhausting experience; I didn't even make it through dinner the night of my debut. I was eating at the team hotel with Mum and Dad, and had to excuse myself and go upstairs. As soon as I put my head on the pillow I was a goner.

I came in at the best moment of Duncan Fletcher's revolution of English cricket. We won the Ashes for the first time in eighteen years. We rode around London in an open-topped bus, and had the best of fun.

By the spring of 2007 Duncan had gone. Peter Moores came in as coach and things changed. Where Duncan had given us freedom, Moores was tapping on our heads like a woodpecker all day, every day.

The captaincy dropped into my gloves the following year. Too much too soon, but it was too good to turn down. The night I got given the job I went out with Jess, my brother and his partner and we had the most incredible celebration. I was so excited. I thought I might be able to influence things.

Before it happened, it hadn't even crossed my mind that I would captain England. But then, anything can happen in cricket . . .

The story?

Somebody got a ban. Somebody else had had enough. I was the last man standing.

First, as punishment for a slow over rate in a one-day international in June 2008, our ODI captain Paul Collingwood was banned for four matches.

With Colly gone, I was asked to fill in as the one-day captain. My experience of being a captain? Zilch. Zero. Nothing.

Since I'd left South Africa, though, everything I'd touched had turned to gold. I was bulletproof. Twenty feet tall. Captain an England team? Was I going to turn it down? No chance.

I consulted with my old mentor Clive Rice, who's a cricketing legend in South Africa, and who'd brought me over to play for Nottinghamshire. Clive said to make a big impression from the start. Ask a lot of questions and pick out the best idea from the answers. Then, if that idea doesn't work, pick the second-best idea and so on. Suited me.

Our main summer Test series of 2008 was at home to South Africa. Michael Vaughan was still Test captain when the series began. On the first day I hit 152 at Lord's. A standing ovation and huge emotion under blue skies. Ian Bell hit an incredible 199 for us – all good.

We drew that first Test, but then had a big defeat at Headingley.

Edgbaston brought more crap: poor Michael Vaughan had been struggling with the bat, and was out for a duck before we collapsed for 231 all out on the first day. The second innings was better, but I had one of those moments: I was on 94 and wanted a six to land the century in style. I hit a ball from Paul Harris straight into the paws of AB de Villiers out near the boundary. Reckless, they said. Reckless and bloody typical.

We lost by five wickets. The series was dead before we reached the final Test at the Oval, and Michael Vaughan's role as captain was being questioned. All the while, Peter Moores was pecking away.

Duncan Fletcher had been a quiet facilitator. He had the ability to quietly influence, and the humility to act as a consultant. I loved the man. He would be your coach when he needed to be, and he would be your mate when you needed that. You could express yourself.

Peter Moores was the coach: full stop, 24/7. He's a nice guy, but like a human triple espresso – so intense. Big things and small things. He loves statistics, and would always go on about them. Averages, strike rates: it was as if a player's worth all came down to the numbers. It drove me up the wall: you play so much cricket and have so much pressure, then there's some guy in your ear setting silly little targets every day.

As the South Africa series went on, Vaughan struggled and Moores seemed to want to expand his influence all the time. He was everywhere.

And nobody was happy. A team needs to be happy if they want to play well. After we had lost the third Test, and the series, Vaughan got the usual kicking in the media. He hadn't been playing well, and England were losing matches. Everything good that he'd done in his five years as captain, everything he had been part of, seemed to have been forgotten.

Vaughan resigned and made himself unavailable for the final Test. It was an emotional farewell, and the skies were less blue now.

With Michael gone and one Test left to play, the ECB were in a bind.

Hindsight: cricket coaches aren't the same as football managers. You might win football matches from the dugout, but you don't win cricket games from the balcony. The cricket captain calls the shots on the field, so the captain and the coach must work out a balance between their jobs. It's best to sort that out at the start.

When Vaughan went, Paul Collingwood was the obvious replacement as Test captain, even though he still had three one-day matches of his ban left to serve. However, about an hour after Michael's resignation Paul made himself unavailable for the final Test. He also resigned the ODI captaincy.

The Oval Test was in five days' time. The ECB were sweating: they needed a captain, and they wanted to unite the captaincy of the Test team and the ODI team. Andrew Strauss, who might have been the conservatives' favourite, hadn't been playing one-dayers for some time, and he'd been dropped for the previous winter's tour of New Zealand.

That didn't leave many options. One morning, I was lying on my sofa watching TV when Sky Sports News told me I was favourite to be the next England captain.

I sat up and said, what?

I was the only real candidate. I was playing all forms of cricket, and playing them well. So I was elected. Or handed the poisoned chalice. Whatever. Even now, I sometimes wake up at night and ask myself, how did all that happen?

It was all very weird. Peter Moores called me and said, I want you as captain. I wondered if he was in a phone box with a gun being held to his head. It was no secret that my relationship with Peter Moores wasn't a happy one.

We went to a hotel in Northampton on a Sunday afternoon to discuss things. The papers said we had 'clear-the-air talks'.

We looked at each other and said, well, we don't have a great relationship, do we? The coach and the captain should really have a good relationship but we don't.

In real life, that's where people say goodbye, isn't it? It's not you, it's me. Have a nice life.

Well, he said, I want you to be captain.

Okay, cool, yeah, I said. Well, we can work on it.

I wanted Moores to sit in the back seat. To facilitate. In hindsight, I don't think he is actually capable of doing that. Moores told everybody that everything between us was great, that KP would be his own man, but he never took his hands off the steering wheel for a moment.

The Test series against South Africa was dead. The last game was just for pride, so I was allowed to pick the team. Might as well be hung for a sheep as a bloody lamb. I replaced Michael Vaughan with Steve Harmison, and gave the first over to Harmison too. I wanted him to know that he had my full confidence as a bowler.

It went well: I hit a century at the Oval in my first Test match as England captain and we won by six wickets. We went on to thrash South Africa 4–0 in the one-day series and won ourselves a trophy. Steve Harmison came out of ODI retirement.

This captaincy business? Nothing to it.

The Ashes were a year away. I had a feeling we had to be thinking long term. We had to start moving in a different direction from the one Peter Moores was pulling in. We had to build towards the Ashes, but I was afraid that Moores was going to run us into the ground before a ball had been bowled in the series.

We had started off well with the last Test against South Africa, but the upcoming winter tour to India would be the real challenge. The first time Moores and I would be together 24/7 would be in India. The honeymoon would be over.

Before India, however, there was the show for dough. In October 2008 we went to the Caribbean to play in the Stanford Super Series. Twenty20 for $20 million. Winner takes all. The games were backed by the now-disgraced billionaire Sir Allen Stanford.

Looking back, Stanford was a sleaze and the series became a farce. We managed to win our two exhibition matches, but in the big one, the $20 million match against the Stanford SuperStars invitational XI, we were a mess. No dignity. We got a ten-wicket hammering from a team that had been together for a fortnight.

Shortly after that humiliation, we were off to India. We lost the one-day series five–nil. The bowlers, apart from Freddie Flintoff, were struggling.

I was feeling the strain. I thought we were sliding towards mediocrity. Moores and I were out of step.

I needed guidance.

3

The Captain and
the Woodpecker

I should have known what was ahead before we even set foot in India. Whatever dial is in Peter Moores's head, it can't be turned down to 'chill'. The man can't relax. I could never relax when he was around. He was always around.

That had been the story when Michael Vaughan was captain. I'd seen Vaughan just getting worn down. He looked frazzled and frayed by the end.

I'd been there when we had to do training sessions following a day of international cricket. On one occasion we trained twice before a T20 night game at the Oval. We trained in the morning.

We had a break. We trained again. And then, after tea, we played the West Indies.

From the beginning, Moores was just relentless. He was a good bloke who wanted to do a good job, but was so obsessed with micro-managing every minute of everybody's day that I thought he risked breaking our spirits.

I remember having a meeting with Moores in Colombo at the start of the Sri Lankan Test series – this would have been at the end of 2007, before I was even captain. I sat down with him and just said, Peter, we've got to stop these team meetings. You're killing me. We're having team meeting after team meeting after team meeting, and I just can't do it. We're talking about cricket so much, but I just don't know what I'm going to do. Something needs to change.

He needed to understand something about modern cricketers. We are on the road for 250 days a year. We wear our England kit on most of those days. There are some days when you don't have to wear your England kit, when you don't have to put on your equipment. Those days are gold dust. They keep you feeling human.

A team meeting might only take half an hour, but for an hour beforehand it's there, looming. You're thinking, I have to go to the team meeting in an hour. I'd better not start anything else. What's this one about? Is there anything that really needs to be said? Then you've got to go to the team meeting, and it turns out it's about nothing. Just clichés, usually. But it stays in your head. You resent the time it took away from you.

All of those meetings amount to a lot when you've still got to practise and you've still got to think about your own game, you need to rest, you've got to get your body right, your head has to be okay and then you've got to go out and play five days of Test cricket. The pressures are tenfold when you're playing international cricket. The biggest comfort on tour is to have your own time. Your own time to relax, to chill, get your head right.

It never, ever ended. People seemed to think that if you want to get better at cricket you have to talk cricket and think about cricket all day long. People on the team would say we didn't talk enough cricket. You know what? If you want to talk cricket, go and talk cricket with your coaches to improve your game; you don't need to involve me in this.

A lot of players don't like team meetings. A lot of people, including coaches, love team meetings. They are a comfort blanket. Don't stand about doing nothing: have a team meeting! It makes coaches feel good: had a team meeting today – box ticked.

You've got to try to find a balance.

Anyway, Moores and I had that talk in Colombo and nothing changed. We went to New Zealand on the following tour, in early 2008, and had maybe one day off in the entire time we were out there.

We'd tied on 340 runs in the one-day international in Napier, and were due to play the decider in Christchurch three days later, but Moores still made us do a fitness session after the game. The New Zealand players were drinking beers and having a smoke on the boundary as they watched, and laughed at us. What the hell are you guys doing?

Peter Moores's theory was that we were training to show them how tough we were. Look at us: we can go train after an international and we will beat you in the next game.

The next game? They thrashed us.

It was crazy. We would get off the plane wherever our next match was, and an hour later we'd be doing ridiculous army-type training, running up hills, doing press-ups and sit-ups and sprints and carrying each other. We were having our pictures taken in our underwear, assessing what our body shapes were like and if they were going to change during the tour.

I mean, come on: we're grown men but we're having some bloke take pictures of us in our underwear.

There was no let-up. If it's Tuesday, this must be Christchurch. How do you know? He told us at a team meeting.

We got burnt out big time.

I remember Michael Vaughan talking to me in Hamilton after a day's play in a Test match. He said he was thinking of retiring from international cricket as he couldn't handle Moores any longer. He was in his head, all day every day.

It starts as enthusiasm, but it soon turns into pecking. In the end, the woodpecker has become a jackhammer.

We lost every single one-day game in India. Then, the start of the Mumbai attacks changed everything; 173 people were killed. The Taj Mahal Palace Hotel, where we had stayed a fortnight earlier, and were due to return in a couple of weeks' time, was at the centre of the tragedy. This wasn't like some remote event we saw on TV. We felt it to the bone.

We were pulled back to England, flown back to London at the first opportunity. Then we waited for the situation to be assessed by security specialists.

In the meantime, there was pressure for us to return to play the two remaining Tests. The ECB had contracts to fulfil and its relationship with India to worry about. It was a really difficult time as I had to convince a lot of players that we should go back. I was on the phone for fifteen hours some of those days in England.

I promised that no player would be obliged to return, but I was in favour of going back. Some of the senior players weren't keen.

In the end, we went to Abu Dhabi to train for a few days while the security requirements for Tests in Chennai and Mohali – which had replaced the Ahmedabad and Mumbai fixtures – were sorted. The series was still pending when we went to Abu Dhabi, but thorough assurances about security were provided when we got there. There were bizarre discussions about where we would be most likely to be killed, who was most likely to kill us, what methods would be used, who would guard us, how they would guard us. We almost had a Duckworth–Lewis method for calculating our own deaths.

The bottom line was that if we were happy with everything, we would return to India. In Abu Dhabi, everything was finally settled. Everybody got on board and we were going back to India.

I admit, at the time I didn't understand why some of the guys weren't keen to return; I couldn't see where they were coming from. I do now: they had kids. They needed to know what would happen if something went wrong when we got back to India. My position was different, so it was easier for me to be a bit gung-ho. My life has changed since then. I know why they were worried.

When we flew into India the security was incredible. We were looked after really well but we didn't play as well as we might have. I failed badly in the first Test, hitting two single-figure scores for the first time in my career. It was also the only time in my career that I'd fallen asleep while waiting to bat. I was completely shattered. To make things worse, tensions were threatening to boil over. I wasn't getting along with Moores, and it seemed that he was starting to irritate some of the other senior players too.

India won easily. Sachin Tendulkar played a remarkable innings, which he dedicated to the families who lost loved ones in the attacks, and to the city of Mumbai as a whole.

I got a hundred in the second Test match but we lost the series.

There was to be a short break after the India tour. We would return home to England for Christmas and New Year, before travelling out for a series in the West Indies towards the end of January 2009. I knew something had to change before we went to the Caribbean.

I couldn't act effectively as captain with the woodpecker on my shoulder, and the players were getting fed up with Moores's coaching. We had been kings of the world in 2005. Under Moores, we had played twenty-two Tests and won only eight. Seven of those Tests had been against New Zealand. We had also lost Michael Vaughan, a great player and a good captain.

I took soundings from some of the senior players while we were still in India, and I got some consensus as to what we should do.

I rang Giles Clarke, the chairman of the ECB, and asked to see him while we were in Chennai. Then I spoke to a few of the senior players before I went to sit down with him. Andrew Strauss and Paul Collingwood were the last two guys I spoke to, just ten minutes before the meeting. We were all in agreement.

I told Clarke that I no longer wanted to captain England because of the relationship with Peter Moores. I gave it to him straight: this can't carry on, so let me step down if you want this guy to coach. He's putting too much pressure on us, he's killing our spirits. I told Clarke that I couldn't captain with this Moores; I'd rather just go back into the ranks and bat.

That was it. I didn't say it's him or me. No chance. Never. If the ECB had complete belief in Moores, that was fine. I would step down as captain as somebody else might work better with the guy.

(What hacks me off about Strauss is that in his autobiography, which came out last year, he claimed that while he was aware that things between Moores and me were difficult, 'it was one battle [he] really didn't want anything to do with'.)

I can't remember if Straussy backed me, but there is no doubt that he was in favour of Peter Moores's coaching style being assessed. He supported me going to Giles Clarke. I suppose he had political reasons to distance himself when he became captain, but he was right at the time. A losing team that is an unhappy team will go into a death spiral unless somebody grabs the controls.

When I spoke to Giles Clarke, stepping down didn't seem like a real prospect. Initially, the ECB were really good towards me, and wanted me to continue as captain. Or so I thought.

After I had met with Clarke, an ECB board member met me in Mohali and gave me a one-page questionnaire to fill out. They wanted to know what I thought the new England structure should look like. They agreed that Moores was a good guy, but not the right man to coach England.

I really thought that, this time, things would change. I'd spoken to the ECB and we'd agreed about Peter Moores. The team had a problem and, as captain, I'd done everything in the right way. I had consulted, asked for a meeting. I'd said that I felt there was a problem, but if the board was happy with its coach I was equally happy to step down. Something had to give.

The board asked me to think about what was needed going forward, and to present the document they'd asked me to fill in as soon as I got back from the holiday I had planned with Jess and our friends.

I looked forward to my holiday and a rare slice of time with Jess.

I came back from India just before Christmas, then in late December I flew to South Africa with Jess and our friends. All was well. We were in South Africa on safari. Good times.

We were in Cape Town for New Year, and I woke up on New Year's Day to find myself all over the media: Kevin Pietersen wants Peter Moores to be sacked.

Happy New Year, KP. Look, it's raining shit outside.

I am now pretty certain who made the leak, but at the time I got angry with Michael Vaughan. I assumed he had leaked the story, knowing I was away in South Africa, because he was disappointed in me.

When Michael resigned, he was asked who his choice of successor would be; I believe he said my name. I was made captain all right, but the fact that Moores and Vaughan hadn't got on wouldn't go away.

I wanted Vaughan in the squad, but Moores liked youth. Vaughan would have brought a steady, calming influence to the team, and with the pressure of the captaincy gone, I thought he could concentrate on scoring runs and helping the team move forward. Moores was bringing in young player after young player, and we needed the experience and talent of a guy like Vaughan to balance that. He might not have been playing great cricket at the time, but he was a huge figure and I felt he would have played through the slump.

So at the time I thought Vaughan was disappointed when it looked as if I hadn't managed to seal the deal for his comeback after all. I figured that he wanted to create an issue in order to get Moores out and allow me enough influence to bring him back into the squad. I texted him angrily, accusing him of the leak. He denied it and we fell out for a while. And it was my mistake. Sorry Vaughany.

I got back to London on 8 January, and was greeted at Heathrow by TV cameras and tight security. I was whisked off through a private exit and into a waiting car. On the way home I phoned Jess, who'd come back before me for the press launch of the *Dancing on Ice* TV show. She said, have you seen the papers? You are being killed.

I should have known. Two days earlier, when I was still in South Africa, I had been told that I was going to be sacked. Hugh Morris, the ECB's managing director, informed me that things had changed: both Moores and I had to go.

It was one of those calls. Do you want the good news or the bad news? Good news! We're going to get rid of Moores. Bad news – you're going as well.

He had an excuse for making us both walk the plank. If they didn't take us both out it would look like they were just acceding to my demands.

Now the leaks made sense. The leaks were tactical, letting the genie out of the bottle.

There had been no demands from me, no ultimatum. I had simply said, let me step down because this isn't working out. Somebody close to the centre turned that into a him-or-me drama for the enjoyment of the press. Tactics. Politics. Bad politics.

Once upon a time, somewhere in the corridors and meeting rooms in St John's Wood, they had decided that I would be too distracted by life to be anything but a figurehead captain. I'd just be happy to have the job title.

Now I'd shown them another side of me. They knew I was right about Peter Moores, and if Moores went and I stayed they risked letting me have more influence than they ever intended to allow me. If I went and Moores stayed they knew there would be no more rides on open-topped buses and trips to Downing Street.

There was no way of getting me back into the bottle, so now I was going to be sacked for the sake of appearances.

Morris was the one who made the appointments and yet he was keeping his job, while both Peter Moores and I had to go.

You are one weak prick. I called him that because I was so angry.

I had a day or two at home, then on 7 January Peter Moores was stood down as coach and my so-called 'resignation' announced as a fig leaf for the ECB sacking me.

By now, the media were camping outside my house. I was

photographed and harassed every time I came and went for days and days. I did an interview with Kay Burley for Sky News and talked about trying to get my head around everything that had happened. I remember saying that I just didn't know how it had all gone so wrong. I didn't.

I had been looking forward to coming back to training after my holiday. The ECB had asked that I present my thoughts on what would be right for the team's future.

But getting the call from Hugh Morris when I was in South Africa – that hadn't been in the plan. Back then, though, I didn't understand how the ECB really works.

Moores had inherited a great team from Duncan Fletcher, but it was clear from our performances that he was turning wine into water. The Ashes were coming around again that summer and we were going to get tonked. The team were deeply unhappy, and I felt my position was untenable. If I was the problem, in the Board's eyes, they should let me step down and leave Peter Moores there. If he was the problem, then they needed to act accordingly. But being seen to sack us both? Hugh Morris inflated his life raft with his own hot air and paddled away.

That was when I realised the world I had walked into when I took the captaincy was full of little agendas and guys with exit strategies. Everyone looked after themselves. I just walked straight into the shit.

When we were able to take England back to India after the Mumbai terror attacks, the media labelled me the most powerful man in English cricket. There were articles saying what an unbelievable effort it had been from me to persuade the team to go back. I should have known that the guys who were really interested in power would hate that: Giles Clarke, and Hugh Morris too.

But I just looked at all this stuff and laughed. Little did I know that, two months later, it was going to turn sour. I looked like the guy who had got too big for his boots. I read all the articles about how I'd lost the run of myself. I was out of control, throwing my weight around and making demands: get rid of this guy or I walk.

The only walking I did was with my eyes shut. I walked right into this mess. I had no agenda, no exit strategy.

I shouldn't have been captain. Tactically I was fine, no problems there, and I wasn't shy either. I'm straight-talking – most people raised in Africa are the same – but the ECB was a different world. There were people there who could talk out of both sides of their mouths and not mean any of it. I was dealing with people who had never allowed their own right hand to know what the left was doing. If asked, they would deny knowing about either hand. And then someone would leak your question to the media.

I was also too young for the captaincy. To captain an England team successfully, I believe you have to have gone through the ups and downs. I'd only done the ups.

You have to experience the down side of cricket. You have to know failure and you have to understand stuff like family, kids, travel, homesickness. You have to understand life.

For instance, I had trouble dealing with Steve Harmison on the trip to India because of his homesickness. He's a very family-oriented person and kids have a huge pull on your heart and head. I know that now. For the modern-day cricketer, with the amount of travel the game involves, that's a huge issue.

I was no help back then. I was unfair, thinking how can you be homesick? You're out here playing for England! I left South Africa when I was nineteen, so what's your problem?

I've known homesickness since then. I've gone through that, and gone through not playing well and just wanting my family to be with me.

And then there was failure. I didn't understand failure. Talk about the circle of life. I spent so much time on the top of that circle that I didn't know there was anything else. When I got the captaincy taken away from me I had a horrendous eighteen months, cricket-wise, and learnt very quickly that there is a down side.

For all of my Test career so far, the media had been on my side. More than that: I could do no wrong. There was only one line of questioning: how great is KP? Brilliant? Best ever? Immortal?

That was all that I'd read. What came after the captaincy was all new.

In my own eyes, I was a failure as captain of England. When it was over I thought I would just be handed my golden balls back, hugged and sent on my merry way back to the life I had before.

Things never go back to the way they had been, though.

4

Wherever I Hang
My Caps, That's . . .

When I look back at it all, the saddest moment came out of the blue. I was at home, packing my bags to get ready for my trip to India and a new tour – the Indian Premier League. England was finished. I took out my Test caps to put them away, and the emotion just ambushed me.

I picked up my first Test cap, something I treasure more than anything I've had from the game.

What a journey together, old pal. I will never wear you again. I will never pour champagne all over you again. I will never sweat in you again. I will never have dust all over you again. I will never get sun cream all over you again. I will never throw you in the air again.

That was a small but incredibly sad moment.

I kept all five of my caps in the same bag. My debut cap, my twenty-fifth, my fiftieth, my seventy-fifth and my hundredth. Five caps, all in one place. They had travelled with me, wherever I went, every mile I have done. Always. Every trip I took. They have been with me all the way. If it had a frequent-flyer card, my debut cap would travel free for the rest of its life. Each cap that joined it afterwards might as well have been stapled on to the previous one. I would lose my mind if one became separated from the others.

Now it was all over, I swapped my bag. I was finished with England. More accurately, England was finished with me, I suppose. I didn't want to carry the England stuff any more. I went to Harrods, walked in and bought a new one. Took my little boy to the posh shop and bought a new suitcase.

There were stickers all over the old bag. All those places and games. For the sake of my head, I needed to change and start afresh.

I didn't cry when I was filling the new bag with everything except those five caps, but I sat staring into space for a long time. Where did it all go wrong? Why has it gone so wrong? And yet those five caps, they don't represent failure. They are the stamps that validate the dream I came to England for.

That's why I value them so much. They had a specific place in my bag where they always sat. They have a place in my heart because of what they mean. When I had to take them out and put them away it was a strange and sad moment. My new bag felt lighter. My heart felt heavier.

Five caps. The landmarks of a very personal journey.

*

I love South Africa. It will always be a special place to me because that's where I spent my first nineteen years, my formative years. And I like to think that my schooling, at Maritzburg College in particular, stood me in good stead for some of the battles that were to come.

The school was incredibly strict. Speak to a senior as a junior and you'd say please at the end of every sentence. How are you today, please? Would you like a cup of tea, please? Seriously. As a junior you weren't allowed to put your hands in your pockets or walk on certain patches of grass. And you had to sprint past one of the buildings, out of respect for its history. As a senior, that all changed: you were the one being shown respect. But by then you'd earned it.

And that's where there's quite a big issue in global sport, I think, where you can have the youngest member of your squad on the most money. Footballers coming in at eighteen and signing a £25 million contract? You can understand how the respect might get lost. But because of my upbringing, I've always been one to respect my elders in the dressing room. When I came in to the England set-up I knew full well that Vaughan, Giles, Hoggard, Harmy, Freddie ... those guys were the bosses. They ran the dressing room. It was quite cool that they were my mates too, but above all I respected them as senior players.

Anyone who has been there even once knows South Africa is a beautiful country that just gets into your blood. It's a place where I will always feel at home because that's where Mum and Dad are. But I have a home and family in England too. My son Dylan is English; Jess is English. I've been in England for fourteen years.

It won't be long until I've spent as much of my life in England as I did in South Africa. It has taken me quite a while to realise that, whatever passport I carry, I will always have South Africa in my heart. And I'm good with that.

I think one of the biggest mistakes I made when I was young was overplaying my Englishness, protesting too much, getting the three lions tattoo and all that stuff. I tried too hard with all that shit. I should have said I am South African with English heritage.

The older I've got, the more I've realised the mistakes I've made. One big mistake was not respecting South Africa and what it stands for. Not respecting South Africa and what the country gave me in terms of living there for nineteen happy years.

When I went back to play in South Africa I was still just a young kid. When I scored my first hundred there I should never, ever, have kissed the England badge on my helmet. I was on a high, and trying to make a point, but it was a silly, thoughtless thing to have done. I should never have judged and nailed the political situation in South Africa just because the quota system didn't work for me. I didn't understand enough.

I was very critical of that system. The side effect was that it brought me to England and gave me opportunities, brought me fame and fortune and a woman I love, a son whom I adore and a great life. I didn't need to shoot my mouth off. I was lucky.

I was lucky to be able to adopt England as my second home. As I have got older I appreciate that, and I realise too that South Africa was my first home and my real home. It was the place where I grew up and a place that left its mark on me.

I regret the way I carried on back then, especially the three lions tattoo I got during the first one-day series I played in South

Africa. When I think of it now I blush. My buddy Darren Gough had just had the three lions tattooed on his forearm, and was teasing me about getting my own done. So one day I went down to the tattoo parlour in the mall below the Sandton Sun Hotel, sat down and asked for a tat of the three lions. I called Darren in his room once the inking had started. 'Guess where I am, mate.'

I was in the tattoo parlour, yes. But I was also in Johannesburg, a South African getting the three lions tattooed onto his arm. Does that make you less South African? More English? Get real, mate. Your skin says nothing about your character.

Not the colour of your skin. Not the ink you have on it.

Graeme Smith, who was captaining South Africa at the time, took offence at my behaviour. He drove it back at me, attacked me. You know what? One hundred per cent, I deserved what I got.

Graeme understood the dynamics of the country a lot better than I did. And yeah, he was well within his rights to say what he did. We had a bit of a dingdong for a few years, but Mark Boucher always said to me, listen, you and Biff are like peas in a pod. Let's sort all this out and you guys will become best of mates.

He was right. We've sorted it all out and whenever I go to Cape Town I hook up with Graeme.

I love South Africa. I love England. My wife is English, my son is English, my mum is English. I live here, my brothers live here. I'll never leave. My future is English, and at last I understand that I am a South African abroad. I have my reminders, all the stuff I was brought up on. It's been harder recently, as in the last twelve months I've given up sugar and have had to relinquish all the

South African sweets that I kept in my naughty cupboard at home. But I've always got biltong in my house, and I put Aromat on every meal. And we have a braai, albeit a gas one.

I am English by choice. I have had to think about it. I chose well. I am English in the way that being English means lots of different things. I am English and I am a South African in England.

Years ago, I thought that I couldn't ever say anything like that because maybe English people would hate me. I should have just accepted that being South African was a big part of me. I should have said, this is how it is.

At last I am very comfortable with who I am and where I have come from.

My mum – from whom I get my English roots – always says that if she had known what would happen when I got to England she would never have let me go. In terms of all the controversy, all the headlines, we are not that kind of people. My family would never be in the media by choice. I have three brothers: Tony, Gregg and Bryan. Bryan has a bar; I own it with him. We've actually just bought another one together. Gregg is a banker at Investec in London. My oldest brother, Tony, is in the north of England; he is the minister of a church. None of the three has the slightest interest in being in the public eye.

My dad, Jannie, is Afrikaner. Mum, Penny, was born in England and moved when she was in her teens, when her dad got a job in South Africa. She met Dad and got married. We grew up speaking English at home, but on Wednesdays Dad would speak only Afrikaans to us. It was his way of not letting it go. He taught us to speak decent Afrikaans, our second language at school, which was good because I was useless at maths.

Mum and Dad were incredible with us, and never missed a sports day. If their boys were all at different grounds on the same day, Mum and Dad would somehow get around to seeing us all.

I never looked like being the standout of the family in sport. My younger brother Bryan was very talented at everything. Rugby, swimming, cricket, you name it. He was a proper star from a young age. He was a better cricketer than me coming up through the age groups, but he didn't apply himself as much as I did. He loved life; I just loved cricket. I was putting in three or four hours every day after school as I was so desperate to become a cricket player. I caught up with him in the end.

Most South African households are religious, and ours was no exception. We went to church as a family every Sunday. I loved it, but may not have absorbed the religious side of things as much as my parents would have liked.

After church on Sundays we would meet up with our friends, the Cole-Edwardes family. We played soccer with the Cole-Edwardes boys, and were all on a team called the Savages.

People sometimes look at me and this image of being a maverick that I have ended up with, and they wonder, did I rebel as a kid? Very quick answer: no. We weren't allowed to rebel. Dad just wouldn't have that. It wasn't an option.

My dad is a proper tough Afrikaner. It's difficult to get things past him. You can argue with him a little bit more now that he's sixty-five. You won't win the argument, though.

We were lucky. We got discipline. And my parents both loved sport. Dad played first-division rugby and squash. Mum and Dad are very active still, and go to the gym three times a week. Dad loves running: he ran the London Marathon a few years ago with Tony and Bryan. Three Pietersens running the marathon together, side by side the whole way, right up to the finish line. That tells you a little bit about us.

My brothers are my tightest buddies. Most days I will speak to all three of them, no matter where I am in the world. I know there must have been times when they despaired of me, but there has never been a time when I didn't feel they were on my side.

One good thing about having a brother who is a minister in the church is that he sees real problems. He deals with real tragedies. To him, I'm a piece of cake.

When we were growing up there were rules we lived by. I still don't swear in front of Mum and Dad. Blasphemy – any kind of blasphemy – was an absolute no-go. They wanted us to study well. Wanted their kids to be the best they could possibly be. That was basically it.

We all played rugby; we all played cricket. We could all swim before we could walk because we had a swimming pool at home, but Gregg specialised in swimming and was outstanding in the pool. He was incredibly talented and should have swum for South Africa. To this day I am not sure why that never happened.

My brother Tony, who was a really good rugby player, was the only one of us old enough to do National Service. He had to go away for a year. I missed out on that, thankfully. Somebody screaming at me and telling me to do fifty press-ups at seven in the morning? I had that before the Ashes tour a few years ago and hated it.

I played some rugby. I was fly half; I eventually grew too tall for that position but I was a late developer. Back then, I was a little skinny guy who never missed a place kick. Thirteen from thirteen in one game. Either touchline, anywhere – I just banged them over.

I never had much strength back then, and was probably missing a few skills as well. I played first-team rugby at junior school, though, and then I played for Natal Schools Under 13s.

It was playing rugby that I discovered I like to practise. There was a rugby field just next to our house in Pietermaritzburg and I would spend hours out there trying to make myself better.

Sport was the centre of life in our house. We would play sport every weekday: on school teams or on our own, brother against brother. Literally every day. On Saturdays we played our team sports and Sundays we'd go to church in the morning and then from eleven o'clock until four o'clock in the afternoon we'd be out, either in the nets or, during rugby season, kicking on the rugby field.

At the age of twelve I snapped my arm really badly. I was on one of those zip wires where you hold on to a stick on a pulley and slide along a rope or cord from a height down to the water. Great fun until the pulley breaks off.

Mum and Dad were watching Gregg play water polo and I went to the sort of adventure playground at the school, got on the zip wire and the thing fell off. I only fell about three metres but I landed awkwardly and broke two bones in my arm.

It was very painful. I was sort of numb and fainty, but that's when I found out my pain threshold was pretty high. I ran about five hundred metres with my arm hanging from just below my elbow and said, Mum, look, I've broken my arm. I eventually had pins and plates inserted after the normal procedure of a plaster cast didn't work.

So for six months I was out and I missed a lot. I came back from my arm injury and started playing rugby again. Six weeks later, I went to take a high ball but a guy hit me and my arm snapped again. I got up and ran off the field, and I said, Dad, I've got to go to hospital – my arm is broken again. I didn't wait for the ref, just ran off straight to the car.

After that I felt more confident playing cricket. It became my focus.

Dad was always very encouraging, and I was always really anxious to impress him with my cricket skills. I learned to be my own PR guy. In the evenings Dad would always ask me, did you get out at practice today, Kevin?

And if I got out I would never tell him. I always said, no Dad, they didn't get me out. He'd nod. Very good.

If I'd got out, he'd insist on having a whole post-mortem. I hated that and I loved getting praise. What kid doesn't? To Dad, practice was everything, and he taught me from a very young age that you don't waste a second of it. I've done that my whole career.

I get out a lot in training now because I try things, but it's still a valuable lesson. I always speak about training your brain in practice. If you train your brain to do the right stuff enough it becomes the norm. Dad taught me that if you guard your wicket with your life in practice that will stand you in good stead going forward.

When it came to sport, Mum was less driven. She was the

more caring, enjoyable, supportive parent. Dad was firmer: not in a bad, forceful way, it was just that he wanted you to get the best out of your ability. He lived that way himself. If he is going to go for a run he runs properly, he doesn't piss about.

I'll be in trouble for my language there.

5

Strauss Composes Himself

Maybe it's because I grew up with Dad as head coach and Mum as assistant, but I have a fairly fixed view of how coaching structures should work.

A good coaching set-up works like an old-fashioned marriage. The coach and the assistant coach act like a mother and father dealing with a child. (Okay, fill in your own joke about me being a big child.) The father is there from time to time to discipline and direct the child; he's the stricter one. The coach.

The mother is there to pick up the pieces. The mother can also be strict but she loves, cares, holds and cradles the kids, and makes sure they're okay. You have a much closer bond with your mother, if I can explain it that way. Your father is more distant, in a loving way. They're still your father, still your mother, but there is that little bit of a gap. Different styles of parenting that complement each other.

The assistant coach needs to form a bond with players. The players need to know that they can go to him. He sometimes goes out with them socially, he listens to them, understands what makes them tick.

The head coach needs to be just a little bit above that. He can come in and out of our world, and be the strict disciplinarian when he has to be. He needs to have the ability to make you feel incredibly good and to fill you with confidence in your job.

When Andy Flower was assistant coach to Peter Moores he behaved more like a head coach.

They were both ridiculously intense. I get tired just thinking about how intense they were.

When I became captain I tried to be more positive towards Moores and Flower, but I don't think I tried hard enough. In my stubbornness I was convinced that these guys weren't the right people to be coaching England. The captain–coach relationship is a huge part of a cricket team, and I don't feel that relationship ever got off the ground.

If I saw Moores or Flower at mealtimes I wouldn't want to sit with them. They weren't pulling out a chair and inviting me on over either.

If I bumped into either of them and said, hey there, what's up?, they'd just stop and say, I'm fine, thank you. They'd give me a suspicious look, like, hmm, I wonder why he's asking me what's up. Is something up? Something must be up if he's asking what's up.

I remember Flower talking to me during the Test match in

Mohali after I'd been to Giles Clarke to tell him things weren't working out. Flower sat next to me while I was waiting to bat and said, is there anything you need from me? I mean, I've been a captain before: if you need some assistance I'm happy to help you. I just said, cool, thank you.

On the face of it, that sounds like a reasonable thing for Flower to have said, but at the time it felt like a corporate move: Deputy CEO Andrew Flower has been designated to use a limited amount of empathy with a talented but troubled employee. And I think that's the polite interpretation of his offer, for it struck me that he was perhaps preparing for life after Moores.

So, when Peter Moores went Andy Flower came to power.

I can't say that a shiver of excitement ran down my spine, for by then I had no time for either Moores or Flower. I mean, as a double act they had burnt us out big time. Flower knew I wasn't a fan, and had expressed the view that if the management was to change, Peter Moores shouldn't be walking into the sunset on his own.

We had come from the coaching set-up run by Duncan Fletcher, Matt Maynard and Mark Garaway, which was very relaxed, very calm, and with no ridiculous training sessions, yet when we worked we worked hard. We worked really hard. We won. We were successful. We were well managed.

The dressing room under them had an atmosphere of encouragement. There was no coach sitting there, writing down everything that was said. Fletcher kept it all in his head. He and Maynard, who I've since hooked up with again for the St Lucia Zouks in the Caribbean Premier League, encouraged me to be positive. They encouraged me to be aggressive. They identified my potential to be a game changer, to take the game away from the opposition. When I did great stuff on the pitch they were all over it. And when I cocked up, they still said, you keep doing your thing, we believe in you. You deliver more often than not.

These are the kind of guys who make you feel happy when you see them. You'd seek them out at mealtimes: you could always sit at breakfast with Fletcher and talk about anything and everything other than cricket.

We could talk to those guys and have an occasional beer or glass of wine with them. They created the space to have a really enjoyable time playing cricket for England. While playing well. We went from that to just cricket, cricket, cricket. We weren't individuals any more. We were components, assets.

We didn't get older or more tired, we just depreciated in value.

With Peter Moores and then with Andy Flower it was frowned upon if you weren't going to train more tomorrow than you had today. If your mind wasn't on cricket, you were dodgy.

If you were enjoying yourself, you were doing something wrong. As I've said, when we went to New Zealand – which is supposed to be one of the greatest tours – we hardly had any time off at all. Not a day off to visit the vineyards or anything like that. We were mentally fatigued to the point where we were bored with cricket, bored with playing for England. It wore down Michael Vaughan, one of the most relaxed, chilled out, free-spirited captains you could ever meet. If you can wear Vaughan down you really must be doing something wrong.

*

I had first come across Andy Flower in the early 2000s, when he was Peter Moores's assistant at the ECB National Academy. He'd finished playing for Essex and had gone to Loughborough as a batting coach, and I got on fine with him, though in truth our relationship never went beyond the odd polite exchange.

I felt a little bit of empathy with him, though, because he had come from Zimbabwe. I think Africans tend to be drawn together, wherever they are in the world. The English do the same when they are away from home.

Maybe that's one of my gripes with Flower. If you're from South Africa or Zimbabwe you understand me. You know that the way I speak and relate to people is the African way. Direct, open, honest – that is how we do it. We cut the shit out of each other to each other's faces and then we laugh.

Somebody tells me I'm one of the biggest tossers he has ever met, so I tell him that if that's the case he should get out more but I can see why he doesn't.

He replies, well, if I was guaranteed not to meet a *doos* like you, yeah, I might actually go out more.

And so on. No backstabbing, no playing political games. We don't carry it with us.

Andy bought into the ECB way of doing things. Glances. Whispers. Politics. Agendas.

When the empathy started to wear off there was still admiration. What he did with Henry Olonga back in 2003 – the two of them wearing black armbands and making their 'death of democracy' statement in Mugabe's Zimbabwe – took guts. He had that in the credit column.

I played against him a couple of times for Nottinghamshire when he was with Essex. Got him out once.

He was a fine batsman, a fantastic player. No question. He had a Test average of over 50 and scored some brilliant double hundreds in India. He was very, very good. He was patient, a grinder, hard working and very stubborn. He fought wars of attrition with bowlers. In fact, the opposite to me in style. I'm a free spirit; I could potentially try to hit my first ball for six. That was never Flower's game.

I respected the way he played. It's a great way to be and I wish sometimes I could have been like that. Maybe I would have scored a lot more runs, but I definitely wouldn't have been as entertaining. I realised early on that Flower didn't respect the way I played the game. He didn't like it at all.

Flower was a grinder. I am a grandstander.

I like hitting boundaries. That's the fun of it. Back in 2006, against Sri Lanka at Edgbaston, I reverse-swept Muttiah Muralitharan for six on my way to 142 from 157 balls. I'd practised it on and off for a long time. I played hockey when I was younger, and I have quite good wrists. And playing courtyard cricket with my brothers we'd bat right- and left-handed, so I don't find it hard to change. A lot of people were trying this reverse dab and I just thought, what the hell, why not take it one step further? If it happens, it happens. It happened.

Muralitharan had set a very, very heavy leg-side field. All his fielders were over there. To me, if you set a leg-side field I'll think, the off-side's there for boundaries. He was bowling off spin into me, I was seeing the ball really well, and it was one of those moments when I knew the time was right. He bowled. The ball landed in the perfect area. And I hit it into the terraces.

Everybody who paid to get in was entertained. A lot of the establishment weren't. But to have pretty much invented a new shot? And to get the MCC to meet about it? It's one of the things I'm most proud of achieving.

'It was the only place I could see to hit a boundary,' I said when I was asked about the shot.

I'd have to say that my best switch hit came two years later, in the one-dayer against New Zealand at Durham. I had 60 on the board; Scott Styris was bowling off-cutters and had set a predominantly leg-side field. And I thought, to hell with it, I'm going the other way here. Styris bowled it at a good pace and I got hold of it – six. Then, a few balls later, I'd moved on to about 70 and we were in a good position, so I thought, I'm going to go again. But Styris held it up, bowled a bit slower so I had to wait. I didn't just change to a left-hander and swing: I had to change to a left-hander, spot the flight, the different pace of it, wait for it and only then execute the shot.

The ball flew. Styris's jaw dropped. And that was one of the very best shots of my career.

I don't enjoy being ordinary. I felt comfortable with that approach under Duncan Fletcher.

Andy Flower would have just looked at me as if I was speaking a foreign language.

Flower was the caretaker coach for the West Indies tour that began in January 2009, just after the captaincy shakedown. Moores was gone, and even though Flower had the tag 'caretaker' we pretty much knew that he was the new manager. So did he.

I love the West Indies but I knew before going out there that the Moores business would leave an aftertaste for the whole trip. I saw Moores and Flower as two parts of the same problem. However, the ECB obviously saw my captaincy and Moores as two parts of the same problem. Now Flower was top dog. He had never been Mr Congeniality, and that wasn't about to change.

There were signs there that Strauss, our new captain, was happy with Flower and they started to build a relationship.

The ECB wanted to present a happy marriage to the public and cricket media because English cricket hadn't seen much happiness since Duncan Fletcher resigned. Vaughan and Moores weren't good together at all. Peter and I never saw eye to eye. Flower and Straussy were both ambitious enough to be happy to make a marriage of convenience work. They were also alike as players, which in fairness helped. Purely technical; left-handers; opening batsmen with similar styles. They did a lot of work together throughout Strauss's career and Flower's tenure as coach.

The Caribbean tour was difficult for me. I was a bit shaken by the way the Moores business had ended. Some of the things written about me at the time were savage. I'd had two weeks to lick my wounds and then we were on the road again.

My morale and my confidence were so battered that maybe I shouldn't have travelled. Jess wouldn't be able to come out to the Caribbean because she was doing *Dancing on Ice* on TV, so it was going to be a long and lonely tour.

I was back in the ranks as an ordinary soldier but I gave it my best. I scored a hundred in our first tour match. Then I hit a 97 in the first Test, but we lost by an innings and 23 runs. I got a silly out looking for my century. I hit two sixes and got out trying to hit the next ball for six to bring up my 100. The media tagged me Dumbslog Millionaire for a while.

The second Test was abandoned and we drew the third and fourth. I hit 406 runs in the four Tests. I did my bit.

I had no great problems with the Strauss captaincy. I say that even now. He did a good job, as he was his own man and he is a very good speaker. He was very articulate, and when he spoke people listened because he was sharp and to the point. Plus, he was able to manage Flower and act as a buffer. That became a real problem later, when Cook had come in as captain.

Strauss knew how to be a conduit from the players to Flower. As soon as Strauss retired I noticed a huge difference in that respect. There was nothing: no bridges, no lines of communication.

But Strauss and I sort of fell out within the first week of that tour of the West Indies. I asked if I could take a few days off in the middle of the tour to go home and see the family. There was an empty week between the third and fourth Tests with nothing scheduled. All the other players would have their partners and family around them. I needed to see the people close to me, the people who helped me through whatever I was going through, but I was refused. No precedent would be set. I just wanted forty-eight hours at home. I was told no.

I had swallowed the captaincy thing. I had come to the Caribbean and gone out of my way to make things as smooth as possible for Straussy. I was working hard.

Now I argued the case with Andrew Strauss the captain rather than with Straussy my buddy. Flower knew that my relationship with him was already on the downward spiral. So I had chosen to approach Straussy instead, thinking that he would understand where I was coming from. He knew what had gone down towards the end of my captaincy.

No.

The straight answer was no. We're not setting a precedent for anyone.

The precedent argument is just bullshit to me, and always has been. Everything that has ever happened had no precedent the first time it happened. Why do people have this obsession with precedent when nothing stands still?

There was no precedent for what I had just been through with the ECB and the media. Nobody on the tour had experienced what I had. My going home wasn't going to start a stampede of guys who had partners booked to come out to the West Indies deciding to go home instead. Players are not normally allowed to go home during a tour but Strauss only had to explain to the team the exceptional circumstances that I was operating under. He only had to say that, rather than leave Kevin on his own when everybody else has their families around them, we are letting him nip home for a day or two so we can get the best out of him when he returns.

I was disappointed by the refusal, but I was really hurt by the attitude. I had made Straussy's life as captain a lot easier by knuckling down despite all that had happened.

A lot of people had thought that I would just withdraw from the tour, having been so royally shafted less than two weeks before we left. I wouldn't do that. I don't run away from problems, I confront them. I'd played by the book as captain, and I decided to play by the book in how I handled things as ex-captain. To go out to the Caribbean was to draw a line under the whole Moores debacle. If I'd stayed at home Straussy would have been flying into a shitstorm from the very start, so I went to the West Indies and I was a team player there. However, I felt the attitude and the refusal to see the bad place my head was in was an effort to slap me down.

Okay, I thought. Strauss made it clear that there was suddenly a gap between us.

Right, Straussy, if this is how you want things to go . . .

By the time we got halfway through the one-day series I was at my wits' end. People forget how much time we spend on the road. Having got home from the previous tour just before Christmas, I had been in the Caribbean since 21 January 2009. We started our first game, a warm-up against the St Kitts and Nevis Invitation XI, in St Kitts on 25 January and played the fifth and last one-day international against the West Indies in St Lucia on 3 April. I was due in India the week after that to play in the IPL. Being well paid doesn't insulate you against loneliness.

After just a couple of weeks in the West Indies I really understood what Steve Harmison had meant back in India the previous year when he spoke to me about homesickness.

For the time when I had hoped to go home to Jess, I arranged for some of my friends and one of my brothers to come over and I rented a villa in Barbados. I took a mini-break and would visit them during the day, then go back to the team hotel in the evening. It let me put cricket away for a while. The break turned out to be shorter than Strauss and I had been expecting when we had our argument: the second Test was abandoned due to an unplayable pitch in Antigua, and things were rescheduled. So, even if I'd been allowed to go home I probably wouldn't have been able to make it, but by then, the damage had been done.

I did an interview with Paul Newman of the *Daily Mail* when we were out in the Caribbean as part of my deal with Red Bull, who were sponsoring me at the time. I'd known Paul for a while, and we'd worked together on my first book, so I felt relaxed with him when we met at a restaurant in Bridgetown. Too relaxed, as I spoke too freely and knew I had, including saying that I felt like 'doing a Tevez' – the Manchester City player had disappeared back home to Argentina a few months earlier. I didn't mean for the Tevez line to be part of the story, but it made a good headline for the *Mail*.

The story caused a predictable amount of fuss. I was very disappointed that Paul hadn't run the quotes past my management or my sponsors, as is usual with that kind of interview. Paul knew the territory and he apologised, but our relationship never recovered. I was moving away from the cricket media guys as fast as I could at that stage anyway, and still had the bruises from my first good media kicking over the captaincy issue. I'd come to realise that the world was a harsher place than I had imagined. The people who built you would destroy you just as quickly.

6

Flower. As in Dour

I'm not 100 per cent sure how the conversation went between Strauss and Flower when I asked for the break in the West Indies. I don't know who was the more hard-line, just that the message delivered to me was very cold.

I do know one thing, though. A marker had been set down. Straussy didn't want to set the precedent of letting a stressed player get home to his family. Instead, a precedent was set in terms of how players' families were viewed generally.

From that point on Flower never relented on the issue of players and their families. It became one of his theme tunes. On the 2013/14 Ashes tour he banned families from coming to Australia until the third Test. It was horrendous.

Flower and Hugh Morris would invite all the wives and

partners in to explain to them why things needed to be the way they were. We needed the space to go and win.

It's not a holiday, ladies.

Jess knew the score and just thought, I am a grown adult with a child. If I want to go to Australia I will go to Australia, and if I want to go I'll go when I want to go.

I said exactly the same thing to her: if you want to come out, just come. Andy Flower doesn't micro-manage our marriage.

This was old territory for Flower and me by 2013. I'd had a couple of arguments with him before the first Ashes Test back in 2010. I said that I totally understood that we needed to gel as a team when we landed in Australia, but I hoped that as soon as the Test matches were under way there would be a chance I could have my family near me. Me, and any of the other lads who felt they needed that.

I knew I would need it. I'm the pantomime villain in Australia. I'm the one getting the boos and the abuse. They basically clean me out for three months.

Flower said no. A stone-cold no.

I never really had a relationship with the guy from then on.

He never understood the pressures of playing the Ashes in Australia. How relentless it is. The Aussie players feed off their media, trawling through the sports pages and interviews for stuff to use when they are sledging us in the field. The crowds in the stands seem to have got the same memo.

Usually, although I can't not hear it, I can ignore it. I've developed selective hearing. So when someone calls me an idiot, or someone calls me a genius, I can laugh it off. But in Australia it's different. They are getting under your skin from the start.

Sometimes it's abuse. Sometimes it's just deliberately annoying, like having a guy screaming *Keeeeeeeeeeeeeeeevin, Keeeeeeeeeeeeeeeevin* over and over again for a few hours when you are fielding. Right behind you. Over and over and over and over again, until you convince yourself that no jury would convict you for killing the bastard.

And in Australia, the pressure doesn't end when the playing ends. The cricket media and the cricket public see the Tests as a blood sport. Everywhere you go, they are on your case. Me especially. Walking down the street I get told, you're bloody shit mate, thirty times a day. I'm just a plastic bloody pom. I'm going to get hit so hard I'll be eating through a straw . . .

Flower missed all that side of things.

He was always happy to think I was the odd one out. I was the one looking for special treatment. I was the one out of step with his regiment.

I was the odd one out because I had carried the weight of expectation since the first century I scored at the Oval back in 2005. That changed my life. Anything I did – bad or good – got headlines.

Mentally, it gets to the stage where this pressure-cooker environment is too much. I need a little freedom. I need the people around me that make me happy. Andy Flower and Andrew Strauss are not necessarily among those people.

I will go to Strauss and Flower and request things because I'm not shy to ask. There are other guys on the team who want the same things and need the same things. I'll ask because I hope they can see behind the headlines and the image to how committed I am and how hard I work on my game. Not a chance.

I get attitude back.

What makes you think you are so different?

Man management: ever heard of it?

I am a bit different. Sorry about that. I'll always be the guy that sticks his head above the parapet. Then the machine-gun fire cuts me down. Rat-a-tat-tat.

In the Caribbean I suspected that Strauss was clever enough to play the long game. He would have to get close to Flower if he wanted longevity as captain, and getting tough on me would earn him brownie points. If you have longevity, you have the ECB in your pocket. They hate change. They'd had no stability for eighteen months, so Flower and Straussy working together was like a big dose of Prozac for them.

There were no other major issues. I think that deep down I had some resentment about what had happened to me. I could see how happy Strauss was to have got his dream job. When everything was going real well for him I definitely had some bad days when I just thought, where did it all go wrong? Why could I not be in that position?

Strauss was one of those players who, when he became captain, suddenly batted a lot better. With all his insecurities as a player he'd managed to get dropped in 2007. He just wasn't playing well enough. As soon as he was made captain his game went to a new level because he knew that his place wasn't under threat, he couldn't get dropped. He started playing really well.

Strauss was happy. Flower was happy. The ECB were happy. Cigars all round, chaps. Two Andys. Let's sell it as two Andys and one happy family. No more bad PR.

I know what people say. Pietersen thought he was the big shot.

He got cut down to size. Flower and Strauss had to make him conform.

I did conform. I went to the West Indies. I was happy to be like everybody else. I never got disciplined for anything in the set-up. I never, ever wore the wrong uniform. I was never late for team meetings; I was always there, always respectful.

Flower was still looking to pick a fight, though. He would come and sit next to me, and tell me that when people were talking in team meetings I needed to look at them with interest in my face. Just to show 'the voice of approval'.

He'd tell me things like this and immediately I would be thinking, why are you telling me this?

You don't trust me. You have no respect for me. You want to grind me down. You slither up to me and tell me how my face should look.

If my body language in team meetings was such a big issue (and I don't think it was, by the way), he should have tried to build a better relationship. He should have given me more freedom, some positive words. Maybe he should have helped me instead of seeing that I was unhappy and treating me like something stuck to the sole of his shoe. But with Flower, it was always about control.

He could have given me responsibility or got me involved in the leadership of the team as a senior player. But he just wanted to neutralise me, keep me on the periphery until such time as he was ready to show me the door.

Andy Flower. Contagiously sour. Infectiously dour. He could walk into a room and suck all the joy out of it in five seconds. Just a Mood Hoover. That's how I came to think of him: the Mood Hoover.

He didn't do socialising. He hardly went out for dinner with any of the players. He hardly ever had a beer with us unless it was when the team were celebrating a personal achievement from the day's play.

Fine, but as a coach he started to dismantle the small things that keep a team together on the road.

One of the traditions in the England dressing room was the fines meetings.

Fines meetings were fun and a huge part of the team's make-up. They were a place where we built relationships with each other.

We would have a fines meeting and I would get hammered there for fucking up on the field or wearing something stupid to dinner or saying something ridiculous – something like that. I'd get fined and made to down a beer. Then it was somebody else's turn. It was all affectionate and fun. We'd laugh all the way through them. For the young guys, it was a great way of breaking the ice.

Those are the kinds of things that guys laugh about when they are away on tour. Those are the times when you get away from the pressure. It takes the heat out of your environment and lets you be human for a few hours.

Andy Flower banned the fines meetings within a month or two of becoming coach.

He apparently said that they made some of the management feel uncomfortable. Well, I don't think the management had ever complained, and there was nothing wrong with the fines meetings. I think Andy felt they were just an arena outside of his control. He hated that.

And you know, the irony is you talk to the older guys who remember Flower on tour and they say he loved a beer.

What happens to people?

I said something to him a few years later, when our relationship had got much worse. I said, you know what, Andy, on some days I can look at you and say to myself, that's the Andy I wish we had the whole time.

Because on some days he was fantastic. He would smile and it would look as if he was enjoying practice. If he thought nobody would notice, he would even look as if he was enjoying people. He could look as if he was enjoying his job.

But the other 95 per cent of the time he was fucking horrendous. They say don't sweat the small stuff. Andy never found any stuff that was too small to sweat over. Or too small to make somebody else sweat over.

7

Show Them
the Money

The Indian Premier League opened for business back in 2008. There were no England cricketers there. We had a scheduling problem.

Since then, a lot of people in English cricket like to explain their attitude to the IPL as an ideological problem.

To me, it's an English cricket problem.

A problem about India.

A problem about money.

The ECB don't really know how to deal with India or money. Whenever the IPL comes up in conversation you can feel the room grow uneasy.

I say that I love India and I love the IPL. Love it.

Under their breath they say, yeah I bet he does. A man like that, he's bought and he stays bought.

Keep the blinkers on, mate. You might learn something if you took them off.

A few years ago I had a talk with Straussy about the IPL. I tried to explain to him how important it is, how the ECB needs to change.

Straussy looked pained yet earnest. I might as well have been speaking to the vicar about gangsta rap.

He told me that I should continue with the IPL, but that I must always make sure that England was my number one. If he had said 'Jesus' instead of 'England', he couldn't have sounded any more like a reverend.

Sometimes, you have to tell Straussy the facts of life.

Well, Straussy, how can I be happy playing for you if I keep getting treated like this? If every time I ask for just a little understanding it falls on deaf ears? I'm not asking for much. I'm asking to occasionally miss warm-up games, one-day fixtures. That's all I am asking for. It's not much. You know the pressure I'm under every time I walk out to bat, even in warm-up games.

I am not a batter who needs runs in the middle to feel confident. I need to train well. I need to know my game is in working order and then I'll score runs. That's why I never attached huge importance to warm-up games. I attached it to the net sessions and physical training instead. But then, when I fail in 90 per cent of my warm-up fixtures the media think that

I am out of form, so pressure heaps on me before a ball is even bowled in a Test series. This is the very reason why I was asking to take the warm-up games off. The Andys knew how well I trained and how professional I was, but my requests didn't get me anywhere.

He gave me that baffled look. I knew what he was thinking.

Young people today . . .

We left it there.

In April 2013 David Collier, the ECB chief executive, urged the Board of Control for Cricket in India (BCCI) to schedule future Indian Premier League seasons so that they would dovetail more successfully with the England first-class season.

I had to laugh. It was like a knackered old wildebeest asking a young lion if he wouldn't mind working a three-day week and staying at least five hundred yards away from the watering hole at any given time.

Hopeful. You might as well ask, even if you have nothing to back it up.

After years of patronising the IPL for being a cross between a bank heist and a travelling circus, the ECB were asking the IPL to trim its calendar to suit England's 'traditional season'.

Tradition, they say.

Player workload, they say.

Blah, blah and more blah. It's India and money.

When the Indian Premier League began in 2008 and the English players stayed away due to scheduling problems, you probably paid very little attention to what went down.

The following year Freddie Flintoff and I were both bought at the IPL auction for $1.55 million apiece.

A lot of people sat up and said, WTF?

If, since then, you have got all your information about the IPL from English newspapers, just a mention will make you shudder and want to go into a dark room for a lie-down.

Almost every English newspaper article about the IPL reads like a health warning to lovers of 'real' cricket. Put all the pieces together and they come across like a 'healthy body, healthy mind' book written back in the days of the Empire.

They say the Indian Premier League is chaotic/problematic/disorganised/disturbing/corrupt/confusing/over-ambitious/over-hyped/over there/a juggernaut/a runaway train/a road to nowhere/often quite amusing/often quite annoying/not real cricket and not bloody going away.

The ECB are trying to tell you that the IPL isn't something you should be interested in. Good old-fashioned wholesome county cricket is enough for any clean-living person. Only grubby bat-for-hire mercenaries go out to India to collect money in that gaudy circus.

I ran away to join the circus in 2009. I saw what the IPL had to offer and said, count me in.

The IPL has a potential audience of a billion people in India alone. Every time you walk out onto the field there are at least forty thousand people watching from the stands. Under the floodlights, no matter where you are, the place buzzes and crackles with electricity and excitement. It's an adrenalin rush. Your teammates and opponents are drawn from the best players in the world. The format is built on aggression and thrills. You are paid better and looked after better than you will ever be at any other time in your career as a top-class cricketer. You feel like you are playing a world game.

The first games I played were in South Africa, for Royal Challengers Bangalore. We beat Rajasthan Royals in the first game and everything was hunky-dory, but then lost the next five matches before I had to go back to England for the Test series. Still, I got glimpses of how well the tournament was run, how brilliant it was for world cricket. How the mix of players and nationalities made it an incredible academy for every cricketer there, regardless of their level of experience.

I have got to make a living. Your career passes you by quickly. The IPL is the future, and in twenty years' time I will be proud to say that yeah, I played in the early years of the Indian Premier League. And playing in the IPL paid for a lot of the life my family will have in twenty years' time.

Some people in English cricket will still be rolling their eyes.

Despite having created and developed the Twenty20 format, England failed to see its potential and the fact is, they are gutted that India has got a hold of the strongest tournament in world cricket. The ECB have been trying to get the genie back in the bottle ever since. That's just the way it is.

County cricket is tradition. It's sedate. It's slow-burn drama on summer evenings. The IPL is a massive rollercoaster action movie. Lights, cameras, action. Colours. Explosiveness. Mad storylines. Scandals. Controversies. Chases. Stars. Brash, in-your-face cricket.

Obviously, if you are producing a Merchant Ivory film you look down your nose at a Bruce Willis blockbuster.

That doesn't mean that blockbuster cricket isn't great fun, that it doesn't attract a huge audience, that the kids who catch it on TV aren't copying the styles and aggression of IPL players. It doesn't mean there's no craft.

The ECB, lacking the imagination to do anything more positive, have settled for drip-feeding condescension out to their media lapdogs. Look at the gaudiness. Listen to the IPL commentators talk it up. Aggers, Blowers – cover your ears, chaps. It's all about money and greed, and it's . . . Dammit, it's somebody else's.

Well, it's just not cricket. Not real cricket.

Remember how mad it was back in 2005?

The ICC runs cricket worldwide. Until 1965 the letters ICC stood for Imperial Cricket Conference. Then it became the International Cricket Conference, and in 1989 it morphed into the International Cricket Council.

In 2005 the ICC upped sticks and moved from Lord's to Dubai. Things have changed since the old imperial days. Big style.

Back then, some people in the empty nest in St John's Wood were too busy to read the goodbye memo. You can't really blame them.

In 2005, when the ICC was 'leaving home', English cricket reached its absolute high point. We won the Ashes after years of failing and the country went mad. Parades. Parties. Poms rule.

That Ashes, the moment that cricket went viral, was actually the last Test series shown on free-to-air television and 8.4 million people watched live when the tension was at its peak. The games shunted the start of the Premiership season into the sidings. We know that because Alex Ferguson said so. Big thing for him to say.

One thing stands out from the TV numbers. In 2005, 25 per cent of the people watching the first session of the first Ashes Test were women. That's about half a million women viewers. For the final innings of the fifth Test they reckon that 39 per cent of viewers were women. By then that percentage equalled 3.25 million women. 3.25 million women watching a game of cricket! That's how cricket caught the imagination in just a few weeks.

Then cricket went to pay-to-view.

Now, the ECB decided to take cricket away from free-to-air television for commercial reasons. For money. If you wanted to, you could say that they were being mercenary. They would say they had to look after the future of the English game.

All very well being popular, but it's better to be profitable.

There have been huge benefits to the deals they have done with Sky. I'm not saying that the ECB made the wrong decision. I'm saying that money is a part of professional sport and we all need to be honest about that. If I look back to that Ashes summer and the victory parade to Trafalgar Square, the media's view of cricketers was that we were better role models than 'spoilt' professional footballers.

It was a moment in time. Cricket will never have that moment again.

Back then, English cricket had something that it's lost. Superstars. Sexiness. Momentum. The right to be called the national sport.

You need stars if you want to grow your game. You need big personalities. You need players' faces plastered on posters in Tube stations and all over the back pages of newspapers.

You need to have administrators with the balls to back themselves to ride the wave. You need administrators who can adapt to the changing personality of the game.

I was catapulted into the public eye in 2005, in the second innings of the fifth Test. I remember reading on the back of one of the papers that morning that England needed a hero. I decided that I was going to be that hero.

I was brave and a little lucky. Three dropped catches – lucky. Fifteen fours and seven sixes – brave. Or cocky. Out there with my buddy Gilo, counting down the runs, counting down the overs. I was dismissed for 158. We drew the Test. We won the Ashes. After that crazy September day my life was never going to be the same again.

My Test career had begun at the very moment when cricket in England became insanely popular. I walked in just when the cricket world was changing, and I had to decide what my place in that world was going to be.

I did that.

I decided that I was going to be a top professional. Live like a pro. Play like a pro. Pack as much experience as I could into the ten years I'd get at the top if I was lucky.

English cricket took the decision to wind its neck back in. I never did that. When it all died down I was left with my head sticking up. A tall poppy, as the Aussies would say. When I felt good I played well. There were some great days. When I felt bad

I made mistakes that stank the place out. I had to grow up in public, which is a laugh until you screw up.

Whatever talent I have, I'm lucky to have been around at a time of huge change.

I love playing Test cricket. I love playing for England. I love to entertain people. I am a professional, and that was the deal in 2005. Money plays a part in my decisions, just as it has played a huge part in the ECB's decisions. Like the decision to allow Allen Stanford to land his helicopter on the hallowed turf at Lord's, bringing with him a box full of cash – $20 million in cash. But I'm straight up about it, while the ECB are hypocritical.

In the not too distant past, again with their eyes on the money, the ECB decided to commit England to seven summer Tests every year.

Why? Money. Quantity not quality. The calendar was being stuffed with more Tests, more tours, more formats. And the ECB were counting the cash and telling players to respect county cricket. County cricket is sacrosanct.

The ECB won't reduce their own schedule because they flogged a television contract to Sky that provides a good chunk of their revenue. In return, Sky were promised seven Tests every summer, as well as T20 games and one-day internationals. County cricket would continue as usual and international players would be told that they had to come home like good little boys to play some county cricket if they wanted to play for England.

It took a long time for them to realise that the public wasn't all that excited about warm-up matches played in the May drizzle against teams who were never really box office to start with. Then the visiting teams began sending apologies to the ECB. The players you might have heard of in our squad? Well, they'll be away playing in the IPL for some of the tour. Those players would only arrive just before the Tests started.

When the IPL came into existence, all the ECB could see was the IPL's money and its own jealousy. So the IPL has become a great global tournament and we have missed the boat. English players should be putting their names into the auction ready to commit to a full IPL season. Look at the guys they would be playing with. You can only get better by playing against the best.

And as usual I find myself isolated. Every discussion about the IPL is a discussion about money. To make things worse, a few of the boys who have put their name in for the auction – Swanny, Prior, Jimmy and others – ended up not getting picked. Their limited availability played a part in that, but it still puts a big dent in the ego. Dented egos are hard to talk to. The attitude afterwards was, well, I didn't really want to go.

Now, when I talk about my schedule, everybody reacts like it's just another outbreak of me, me, me, the greedy mercenary.

The gentlemen of St John's Wood just don't understand the players. It always comes back to the IPL and the feelings the gentlemen have about it. If KP plays in the IPL he's obviously a mercenary. If KP is a mercenary obviously everything he says about anything is about making money in the IPL.

So anyway, what was your question, Mr Pietersen?

If I am the mercenary that many people say I am, I would have scrapped my England career years ago.

I am still very proud to have played Test cricket. I've had some great, great days with England. I was extremely fortunate to have been given that opportunity. I didn't have that chance in South Africa because of the politics so I came over to England and I have been able to fulfil a huge ambition. It's been an incredible journey.

I won't be able to do this when I am fifty years old. When I am fifty nobody will give a shit about how I am doing. Money doesn't drive me. As I get older I want to maximise my earnings, but it isn't the most important thing. After England ditched me I was able to play the full six weeks in the IPL. I got a decent Caribbean contract and a good offer for the Big Bash in Australia. My income from playing cricket tripled.

I'd still prefer to be playing Test cricket for England, to be looking forward to a World Cup with England.

A few years ago when we beat India, I remember telling one of the players that we were in a position of strength with the ECB at that time. I said we should demand to be allowed to play the IPL schedule. Why should we be the only players in the world who can't finish playing an IPL season? It's like our mother calling us in from the green before it even starts to get dark. The rest of the world stays out to play.

He wanted to know what would happen if we didn't get picked by England again.

Jimmy Anderson is one of the top bowlers in the world. Swanny was the number-one spinner. If we go to the ECB and say we would like to be looked after here, this is a great cricket opportunity and a great earning opportunity, are they really going to drop us all?

English players want the IPL, but they are so afraid of not being selected that they won't rattle the cage.

*

Andrew Strauss went to the IPL 2014 final. He was there in Bangalore for the showdown between Kings XI Punjab and Kolkata Knight Riders.

What he saw blew his mind.

In an interview after the final, he said that he thought the IPL was 'a brilliant thing to have happened to cricket. You look at the calibre of the players who are playing here and it is really taking the game of cricket forward . . . It's been a fantastic addition to the game. To sample it in the flesh is to figure out how good it is.'

Straussy took the blinkers off and liked what he saw.

Enough said, for now. That's the money discussion. There's another side to the IPL, but that's for later.

8

Every Step You Take . . .

Over all the years that Andy Flower coached me, I was never made to feel good about the job I did.

Not once.

After a while I realised that, for me, there was very little fun left in playing for England. There was no joy. The only contentment I had was batting. Just practising by myself and batting when my turn came.

That was the way I dealt with things.

After that first West Indies trip in 2009, Flower let the dressing room become home to a clique. He had the inclination for control, but he didn't have the personality for influence or empathy so he let the dressing room decline. It was a slow process, and to be fair to Andrew Strauss I think he saw what was happening and did his best, but the dressing room slowly became the territory of those biggest mouths among the bowlers – and a wicketkeeper.

They ran an exclusive club. If you were outside that clique, you were fair game for mocking, ridicule, bullying. That's what those guys did.

In the first couple of years it didn't affect me directly. I was a senior player and I could give as good as I got in there, but it hurt the young players, especially the batters.

Let me explain what I mean by bullying. It's schoolyard stuff, which for a gentleman's game is pretty ridiculous. It's picking on players – particularly the younger ones – publicly, in the field, and then taking it back to the dressing room and giving them an earful there as well. A guy could make one mistake, fumble a ball, let a batsman get off the mark, and boom: what the *fuck* are you doing? For *fuck's sake! FUCKING WAKE UP!* All accompanied by wild gesticulation and faces like thunder. Once that player's card was marked, they couldn't do a thing right. Every time they made the slightest mistake it would come out again. Even their positioning in the field would be directed by the sort of pointing that means, if you get this wrong I'll let you know you're a fucking idiot, and I expect you'll get it wrong, because you're a fucking idiot.

I'm not saying bowlers don't have a right to be disappointed if their fielders mess up. But look at any other national team and I guarantee you'll be far more likely to see a shrug, pursed lips, a hand thrown up in despair, at most quiet swearing, before the team moves on. Next ball. Other national teams don't find themselves in a situation where a young, talented player confides that he's actually scared to play for his country because of the abuse he'll get for his fielding.

I've faced some of the most aggressive bowling attacks in the world, but as I've told bowlers from my own team on numerous occasions, I've never felt more nervous playing cricket than when I'm fielding at mid-on and I've thrown the ball back to the bowler when he's walking to his mark. I've laughed with them about it: mate, I don't even feel that intimidated when I'm waiting to bat. And that stems from the abuse the bowlers and wicketkeeper have given fielders over the years.

And what are the opposition thinking when this is all going off? Fucking hell, the guy's abusing his own teammate. OK, he's upset with him. That's good. That's something to play on.

To the outsider it probably isn't obvious, but bowling is a more macho business than batting. When you go out to bat you are basically on your own. You find your zone, you shut everything else out and you try to see the ball and then hit it. The bowler can make you look like a hero or a clown.

Bowlers do their work in the field with their teammates all around them, and they create the atmosphere for sledging. Bowling can be creative, but it is basically destructive. You want to get that guy out of there. In that scenario, the bowler is king while he has the ball. The field sets as he wants it to be set. He chooses what he is going to deliver and if it comes off he's the big guy. If it doesn't, if somebody in the field makes a mistake, drops a ball, reacts slowly, he can turn on them.

The dominant clique in the dressing room was made up of Graeme Swann, Stuart Broad and Matt Prior. And although Jimmy Anderson ran with them, he wasn't in the same league because at heart Jimmy is the nicest bloke in the world. I generally have a really good relationship with him.

Jimmy is an introvert, and he needs an extrovert to attach himself to, somebody who will bring him out of his shell. He did it with Freddie Flintoff in his early days with Lancashire. He was tight with Freddie when Freddie was big in the dressing room. Then he got really tight with Swann, because Swanny was the extrovert, the loudmouth. He was also the one who picked on players.

The clique were extrovert and loud, and turned the dressing room into a batters v bowlers environment. The batters were guys like Ian Bell, Alastair Cook, Jonathan Trott, Eoin Morgan, Joe Root, Ravi Bopara. None of those guys would say boo to a goose. It's just not in their nature.

As a result, they would just take the abuse on a daily basis: Move! Fuck, come on, for fuck's sake! What the fuck are you doing? But then, in a Test match against Bangladesh, Trott was at deep square leg and just cracked. He started swearing right back at Prior and Swann. Just shouting *Will you fuck off? Who the fuck do you think you are?*

I'd been wanting to ask that question for some time. Trotty screamed it there and then, in the middle of an over in a Test match. The constant abuse and ridicule, even during a game, had just made him snap. The Bangladeshis, who thought they had heard it all with the abuse coming from the bowlers, just stood and looked amazed as Trotty returned fire.

The success we had covered the cracks for a long while but it couldn't last. There are so many different elements that make up a team; you have to respect everybody or the whole show will fall apart.

I have always thought that the team I came into, the side that was number one in the world just a few years ago, had it right. There was a strong culture of support and respect, and everyone worked together in defined roles. We had guys like Alastair Cook and Andrew Strauss who were solid players. Strauss was a little bit more attack-minded than Cook, but Cook would bat all day. Trott could also bat all day, grinding the bowlers down, and my role would be to destroy the bowling attack on my knock.

I had to alter the course of games and change the pattern of sessions and when that was all working well it was fantastic.

I was never going to change the way that I played. Never. I look at my numbers now and they're not that bad, not that bad at all. If I played that badly I wouldn't have played for so long and I wouldn't have had the career I had.

But things changed, the atmosphere deteriorated and the dressing room quietly isolated me. It got inside my head. All of it. An empathetic coach would have seen that. I've worked my way through bad times before. Flower didn't want me to play better, it seemed – he just wanted me to play his way. If I played his way he was happy, and if I felt diminished in the process so be it.

I tried to tell him that there was a better way. I have always been willing to work hard on the flaws in my technical game. If we can talk about nuts and bolts I will talk cricket for hours. I will work from dawn to dusk. What I can't be is someone else.

2009 was one long grind of a year. After the Caribbean tour and the IPL, the big days were just going to keep on coming. Two home Tests against the West Indies and a one-day series. Then the World Twenty20. You would need a magnifying glass to see the little cracks in the schedule where we were supposed to live our home lives.

After the West Indies Tests I picked up an Achilles problem and missed the one-day series as a result. I hate being injured, but the interruption gave my head the break it needed. I sat on the balcony for our infamous loss to the Netherlands in the World Twenty20, but found a bit of form in the games against Pakistan, South Africa (well, not so much), India and the West Indies. It wasn't a great tournament, but I was top scorer. Who knew that within a few years that sort of modest achievement would become a sackable offence?

My injury meant that I was more or less out of Test cricket until the end of the year. By then, my world had changed.

Jess and I met through her manager. During the 2005 Ashes there was this girl, Keedie Green, who would sing an operatic solo for the team as we walked out. Later in the year we ended up doing a music video with her performing 'Jerusalem' for a charity single. Garry Wilson was Keedie's agent, and we got friendly. One day I said to him, half joking, you must have some single girls on your books, mate, and he said, well yeah, Jessica Taylor from Liberty X is single.

I asked her out to dinner and the rest is history. Or none of your business!

We just got on really well. We're quite different in a lot of ways, but we understood the world we each lived in.

Jess is a real Lancashire lass. Liberty X, the pop group she was in, started out in 2001, and they worked non-stop. They had an illustrious career, winning a Brit award, and became really famous. When we met, the band's career had just started tapering off, but they'd had a really long life for a pop group. It was simple: they loved what they were doing, and brought a hell of a work ethic to it. They put in some hard yards, kept making great songs and built a really loyal following – I liked them long before I met Jess.

When I met the rest of the band and all the people around them I could see they're just really nice people. That's one of the things I like about all of them: they are incredibly nice, respectful people. No bullshit.

They're all married now; they've got kids and are all good family people. Normal people with no airs and graces. For the level of success that they've had, you would have thought that one or two of them would have got hopelessly lost up their own arses by now, but they haven't. Instead, they are fantastic, generous people.

So, were there any thunderbolts? Arrows through the heart? Was falling in love like being bowled with a body shot? Almost. I thought from a very early stage that I had met the one because Jess just got me and I got her. There was never any awkwardness. There was never any of that game-playing, that treat 'em mean, keep 'em keen sort of thing. We just clicked immediately and talked like old friends from day one. We still do.

We got married in Wiltshire in late December 2007. Darren Gough was my best man. He had got me into so much trouble over the years it seemed right that he hand me over to a more sensible world.

While I was recovering from my Achilles injury in 2009 Jess gave me a bit of good news. We were going to have a baby some time during the 2010 World Twenty20.

She may not have actually mentioned the World Twenty20.

9

Let Me Through, I'm a Left-Arm Spin Doctor

The Ashes were next, the first home Ashes since the madness of 2005. There was no national frenzy this time. We started the series in Cardiff, and by the time we had finished the second Test at Lord's I was just a footnote.

I missed the cricket, but not much else. The interest levels were nothing like they had been four years earlier. In summer 2009, the country just kept on doing whatever it had been doing.

I really just struggled through the first Test with my Achilles injury. I batted nicely in the first innings, reached 69 and then got out when I swept a ball and it hit my helmet. The ball just came off my helmet, looped up in the air and was caught at short leg by Simon Katich.

I woke up the next day to all the papers saying it was my fault. I should have got a hundred. I knew by then that things were never going to be easy between me and the media. Since the captaincy stuff I'd stopped being a good thing. I was now a bad thing. The papers had to remind people of that whenever they could – just a public service they provide.

I hadn't scored a Test hundred since we were in the West Indies in early 2009. Now I'd thrown one away, just like that. And I was limping around like somebody who had been shot in the foot. They were sick of me.

I remember at the end of one day's play in Cardiff I went and got an epidural injection in my back, hoping it would help. It did bring down the pain a little but it couldn't do anything to stop the media gunning me for getting out on that 69.

I limped through the second Test and that was it. Kaput.

After the second Test, I suspected that I needed surgery on my Achilles. I did some tests with the ECB's head of physiotherapy, Mark Young. Mark is an Australian, but I've never held that against him. Anyway, after those tests I was booked in for surgery at a hospital in north London.

A leading surgeon broke off his summer holiday to come and work on my Achilles. Mark was there, taking photos of the surgery as it was going on, asking the surgeon about this and that.

I was there on the bed, my leg numbed but otherwise fully conscious, thinking to myself, let him get on with it.

The surgeon seemed like a nice man, and I was confident that the surgery would be successful.

The job got finished and I was bandaged up. Everybody seemed happy. I got a pair of crutches. Signed a few things. Mark Young said, okay, I'll call you later – we'll sort out some rehab and left. Shortly after that I realised that nobody had organised a way for me to get home.

I had to get on my crutches and hobble out on the street to hail a black cab, while carrying my stuff in a bag. I had to manoeuvre my freshly operated leg into the taxi, then swing it back out when we got to my house. Then I had to ask the taxi driver if he wouldn't mind helping me into my house.

Jess was appalled that I'd had to find my own way home with no help. I'm not saying I expected the red carpet, but I'd assumed that something had been sorted. I guess everyone thought that too.

Then the pressure came on to get me rehabbed as quickly as possible: it was the middle of the Ashes series, and the hope was that I'd be back in time for the last Test. So, three days after the op we set to work on various exercises: calf squeezes, foot slides. Then within a week I was back at the gym – walking drills, high-knee drills, side-to-side drills. I was there for three or four days on the trot, and every time I worried about the amount of blood that seemed to be seeping through to my socks and trainers. By this time the wound was dressed with a standard plaster, and part of that stuck to the raw flesh. It didn't look, or feel, right.

The surgeon was so concerned about the slow pace of my recovery he twice postponed the removal of the stitches. And more than two weeks after the original operation I was still having serious problems. One day, after the stitches were finally taken out, I walked out of my house and within minutes was bleeding profusely. I rang Nick Peirce, the ECB doctor, and told him that I was panicking.

He told me to get myself down to Lister Hospital right away. At the Lister, I was seen by a specialist, a great guy who knew ankles and enjoyed cricket.

He knew who I was, and the recent history. He cleaned the wound up and then looked me in the eye.

I should let you know that this could be the end of your career.

I just went white.

He said that he could actually see my Achilles tendon through the wound. We needed to sort it out sharpish.

He put some special tape and a dressing on the wound, and after that I had to go to north London every second morning to see a plastic surgeon and get it checked and re-dressed. I did that for quite a few weeks, because the wound got infected.

The injury was supposed to be a four-week deal. Instead it took four months, and I was so lucky I ended up at the Lister and they set me right.

At the time, I was living fairly close to Frank Lampard and we had become friendly. I remember looking forward to telling him about the black cab business just to hear what he would say. Frank Lampard, Champions League finalist, needs an operation and Chelsea leave him to get a cab home on his own! The cab driver gets him into his house. And then his rehab causes problems, leading to a panicked visit to hospital?

Around that time I concluded that I must just be a piece of meat to the ECB. Nothing special. That got me thinking. You know what? You need to do this for yourself and the people you love. Your career could have ended just there. You make the most of the extension that you have been given.

And that's the advice I give to young players: look after yourself first. It could all end tomorrow and nobody will remember you the day after that.

I was back playing towards the end of 2009, when we went to South Africa, but I had a bad tour. I'd had quite a long layoff, and it was taking me a while to get back into my game. People complained about my concentration, and the frustration built. I got harder and harder on myself when I needed somebody to remind me that playing in South Africa would always be tough for me mentally, that the South Africans were a fantastic side and that it would all come back to me if I relaxed and believed in myself.

By the time we got to Bangladesh in the following March a new theory was unravelling in the media: left-arm spinners are to Kevin Pietersen what kryptonite is to Superman.

Bangladesh was an unusual tour. Jimmy Anderson didn't travel as he needed to rehab a knee injury. Bring taxi money, mate. And Straussy, our captain, stayed at home because he needed a rest.

I didn't begrudge him the break, but it was interesting to see that concern for the mental wellbeing and energy of players was a selective thing. One senior player can't take a two-day break during a tour. Another senior player, in fact the one who refused the break to the first player, stays home from a month-long tour to put his feet up and get his head right.

On second thoughts, maybe I did begrudge him the break.

The media asked a lot of questions about my problems with

The innings that catapulted me into the public eye. And the celebrations that followed

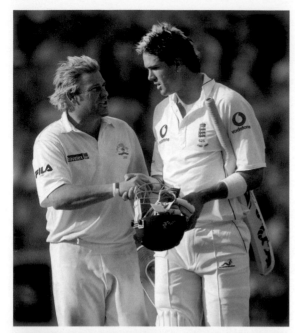

Ups and downs with Warney. Shaking hands and savouring the moment at the Oval in 2005 . . .

. . . then falling out a little over a year later

The drawn first Ashes test of 2009 in Cardiff – I scored 69 in the first innings

But I struggled through the second Test, then my Achilles problems really started. Ashes over

Heading for my highest Test score of 227 at Adelaide in 2010. And I took
Michael Clarke's wicket – the icing on the cake

Me and Cooky at Trent Bridge, during the first Test of the 2013 home Ashes

A match-saving innings of 113 at Old Trafford in 2013

The last time we had our hands on the urn. The Oval, August 2013

One way to quieten an Aussie crowd: catching George Bailey on 7 at the WACA in the third Test of the 2013/14 series

Boom. Not bowling to the left or right any more. Facing the new Mitchell Johnson at the MCG: he was nasty, aggressive . . . and sensational

Leaving the field at the SCG in January 2014. My last time in an England shirt. For now

left-arm spinners, and I knew there was some truth in it. I had a definite weakness when playing against them. My technique couldn't cope with the way the game was changing. Guys like Yuvraj Singh, Abdur Razzak, Sulieman Benn, Shakib Al Hasan or Paul Harris smelt blood whenever I came to the crease.

Whatever the reason, my form had skipped town on the express train. I had struggled in the first warm-up, and in the one-day series I kept getting out to the same bowlers. By the time we finished the first innings of the pre-Test warm-up (where I was out for a very cheap 2) I had a grand total of 69 runs from seven innings in Bangladesh. I was going out of my mind.

I found it helped to talk to guys like Mark Garaway and Mushtaq Ahmed, but with Flower I increasingly felt frozen out. Every time he looked at me I could feel his frustration. The media was sniping about whether I could still cut it. I was beginning to wonder about that myself.

To solve the problem, I decided to put myself in a high-pressure zone. I got a load of left-arm spinners, just kids, to bowl to me in the nets. England had no left-armer in the team so I had to go and find a few and show them what to do. I knew I was struggling, and had become a new form of prey for spinners. And yeah, they kept getting me out, but I kept working at it. I obsessed until, finally, I found a way out of that forest. It was a long process that was far from finished by the time we left Bangladesh, but things were improving, at least.

In terms of cricket specifics, there was a reason why I had started to struggle with left-arm spin. The ICC was in the process of introducing the Decision Review System (DRS). It had been officially launched in November 2009, during the first Test between New Zealand and Pakistan in Dunedin, but for cost reasons its use around the world was patchy for a while. The word was that you could be given out if a bowler queried an umpire's decision. It was a boom time for bowlers, especially spinners. As Swanny said, 'I wasn't a fan until I realised I could get fifty more lbws.'

If the bowler made a query the officials would go and check the replay on television with this new technology. I'm a tall guy who had always been able to get a big stride out and sort of play spinners with my pad and bat together. Being so tall, the umpires would think, you know what: there's such a long distance to travel between where his front foot is and the wicket, there's some uncertainty. We can't definitely know it's going to hit the stumps so it's not going to be out.

When the umpires started giving guys out at that distance I knew the jig was up. Umpires were getting more and more confident about giving batsmen out on the front foot. I learnt to remain inside the line of the ball. I'd always hit a lot of runs on the leg side, but now I started playing the off side. That gave me more room than I'd had before.

By the time of the first Test in Chittagong I was still a work in progress but I hit a 99 in my first innings by staying more leg side of the ball. Razzak got me out before I reached the comfort of a ton.

I had to change the whole style that I played. It was a huge shift but I got through. I hit rock bottom once or twice and thought, shit, I don't think I can overcome this. Is this going to be career-threatening? Is every bowler with a left arm going to decide I'm a soft target? How am I going to be able to do this? The flaw in my game was being exploited by the opposition. It was also being picked over by the media vultures.

So I spent hours in the nets trying to make sure that I could find a way. Later, when I went back to the IPL, I spent time with other batsmen – Rahul Dravid in particular. Rahul is one of the greatest players of spin the game has seen. I realised how lucky I was to have to come to the IPL.

The IPL, if you are open to it, can be like a university: you will learn things from different cricket cultures if your mind is open. But . . .

Don't get me started again.

10

Friends

When the 2010 Bangladesh series finished I went back to India and the IPL for my second season with Royal Challengers Bangalore.

I was excited to be going back for many reasons.

I had captained RCB the previous season and we'd not done well. I had loved the whole IPL concept, though: it was lots of fun and very different from international cricket. The play was serious but with it came a lot of enjoyment. I got up every day looking forward to going to work as a cricketer. There is a culture in India that appreciates it if you double down and go for the big shot. It's a game of cricket, not economics. Not life or death. Take a risk. IPL crowds don't want to see you batting out singles as you pick and choose which balls to hit. Life is too short.

In the IPL there are lots of chances to shoot the breeze with cricketers from other places, to learn from them. You are building relationships with guys you have played against in Test matches or World Cups. You thought some of these blokes were weirdoes. More, you plain didn't like them. Then you go and play with them in the IPL and you think, fucking hell, this guy is actually a good friend. How did that happen?

Going back to Bangalore in 2010, the great Anil Kumble was going to be our captain, playing his final season in his home state. Another little scribble in the diary for the grandkids: I played on Anil Kumble's team. What do you mean, you don't know who Anil Kumble was? Let me tell you . . .

I was looking forward to seeing the guys. I could talk about money and the IPL all day to you, but for the friendships alone I would play for free.

I've built all my relationships with foreign cricketers while in the IPL. That doesn't help in the England dressing room, where people like to say things like, right let's sort this bastard. I find myself saying, who? No, no, no, he's a good guy.

The England guys don't have many relationships with foreign players unless they've played with them in their county cricket set-up for a couple of games. There are not many of those friendships.

Whereas I have friends in literally every single international team around the world. Guys I can call up and just say, hey bro, what's up? If I am in town or they are in London we'll meet and have dinner.

You just absorb so much joy and wisdom from experiences like playing cricket in a different culture. The IPL has many international players, but most are Indian. As cricketers they are free spirits, playing in a country where you don't need a licence to be a free spirit. They play the same way that I play. They love cricket for what cricket is, but they also know that there are a lot of things outside the game that have more value and offer a lot more enjoyment. I love them for that and for not being all buttoned up and uptight about it.

The friendships are valuable in themselves, but I also enjoy being in India for what I can learn from other cricketers. I'll ask a question about a shot or a good knock, and every time I'll get an answer that gives me something to work on, something I had never thought of before, a new way of seeing a shot or understanding a play.

During the Bangladesh series I'd worked hard to adapt my game to the increased threat of left-arm spinners. The IPL was a safe haven in that regard, as India has never adopted the DRS system. I think they see human error as part of the fabric of cricket.

The guy I spoke to the most about the problems I was having was Rahul Dravid. Rahul was a great and heroic Indian batsman in his day. He is also a genius at dealing with spin bowlers. Our conversations and emails were a private masterclass from a genuine guru. Rahul improved my cricket and helped me develop the way I think about the game. His generosity will stay with me always.

In that spirit, I'll share something and hope my friend doesn't mind: an email Rahul sent me some time ago as part of our conversation about playing different spinners.

Can you treasure an email? I treasure this . . .

Champ,

I'll start with a disclaimer: I have not batted against the two of them [two Bangladeshi bowlers we had been discussing] and also have not been able to watch any of the cricket in this series. So, if some of what I say makes no sense or is not relevant or practical against these two just ignore. As we know, giving advice is easy, but until you have actual experience it's hard to get a real feel of what's the correct way.

They do bowl quicker and if the tracks have been turn- ing then it's always going to be a challenge for anyone.

Against guys who bowled a bit quicker (and I grew up playing Anil) I would look to go forward without commit- ting or planting the front foot. What can happen is we look to go forward which is correct but because we are so keen to get forward and not get trapped on the back foot sometimes you can plant that front foot too early. It sends the timing all wrong and forces your bat to come down too quickly (because once your foot is planted it is a signal for your brain to deliver the bat) resulting in you pushing at it rather than letting it come to you. Also then if it turns you are more liable to follow the ball rather than holding your line and letting it spin past. (Nobody counts how often you get beaten.). Also that results in what we call 'hard hands', which is nothing but pushing out. If your transfer of weight brings your bat down then that's per- fect because it always puts the bat in the right place. (I have in fact struggled a bit with that in Aus as my timing has been a bit off and has led to me pushing out at ball and created a gap between bat and pad.) That's the bummer with timing – it's impossible to teach or train.

Anyway, all this stuff is happening in the subconscious and you can't think about it.

You can practise a few things though – in the nets try and pick up length from the bowler's hand, that will force you to watch it closely. Look to go forward but recognise that a lot of the scoring opportunities are off the back foot, so while you're looking to go forward you are not committing, the key word is looking, you are ready to rock back and pick up some runs if you can.

One good practice is to bat against Swann and Monty without pads or with just knee pads (maybe not a day before a game!). When you have no pads it will force you, sometimes painfully, to get the bat forward of the pads and will force you to watch the ball. Also the leg will be less keen to push out without any protection. My coach would tell me you should never need pads to play spin!!

KP, you are a really good player, you need to watch the ball and trust yourself. You'll be able to pick up length and line and spin a lot better if you're calm and trusting at the crease. Under stress we miss vital clues especially early on. If you get beaten and it spins past you so what ... you're still in, and realise that you'll pick up the next ball better if you can forget the earlier one. Don't let anyone tell you that you can't play spin, I have seen you and you can!

Anyway, I probably rambled on too much ... all the best, go well!

Rahul

Help through encouragement and wisdom? He had me at Champ. If you love cricket you'll know why I often read that email and smile to myself.

So, the IPL is a runaway train: yeah, yeah. As the song says (sort of), people hear what they want to hear and disregard the rest.

People hear that the IPL is the most watched Twenty20 league in the world. That means gold-rush money. Dollar numbers blasting through the roof. Sony bought the broadcast rights out the gate in 2008: ten years for $1 billion. Pepsi became the second title sponsor of the league in 2013, at $72 million for five years.

But come at it from a different angle.

Usually when I speak about the IPL in England the response is the same. Money and mercenaries, yadda yadda yadda. An auction? How could you demean yourself?

Well, the auction system is a drama in itself. It's hype. It's show. It's brutally honest. Players submit their names and they put in what their minimum reserve price is. As soon as your name comes up it's like, right, Kevin Pietersen starts at a hundred thousand dollars!

You've got all the owners in the room, putting up their banners: two, three, four hundred thousand, a million dollars and so on.

At the February 2014 auction, it was between two teams bidding against each other for my services. I started at a reserve of three hundred thousand dollars, but the rival bids got me up to $1.5 million.

At that point, Delhi Daredevils played their 'right to match' card. They'd released me the previous month to free up money for the auction, but on the day they were allowed to keep up to two players from the previous season if they used their 'right to match' cards. Each team has a spending cap, but if you retain players that cap goes down, and the system encourages the franchises to keep the sixteen designated marquee players in circulation. So, by releasing me before the auction they were able to go fishing for something different if they saw it. If Delhi and I were a sitcom relationship we were 'on a break'. Free to see other people.

So the other two clubs took my price to $1.5 million, then Delhi just said, sure, we'll have him back – here's our card. They'd had a look at what was on offer and they had come back to me, and had to pay $1.5 million. On a different day they might have been able to buy me back quite cheaply, but that's just the way the biscuit crumbled.

The system puts a price on you and some people find that a bit brutal, but there's a price on everything you do in life. As a professional, the sooner you realise that you are a piece of meat the better.

I've had good friends on county sides who thought they were loved and appreciated, and who were happily planning their future having been promised a new contract was on the way. And then one day they've had the rug pulled from under them in the most two-faced manner.

The IPL is professionalism taken to its logical extreme. All the bullshit and hypocrisy have been burned off.

And here's the weird thing. In that professional environment there are more honest friendships and more mutual respect than in our own daggers-and-whispers professional culture. They've moved closer to the civilised heart of the game.

Meanwhile, friends in the IPL all ask me the same question about England:

Kevin, how the fuck do your blokes talk like that to each other on the field? Is that okay?

I find it pretty sad.

The social price of being in the IPL has been high. A lot of resentment has festered in the England dressing room. Money is the obvious thing, but the friendships irritate the other England players too. I don't blame them, but I do blame the management for never dealing with it.

As soon as you get out to India for a new IPL season all the captains have a meeting with the heads of the BCCI and the IPL governing body, and then we all go on to a social function together. So from the start we're spending hours in each other's company: Shikhar Dhawan, George Bailey, MS Dhoni, Shane Watson, Virat Kholi, Gautam Gambhir, Rohit Sharma and myself. We're all together, just hanging out and swapping stories for the guts of a day. I am in my element. Loving it.

I get back to England and I begin a story: So me and Virat Kholi and the boys . . .

Eyes glaze over.

The IPL has given me the kind of experiences that I hoped for when I left South Africa. I've built friendships and had adventure. I've had so much fun that the experiences with England, which I had always yearned for and will always be proud of, often seem to have happened while I was wearing a straitjacket.

Even just sharing a hotel with the other foreign players in your squad is an experience. We eat together. We swim together. We train together. We aren't locked down like children. We don't get the cabin fever we get from being on tour with the same huge international squad and back-up staff all the time.

We are professionals and friends together for a few weeks in a great environment. The league is throwing up match after match, incident after incident, things that interest us and affect us, but which might be happening to other teams. We're not the only show in town. The pressure is different that way. Almost enjoyable.

When other IPL teams visit us to play, or when we are on the road, we have dinner every evening with players from everywhere and anywhere. The experience has changed me. With England, I was working in an environment that never changed or wanted to change. In England I was given a media image back in 2005 and was never really allowed to outgrow it. I look back at the blond streak in the hair, the silly outfits, the coming out of nightclubs hammered, and I think, what the hell were you doing? But although I haven't courted the media for however many years now, I think people do still have that impression of me.

In due time, back in England I would walk into gunfire for having friendships in the South African team, but for me those friendships are a part of life. They have changed the way I feel about cricket.

Funny for a mercenary, but in fifteen years' time I won't be sitting back counting my money and wishing I'd done better. I'll be enjoying those friendships and memories and knowing that I couldn't have done better.

*

In the third Ashes Test of the 2013/14 series, David Warner went really hard at Matt Prior. I had been a teammate of Warner's at Delhi Daredevils, and got to know him really well – I got on absolutely fine with him. People in the England dressing room hate him, but I realised (with a bit of a guilty conscience) that I quite liked the bloke.

So, when it got hot and heavy between him and Prior I stepped in. Warner felt that Matt Prior was personally abusing him, saying things that were over the line. I said, yeah, but Dave, you shouldn't have said the shit you said about Trotty earlier. So, guys, just calm down.

Fine. I knew, though, that from the England point of view the dressing room felt that I wasn't on their side while we were hammering those bastard Australians.

I find it all so childish.

Back at the Oval in 2005, when I'd just made my maiden hundred in the fifth Ashes Test, Shane Warne came across the grass, shook my hand and told me to savour the moment. He was an Aussie, but he was also a friend and a mentor. I treasure that moment.

I had got 158 runs in that innings, and over the five Tests he'd taken forty wickets. We broke each other's hearts on the field that summer, but we remained friends.

The return series didn't start until November 2006 in Brisbane, and by then Warney had been ordered to withdraw his friendship. He was actually told that he wasn't allowed to be friends with me during the series. Proper, proper madness. The Aussies decided they couldn't have their great verbal volleyer chatting with the poms' star player, carrying on like it's just a bloody club match. And he obeyed, absolutely, though he didn't feel good about it.

He threw the ball at me twice in the first innings in Brisbane. He almost hit me both times, and I lost my rag. One of the very few occasions that I've ever lost my shit on a cricket field.

I swore at him fluently. I called him an arsehole. I said, who the fuck do you think you are?

I advised him as to his safety: stand in my way and I'll fucking run over you.

I proper went to town on him.

That's how bad it was. I let myself down, and Shane and I let our friendship down. There are people who still think that sort of carry-on is the proper order of things. It's not.

I had sensed it was coming. As opposed to KP or Kapes or any of the other nicknames I have, Warney always used to call me PK. But that day, on the steps leading out to where the team vehicles park at the Gabba, he just walked past me and said, morning Kevin. Cold and formal.

I knew things were different, but I was batting well: I'd just got a century in Sydney, one of my only hundreds in warm-up games. The reason I'd played so well in that game was because the bowling attack included Glenn McGrath, Brett Lee and Stuart Clark from the Test-team attack. I was up for it. I mowed it. I was ready for war.

Now Warney of all people was giving me the cold shoulder. A minute later and he's throwing balls straight at me.

He told me what happened afterwards, when we finally hooked up and continued our friendship. It was not just his mates but Cricket Australia who had told him why he was there. Not for friendship or sporting gestures. They needed to destroy us, and he had to be on message. I was identified as a big weapon for England. He was their big weapon. No more Mr Nice Guy.

So he went at me. I defended a ball back to him and he picked the ball up, then when I sort of looked away I heard Adam Gilchrist, their wicketkeeper, say, watch it, and as I turned the ball flew straight past my head.

Fuck you, Warney.

He just turned around and walked off. He was trying to rattle me because I was batting well. He was obeying orders.

Each and every time I got a single that day I'd run down the wicket and get in his grill. You fucking arsehole, Shane, fuck you. Who the fuck do you think you are, fatso?

I mean, yeah, there was a lot of swearing. I'm not proud of it, but anybody who knows me knows that I fight my patch like a honey badger if you put it up to me. The fact that it was Shane putting it up to me made things ten times worse.

Neither of us felt good about what had happened. It was pathetic. And it was a hard lesson learned.

England got sucked into the war. There was a moment when I went to sweep a ball from Warney and he bowled me out behind my legs. Said it all. We lost the series five–nil.

The way cricket has changed in recent years has brought about new friendships, and this now means there's a big difference in Test cricket and how it is played. We all want the bragging rights, we all want to win and the intensity is higher than ever, but so is the respect we have for each other and for the game.

What is cricket about? Warney and me screaming at each other like two drunks, or quietly learning from a guy like Rahul Dravid?

As my brother might say, there ends the sermon for today.

11

I Am Like a Hurricane. Not

The 2010/11 Ashes series in Australia was coming down the tracks at us like a runaway train. In preparation, the caring people who create our schedules did everything they could to grind us into dust. Between January and March we played six Tests in the course of our tours of South Africa and Bangladesh. Then to the Caribbean for the World T20 in April. Home for two more Tests and a one-day series against Bangladesh. Then, for some reason, five one-day internationals with the Aussies before Pakistan arrived to play four more full Tests and a five-game ODI series in late summer.

I headed for the Caribbean after my little window of pleasure in the IPL. My mood had picked up, and while I was slow to start with, as the World Twenty20 wore on I felt happier and happier with my own world. I played well in our matches against Pakistan and

South Africa. We were through early to the semi-finals so I could skip the final group match against New Zealand. Other business.

Dylan was born on 10 May 2010. The ash cloud meant that I had to fly from Barbados to Trinidad to New York to London to be there. There was a bit of grumbling about me leaving the team, but I think anybody with a bit of power had the sense to know that I would be going whether it was a meaningless group game or the final.

I got home in time for Dylan's birth. I had one perfect day with Dylan and Jess and then did the whole four-thousand-mile trip in reverse. I would have travelled forty thousand miles each way on a camel. It was so worth it.

I played well when I got back out: semi-final against Sri Lanka, final against Australia. The groove went on.

The hype was all about them. Australia, Australia. We'd never won a World T20 final, but I knew that I was batting as well as I'd batted in my life. I had a son. And I was walking out to bat feeling on top of the world.

A lot of the way I bat in games is down to the way I train, the confidence I get from going out and hitting well in the nets. If I'm going well there, I'll go out and score runs. And I train hard, so that when I go to bed the night before a match I know that I've left no stone unturned, I've done everything I can to make sure I can be successful the following day. I remember having throw-downs in the nets before the T20 final in Barbados, and I really was just hitting every ball wherever I wanted to. So I went out there, and we needed 140, 150. Craig Kieswetter was whacking it at the other end and every ball I decided to hit, I hit. And we won with three overs to spare.

World champions. I was Player of the Tournament.

We had a drinks reception afterwards with the ECB, but the lads just wanted to get to the rum in Harbour Lights. Get yourself a taxi. Get to Harbour Lights. You're in the Caribbean. Sea, sand, sun . . . and rum *everywhere*. The boys were on a high, supporters were there, the Aussies were there, our management were there. It was probably the best night out I've had in the game. The flight back the next day was horrendous. The boys were not in a good place at all. But no one gave two hoots.

There was a lesson there that a distracted donkey could pick up. I was a very happy man, and I do well when I am happy.

That being said, when I got back from the Caribbean life with Dylan and Jess absorbed me completely and that sort of blurred my focus on cricket for a while. That's the way it should be. I think it's only natural for your focus to be taken away from your profession when you become a parent, and I certainly felt it and I had to pull myself back into shape.

People talk about it and you hear about it, but the experience of becoming a dad is just somebody else's boring story until it happens to you. Then the world changes. Wow! Why did nobody tell me about this?

You experience things you didn't really know about before. The whole world seems different. All the selfishness you've had goes out the window now it's kid, kid, kid. Everything else shrinks. Nothing else matters.

I noticed the change in strange ways. I'm always punctual. I just don't do late. It's about respect and I was taught from a very young age that respect is key. One day that summer, though, I got a call from the ECB media manager. There was a Test coming up. He said, where are you, Kevin? I hadn't a care in the world. I thought he was just asking out of interest.

I'm at home.

You were supposed to be here at Lord's ten minutes ago for media.

Shit.

My head was like a burst bag of shopping. All over the place. I wasn't sleeping much, or getting much quality practice because of the tiredness that consumes new parents. I didn't just want to be some father figure for Dylan. I wanted to be the best dad ever. Nothing else was getting through to my brain.

That whole summer was a frustrating one. I had been getting less enjoyment from being around England, but now things were getting even tougher as I had to leave Jess and Dylan to go away to the England environment. I hadn't hit a century in a long time. Not being a defensive player, I know that hitting centuries is what puts the bread on the table. I was starting to worry that England would drop me. When I start having worries like that they fulfil themselves. I'm worried that I am not playing well enough so that makes me play poorly and so on.

Finally, it happened. I was out for a duck in the fourth Pakistan Test at Lord's. Not long after I took that walk of shame I was lovingly dropped for the one-day series. My form had been patchy, but I'd put together a scrappy 80 in the first innings of the second Test and hadn't been needed to bat in the second.

Anyway, they were dropping me and I'd never seen Andy Flower smile so easily.

They called me to a hotel in London. I asked what I was there for. I remember the smile breaking out on Andy Flower's face as they told me. Dropped. Lollipopped. I told him it was good to see him smiling for once.

I had a conversation with Flower then. Is there not a better way of doing this? How are you going to report this in the media? Are you going to say you are leaving me out to rest me or are you going to say you have dropped me?

No. We're going to drop you and we'll say so.

The Aussies went to town on it that winter. Every time I had it thrown in my face I just thought, Flower, you dick. It would have been so easy for you to say you were giving me a rest from a packed schedule. It had been done before.

As usual when I am playing badly or stuck in some bog full of controversy, I had to remind myself that everybody was entitled to their opinion. And I had to put up with the fact that everybody felt that I was entitled to their opinion too.

Dr Geoffrey Boycott, the specialist in suggesting remedies for delicate situations, trumpeted that there was nowt wrong with me that some good old county cricket wouldn't cure. All the nodding dogs in the ECB agreed. Two spoonfuls of county cricket would be just the thing.

For various reasons, my relationship with Hampshire was at a low point just then. Apart from the three-hour round trip to the Rose Bowl, the main problem was the ECB scheduling. The Board had taken virtual ownership of players on central contracts. For all the lip service they paid to the charms of county cricket they didn't really take into account whether we were available for our county sides or not. My absences hadn't made any Hampshire hearts grow fonder.

Earlier in the summer, Andy Flower had instructed me to play some county cricket. England wanted me to get in some practice in Hampshire's CB40 match against Kent ahead of the first Test at Trent Bridge. Rod Bransgrove, the boss at Hampshire, resisted: I'd already let it be known that I was planning to leave Hampshire, and he couldn't see why he should dump a regular player for the benefit of a guy who was never there. He stayed loyal to his guys, and I could see his point.

I was having lunch at our local wine bar with Jess when I messaged Shane Warne with my frustration:

Done for rest of summer!! Man of the World Cup T20 and dropped from the T20 side too. Its a fuck up!!

Somehow, instead of direct-messaging Shane the thing went up as a tweet.

I knew immediately. I got that stomach-lurching feeling, and put my fork down halfway through my starter. I said to Jess, I need to get the bill here, I've fucked up. I walked the hundred yards back home, headed up the stairs and sat on the top step, just crying. How on earth have you done this? Typically, Jess calmed me down. Mistakes happen, she reminded me. Let's just deal with it now.

I felt ashamed that it had gone public, and got it down as soon as I realised, but I had played right into their hands. Geoff Miller of the selection committee went straight into his elderly brigadier-general impersonation. I'll talk to KP. Whether there is an apology or not, I'm sure Andy Flower will have a word with him. I don't like that kind of language – and I don't use that language at all. I don't follow Twitter and I'm not a great believer in that kind of thing. I don't think it is necessary. What I do is select sides with my co-selectors that we think is right for England. My priority is the England side, and it is not about individuals. We make our decisions honourably and loyally for the England cause and we'll continue to do so.

Yes, yes. Quite.

So anyway, the ECB announced they were dropping me and sending me on a sort of blind date to play cricket on loan with Surrey.

Beautifully handled as usual.

Kevin is a world-class player but he does upset people wherever he goes.
GRAEME SWANN, 2014

Now, when an expert like Graeme Swann passes comment about me falling out with people wherever I go, I reckon he is shooting his mouth off based on three things that he has only read the headlines about. Leaving South Africa. Leaving Nottinghamshire. Leaving Hampshire.

So here goes . . .

I wasn't such a great prospect when I left South Africa. I was a fairly late developer. I played for South African schools, and Natal. When I came to England, I was an off-spinner who batted a little bit down the order.

I did a lot of work on my game back in my teens with my best friend Grant Rowley. I was all right at most parts of the game, but lacked physical strength with the bat. Grant and I would go down and spend hours bowling to each other every day. I would bat and he would bowl, then we'd switch. We would run along the beachfront and swim; we'd work for five hours every single day and then play club cricket on the weekends. Grant was a very good batsman who bowled a little. Very talented. He played first-class cricket for Natal and for North West. He's still my buddy, and when I played my hundredth Test he flew over to Brisbane to be there.

In South Africa I came under the influence of good people: Graham Ford and Shaun Pollock. Graham has known me since I was five, and was my mentor when I was growing up. He noticed I had something, and was the one who said, get out of South Africa, the political system won't let you play here.

Shaun Pollock, who was playing for Natal when I was there, said the exact same thing. I had some good friends in the Natal set-up. Robbie MacQueen and I were close. I was pals with Kyle Bender and a guy called Craig Tatton. They were spinners as well, so it was a tricky time. I wasn't up to their standard, but I was developing into something good. When the quota system came in, I just wasn't good enough yet.

Natal tried to keep me. They eventually set up a meeting with Ali Bacher, the head of the United Cricket Board of South Africa. I hoped he would give me some sort of guarantee or hope about my future in South Africa. He couldn't give me that.

I had started batting really well in my last couple of seasons in South Africa, and Clive Rice had noticed me playing for South African schools. Clive was the Nottinghamshire coach at the time, and along with Doug Watson he arranged for me to come over and play a season for Cannock, just off the M6 in Staffordshire. I did fine with the bat but I was poor with the ball. I had a trial with Nottinghamshire and Clive offered me a three-year contract to play at Trent Bridge, so I had a decision to make. I was contracted to Natal for the 2000–1 season, but it was an uncertain future, whereas I had a three-year offer in the UK where, if I made the most of my opportunities, I could possibly make a career out of cricket. Playing under Clive was also a huge draw.

Now, I was a kid who had left a tight family set-up and travelled halfway across the world to play cricket.

I was asked about quotas constantly in interviews, and how the system had worked against me. South Africa didn't see the big picture back then. Neither did I. I said too much without understanding enough.

Throwing players straight into the Natal side, straight into the Western Province side, straight into the Transvaal side, when they weren't ready? I think the quota system was unfair on them, as much as it was unfair on the guys who were ready.

South Africa was very keen to change, but change doesn't happen overnight. They had to get the process right, which is to start the development end of things. That needed to be tilted towards funding places that had never had development schemes. With that right, the end result will be a lot more meaningful than if you just say, I am going to use quotas so it looks to the world like we've fast-forwarded to the end result.

If I want to get a hundred runs tomorrow, will I succeed if I just think about the number one hundred? No. How am I going to get that hundred? Working shot by shot. For South African cricket, the development process needed to be the same, working bit by bit, player by player.

I wasn't happy that I missed out. I didn't realise how lucky I was that I had an alternative. I had the benefit of having a British passport and, with it, the chance to make a future for myself in cricket. I left behind guys who were better than me but who didn't have that chance. I know that for a very long time black players in South Africa missed out. They were invisible. I was very fortunate to have the chance to go to England. But when you are twenty you don't see it like that. I have moved on, and so has South Africa. I always felt that the way forward was to put resources into the development of talent in those communities that had never been given a chance. Quotas are gone and the talent is coming through.

Back then, I saw mainly my own situation. Now, I think we all see a country that was trying to deal with a horrible past.

I was with Nottinghamshire for four years, and then I left. The story goes that I fell out with everybody, and then when there was nobody left to fall out with I walked out.

Didn't happen.

Clive Rice was a great early influence on me. He gave me incredible self-belief and encouragement. I will always remember the first chat we had when we arrived back in the UK after a short pre-season in South Africa, and how Ricey told me that I was going to bat at number six for him all season and how he wanted me to score him a bucketload of runs. This was the kind of security and confidence that I needed at that time. I certainly repaid his confidence, with 1275 championship runs in my first season. I was scoring at a rate of 82 runs for every 100 balls. I topped Notts's averages chart on 57.95 per innings and we reached the semi-final of the Benson and Hedges Cup.

I became close friends with Richard Logan, who left Northamptonshire and joined Notts at the same time as me. We were the same age and had similar interests. Notts had put me up in a house with a lady from the club, but I never felt quite comfortable sharing a house with her so Logie invited me to stay at his, and that's how we ended up being the greatest of buddies. I will always be indebted to him for the way he took me under his wing and helped me get into the swing of things at Notts.

The next season Notts sacked Clive Rice while he was at home in South Africa looking after his dying father. I absolutely hated the way the sacking was done: I thought it was totally disrespectful. When Clive had gone Mick Newell was promoted from the second team and immediately dropped me to the seconds. I wasn't scoring as I had been, but I thought that with the runs I had scored previously I was at least going to be given a bit of a chance. Instead, I felt that Mick was flexing his muscles and trying to make a point. Not a great start to my relationship with him. He had his favourites like Paul Franks and Guy Welton, and I don't think he enjoyed a little South African kid coming to Notts, doing so well and being looked after by Ricey.

I played a couple of second-team games, came back into the first team and scored four back-to-back centuries and then, not long afterwards, broke my leg diving for a catch against Glamorgan in August 2002.

That same month Notts brought in Stuey MacGill, the Aussie bowler, and he promptly took forty wickets. Stuey is the sort of man you don't meet every day. He was a good influence on me. He was an incredibly positive cricketer, something I loved, and would always attack when he bowled. It was Stuey who took me to Sydney with him to play grade cricket one winter. A great learning experience.

Notts were promoted that year and all was good, but then in 2003, the final year of my contract, we were relegated back to Division 2. I didn't enjoy that season at all. Certain players seemed to be okay with losing as they were still collecting a healthy wage every month. That wasn't in my make-up. I didn't want to go back there with them. I wanted to continue playing in Division 1, because that's where the most testing cricket is played. I certainly felt that there were a lot of players just looking after themselves, who were happy in their own county cricket comfort zone. That wasn't me. I don't do comfort zones, and if I feel you are the kind of person who enjoys the comfort-zone way of life I tell you. Why would you not try to be the best person and player you possibly can be? Why can't you push yourself? Why can't you set goals that are sky high? These are things I don't understand about some people. You only get one chance at life. Try to be the best you possibly can be. Don't hide behind others and plod along. Think big, achieve big is my mentality.

On the last day of the 2003 season I told Jason Gallian, the captain, that I was intending to move on. I had topped the averages for three years in the batting department, and now we were going back to Division 2. It didn't go down too well with him, but then it was never going to be a great conversation. I went off for dinner. Famously, Jason threw my kit off the balcony at Trent Bridge. I got a call from my buddy Bilal Shafayat the following morning. Guess what happened to your kit last night?

Bilal went and picked all my kit up for me.

We weren't best buddies, and I think we both know Gallian wouldn't have had the balls to do it if I had been around. It wasn't a big deal, but it's easier to write that Pietersen caused a trail of destruction. I think that me confronting mediocrity throughout my career has earned me this reputation of being destructive. Some people don't like hearing the truth and would rather make out that I am the problem.

Not long after this I got a call from Rod Marsh, who was in charge of England's cricket academy at Loughborough, inviting me to spend the next six months there.

I threw myself into it, commuting from Nottingham each day, getting up at five in the morning and getting home late at night, and I loved it. Again, I got plenty of encouragement. Then, early in 2004 a bunch of us from Loughborough went off on a tour of India. I got off to a slow start, but found my way into it. Once more, all Rod and his people did was give me confidence, and I scored four centuries and a 94. I got a crash course in playing spin bowlers. I learned about tour life.

By the time I came back from India I believed that I had a good chance of being picked to play for England when my four-year residency requirement was fulfilled in just under a year's time.

I went back to Notts and decided to just grin and bear it for another season.

It was a tough year. I wasn't isolated in the dressing room, but it wasn't a good place to be. Stuey and Richard got me through. David Hussey from Australia was there at that stage and he was a friend too. I wasn't happy, but I had a target now: I had to keep my form if I was to play for England. I scored 965 runs that season and we got promoted again.

The club had told Richard Logan that they would be sticking with the players who won the promotion. A new contract would be coming his way. They then went back on that promise. Clive and Richard had both looked after me at Nottingham. I arrived in the dressing room as a kid from South Africa, and adapting to life in England was often hard. I needed some good friends when there were guys like Paul Franks, who enjoyed going around singing 'I've Never Met a Nice South African'. I'm not trying to bag Franksy here: I think he genuinely thought it was funny. And maybe for the first hundred or so times it was. But I did feel that I stuck out like a big sore South African thumb, and so those friendships I made meant a lot.

When Richard had been promised that contract I had said, okay, cool, we'll both stay at Nottingham. When that changed I said, okay, then I'm leaving the club as well. Enough is enough.

People say to me, but you were causing trouble as long as you were at Nottingham. Scratch the surface: in the end, I was looking after my guy who had looked after me. All I was doing was being loyal to my best friend in an environment where there was no loyalty to Clive or Richard or me.

When I finished at Nottingham I backed myself to do well wherever I went. I looked for a new challenge.

Shane Warne was desperate for me to come to Hampshire,

where he was captain. Rod Bransgrove, the owner, had turned the club around. He wanted me. I met Paul Terry, the coach, and I liked what I heard. Everybody was friendly and ambitious. The wicket wasn't great but the place was nice and the offer was good. I signed on the dotted line.

Richard had also signed at Hampshire, so we left together. At Notts we had lived together in a three up, two down. Us two and a guy who played hockey for England, as far as I remember. When we got to Southampton Richard and I shared an apartment, and he has remained my closest friend. We are incredibly tight even now, and he runs my cricket school in Dubai.

I think if you look at my record, my friendships last. My first tour with England was to Zimbabwe at the end of 2004. As on previous tours the management decided we'd operate a buddy system. My buddy was Ashley Giles. Again, still a mate.

Simon Jones and I really clicked immediately there, too. Now there's someone who deserves more plaudits than they'll ever receive for their England career. Jonah was one of the standouts in the 2005 Ashes series, taking wickets that were as valuable as any performance by me, or by Freddie Flintoff. But then he went down with injury after injury and didn't get to reap any of the benefits of being a key player in the series that transformed cricket in this country.

I don't mind pissing off other people if I'm loyal to my family and close friends.

Next question. Why did I leave Hampshire? What was the falling-out there?

There was no fight or falling-out.

Things were going well with England and I was tipped to play in the Ashes. I did a lot of work back then with Matt Maynard, the batting coach under Duncan Fletcher, and he encouraged the aggressive side of my game. (Both are still friends of mine, funnily enough.)

My England commitments just snowballed through 2005. I made the one-day team for the tour of South Africa early in the year. Those seven matches back in the place I grew up were a huge test of my character. In my second match, in Bloemfontein, the entire South African crowd turned its back on me as I came off the pitch. By the seventh, in Centurion, I was leaving the field to a standing ovation.

I learned a lot very fast. I worked with coaches and a captain who protected and encouraged me through that. At the Wanderers Stadium in Johannesburg, just before the first game started, Michael Vaughan called us into a huddle. If anybody on the field gives Kevin abuse, they get it back tenfold. If one of us is abused, all of us are abused. I loved him for it.

I remember walking out to bat at the bullring, as they call it. The boos were deafening. The crowd was so aggressive, so intimidating, so full of hatred I felt that if they could've got on to the pitch and physically harmed me, they would. I played and missed my first ball from André Nel. A good ball. But I kept it simple. Watch the ball. Watch the ball. Watch the ball. And after five minutes of concentrating on my processes, and with Vaughan's support from the other end, I'd calmed down. I ended up with 22 not out before rain put an end to the match. And that twenty minutes laid a foundation. I knew that if I could get through that, I could get through anything.

Then that second match at Bloemfontein, where the crowd turned their backs. They'd put up signs on the scoreboard: Welcome home, KP. Stuff like that, the digs, spurred me on. I thought, you know what? I need to do something special here. I got my first one-day hundred. Then, two more in the series. (The first of them remained England's fastest one-day hundred until Jos Buttler bettered it in May 2014, and I'm happy to relinquish the record to someone as entertaining as him.) I was named Man of the Series.

I loved being there by the end. I was playing as an international cricketer where I'd grown up watching international sport. I could remember being a helper in Durban as a teenager, a net bowler when the international sides came. I'd see them arrive on the coach, putting their stuff in their changing room, and think, that must be amazing. And then one of my first international experiences was with England, in South Africa, going to those same changing rooms.

I loved all my mates watching. I loved my family watching. I was playing good cricket. I was part of a team that protected me and encouraged me. I clung to that back then. I miss it now.

The price of settling in with England was that I had a bad start at Hampshire. A few months after the South Africa tour I played in a one-day series against Australia and had a fantastic run, then was picked for the Ashes and things went mad. In three years I played something like six games for Hampshire.

So when the crunch came in 2010, Hampshire stuck with the guys they had a relationship with. What else could they do? I did my training at Lord's and was very rarely able to take a spin down to the Rose Bowl. The longer you are out of a county dressing room the harder it is to step back in.

The ECB shifted me to Surrey, and I'm happy there. They have been brilliant to me during the last year or so when the shit was raining down. I have no hard feelings about Hampshire at all. They were good, progressive people. They didn't know and I didn't know how life would go after the 2005 Ashes.

That's three exits. I made mistakes for sure but there's no trail of destruction, no place I wouldn't go back to. No blood feuds but thanks for your input anyway, Swanny.

I played my first game for Surrey against Worcestershire at the Oval. Nice welcome. Mediocre innings. I played again a few days later and was enjoying the environment at Surrey, having people believe in me. I hit 116 off 105 balls that day against Sussex and hoped I was starting a streak, but it was back to the old nightmare when we played Glamorgan and Gloucestershire in our last two games of the season.

We just about managed to float away from the bottom of the table but I knew I needed more.

I packed up my troubles (and my caps) in my old kit bag and headed home.

12

Two Two Seven

There was light at the end of the tunnel when I played for Surrey, but I was still struggling for form. My technique wasn't right, but nobody in the England set-up was picking up on any problem. Not my unhappiness. Not anything technical with my game. I could have sorted it if I had an empathetic coach around me. If.

At the end of that loan deal to Surrey I flew to South Africa. Graham Ford, my old mentor, signed me to play for Natal, or the Dolphins as they are called these days. I was to play two four-day matches. And, being a mercenary bastard, I was to play them for free.

I had a good time. My first game at home was literally at home, as we played the Warriors in Pietermaritzburg. It went okay. The second game was in Durban against the Titans. One innings and out for a duck.

The real bonus, though, the headline act on the main stage, was up next. Just getting to work with Graham Ford made the journey to South Africa worthwhile. Here's a man who knew everything about me and who cared.

From the time I had hit my last hundred back in March 2009 Andy Flower must have noticed my decline and my confidence ebbing away over the next fifteen or sixteen months. But his only solution to my declining performance was to drop me, which just demoralised me further.

Was that the same sort of progressive thinking that would eventually shove the entire blame for England's collective failure in the 2013/14 Ashes onto the lap of one injured player?

I went home and I sat with Graham Ford and talked. We went to the nets and within a few balls he had sorted me out.

Fordy looked at me and told me that I was still a great batsman, but in technical terms I wasn't getting my head into the ball any more. I was standing and playing from the crease, and I was using my hands more than my head. It was a bad habit and no one else had picked it up from watching me.

Fordy said, you're not doing one of the things that made you so successful, which was getting your head into the ball and making sure that on contact your head was as close to the ball as possible, whether you're on the front foot or on the back foot.

It made sense as soon as he said it. When you do that it gives you power, it gives you control and it helps you align yourself to hit the ball into the areas where you want it to go. The closer your eyes are to the ball the less peripheral stuff is going on. You just read the ball better. It's like a boxer: he's always boxing better when his head is forward. When he's on the ropes he's nowhere.

After three or four balls with Fordy I felt like this big burden had been lifted off my back. Gone. I had come to South Africa with the intention of trying my hardest to forget all the nonsense that had gone on and to try to get myself back to where I was.

I had enjoyed playing with the Dolphins, but Graham Ford had given me back my game.

The Ashes in Australia. I've said before that the England team never ends, never rests. Even if you get dropped, the next long haul is still coming at you. Australia in the Ashes series of 2010/11 weren't the Australia of old. They weren't the giants we had taken down in 2005, but the fact remained that we hadn't won a series on their turf since 1986/87. South Africa and India might have overtaken the Aussies in terms of world rankings and respect, but Australia were the ones we wanted to beat and every English cricketer wanted to be a part of it if we were going to turn them over in Australia.

We started with a warm-up against Western Australia in early November, and weren't going to be done till the end of the seventh one-day international on 6 February.

They have a chain of shops in Australia called Harvey Norman, and a big part of their advertising is that they claim to offer 'zero interest'. Guys sometimes call me Harvey Norman because I have zero interest in warm-up games and exhibitions. What you do against Western Australia in November won't be remembered if you fly home empty-handed in February. I hit 58 against Western

Australia. Then, more true to my history, a 35 and a 5 in the other two warm-ups.

First Test: Brisbane.

A couple of days beforehand Surrey confirmed that, having had me on loan, they were now signing me permanently. Good. I was missing Jess and Dylan, so any happy news from home was welcome. I made 43 in the first innings. Not much to say except that it was Peter Siddle who did me yet again. Give me a war with Mitchell Johnson or Morné Morkel any day of the week.

Siddle bowls with the patience of a robot. Just very tight lines. I dig in and tell myself that, okay, this will be ugly but I'll get through it. It takes so long to build the numbers, though. He never seems to gamble. He's never bowling for the jackpot. The longer it goes on the more shots I try to make. Maybe if I start hitting a few big numbers they will take him away. Then the valve pops: I see a ball and have to try something. The next thing I know, I'm taking a walk. Time after time he does me. I know what he is going to do. He does it. Suffocates me. I clearly remember saying to myself after the tenth or eleventh time Sids got me, this cannot happen again. I have to be more patient and beat his game. I did that for the rest of that series.

I don't get to bat in the second innings. Rain affects play and we end up with a draw.

Second Test: Adelaide Oval.

Four years ago Shane Warne put us to sleep without a struggle in this place. Just killed us. For this Test there is no Warney and they have dropped Mitchell Johnson, who is the World Player of the Year. After we take three wickets for two runs they are probably wondering about that one.

When we bat Cooky is at his best, dogging out 136 not out by the end of the second day. I have clear memories of the morning of the third day. After twenty-one months I reached a Test century again. Did I think about England, and our redemption in the Oval coming with my own redemption?

No. I just said, at last.

The relief. About a thousand pounds of pressure dropped off my shoulders. So much for playing in the style of Andy Flower.

It was history. I passed the hundred mark and kept going. Two hundred. Maybe I'll retire before they get me out. Two hundred and twenty-seven. Caught by Simon Katich and bowled by somebody other than Peter Siddle. Take a bow, Xavier Doherty. Just a small bow. It was 227, after all.

I got to bowl on day four. Took Michael Clarke's wicket. He had been batting beautifully and he was the wicket we needed to win the game. I suppose it was just my time; normally Pup would smash me everywhere, but this time he was mine. We were leading the series one–nil.

Third Test: Perth.

Mitchell Johnson is back and this time he is pissed off. He takes six of us out in the first innings. He hits me for a duck. After three balls. My 227 seems a long while ago all of a sudden.

As I say, give me a slog to 43 with Peter Siddle any day of the week.

In percentage terms the second innings went much better. I

was caught by Shane Watson for a massive three. England 123 all out.

At least it was over quickly. One–all.

Fourth Test: Melbourne.

I spent a lot of time over Christmas in the nets, trying to get my head right. Literally. I knew that what Graham Ford told me in South Africa worked for me. I knew I had to get into a groove with it and get all the old confidence back. When I felt the pressure to play defensively or when I started getting down about being away from home on a long tour, I'd get a little bit tentative. I'd take a fraction of a second longer to react to the ball I was seeing. Then I was late and my head wasn't where it needed to be.

Graham Gooch took me in the nets most days; he's a really nice man and we had a good enough relationship. Andy Flower never really coached me beyond telling me what he wanted and wearing a vinegar puss when he didn't get it. Gooch was good at motivating me, but he's a mechanic and I needed someone to help me keep my head right. Also, I've never liked the tool that Goochy uses in practice.

He calls it the dog stick – it's a bit like one of those things people use to throw balls for their dogs. A stick with a cup at the top to hold the ball, and he uses it as a sidearm ball thrower. It's better than a machine in that it's not predictable, but I just don't like the thing. It might have looked like I didn't like using Graham and I was being uncooperative, but I just didn't like the dog stick.

I used Mushtaq Ahmed a lot in nets too. Mushy was contracted to England as a consultant and on tour we'd have him for about twenty days. I always got a lot of energy whenever he was around.

I generally don't need too much technical advice (apart from my head) because my technique is not actually that good! The sessions with Fordy in South Africa had been an exception. Generally, I just need confidence and self-belief and positivity. I don't need someone who is going to challenge me to break down my batting movement the way golfers break down their swing. I don't want a mechanic to tell me I shouldn't be doing this and I should be doing that. I need someone to come along and tell me that I'm playing like a million dollars. Then I get confidence. Basically, I'm very shallow!

When I get that good feeling going I get rhythm in my batting. I can hit anything. When I work with Flower, or less so with Gooch, I just get stressed. They try to turn me into the batsman they think I should be. The batsman I would be if I had their personality. They were both relentless with their work ethic. They have more in common with each other than I have with either of them.

There's no point trying to make a high roller into a card counter. It's a waste of time. If you aren't giving me confidence, you aren't giving me enough. That's my drug.

We started on Boxing Day and the Aussies staggered about like they were hung over. All out for 98. We ran up 531. I hit 51 before some guy called Peter Siddle got me lbw. No need to put on the pads for a second innings. 2–1.

Fifth Test: Sydney.

It was about this time that I realised I had gone off cheese.

Matt Prior and I met at the academy in Loughborough back in 2002. He was Sussex, I was at Nottinghamshire and, yeah, we were good buddies. He seemed smart, and he had some African heritage too. He lived in South Africa until he was eleven – born in Johannesburg with a mix of South African and English parents, I think – so there was a connection there.

A little over a decade later, and that connection's history. I'm the one who's always being labelled as the uncontrollable individualist, the egomaniac, the arrogant, flash, materialistic South African. But when I close my eyes in the dressing room I can't help wondering why. Every tour I hear Prior getting louder and louder. Pump up the volume. Pump up the volume.

He is dominating the place, and has taken to referring to himself as the Big Cheese (or, informally, Cheese). As in, the Big Cheese is pleased with how he played today. The Big Cheese has earned some beer tonight. Cheese went out last night. Cheese went to bat today. Who does that? I don't know how he got the name, but he'd started using it a lot.

Seriously. How the hell am I even on that level with ego problems? I'm nowhere near it. What always surprises people when they observe the England team on tour is the amount of time I spend alone. I like my downtime. I need to escape other people. There are lots of days when I need to escape the Big Cheese and his followers, the little Baby Cheeses, as they try to run the dressing room.

But when the media give you a tag it sticks to you forever, and every story about you is spun to fit. I got a lot of attention after 2005. That's just the way it was, and that's the way the media work. You have to be the same person when your life went mad in 2005 as you are years later when you have married and had a child.

I hear the way the Big Cheese and the little Baby Cheeses talk in the dressing room, the way they go about their business and the stuff they say to other players both on and off the field, and I realise how little the media know about what goes on inside a team. If you transferred the way he criticised people who'd made mistakes on the field to a playground or a workplace, this behaviour would be labelled as bullying.

Prior has always played the media game cleverly. And he does the managing upwards thing well. The schoolyard bully who is also the teacher's pet. You see him shyly smiling to himself as he is described as 'the heartbeat of the team', 'the voice of the dressing room', 'the moral compass of the England squad'. Please! The only description they got nearly right is the middle one. He's not the voice *of* the dressing room but he's definitely the voice *in* the dressing room. On and on and on.

I'm the one who's always getting hammered here. Why? I'm the easiest to take shots at. Meanwhile, a guy who calls himself the Big Cheese is strutting around the dressing room, showing off his new clothes and telling everyone about the amazing nights out he has. Out on the field, where he is described as 'vocal', he spends his time sledging his own team worse than the opposition sledge them. Every dropped catch is a personal insult to the Cheese.

Here in Australia the Cheese is having a good Test series. We know because he tells us all the time. Top Cheese. Straussy doesn't seem to mind what goes on in the dressing room: we are winning. Success papers over all cracks. I'm thinking, that son of mine could coach this team from the buggy. So many guys are on fire at the same time. Australia are so bad.

The real test is when things go badly and the pressure starts.

We are going to win this series. That will be enough for now, but anybody with a brain can see that under the surface all is not well.

We don't even need a second innings in Sydney. I hit 36 in our first innings but it's a small drop in an ocean of 644 runs. Australia have just rolled over and died in front of their own people. This must be the oddest Ashes series ever.

We go from the Ashes high into a couple of T20 games and seven one-day matches. We win a game in each format, and by the time we are going home the Ashes magic is gone and forgotten. There are cracks. I have to sort myself out. I feel my game is getting better but there is no consistency at all.

After a good day with the bat a voice in my head says, hey, you're an off-spinner, how exactly did you do that? You're a conman, Pietersen.

A conman, and now you've been found out.

That's where the insecurities come from. If I don't know how I did it, I don't know for certain that I can do it again. I can't be sure that I didn't just get lucky. Fordy's advice in South Africa had an instant effect, but some kink in my brain had me pushing too hard with it.

I have to find a middle ground. I'm taking too much to heart. Somebody calls me a genius – I laugh and say shut up, fool. Somebody calls me an idiot – I laugh and say the same thing. Shut up, fool.

After those bad days when I have played a shot so terrible I can't explain it, I stay away from all media. No newspapers. No TV. And I don't need two million Twitter followers reminding me about it for three or four days.

My game is bothering me and the dressing-room politics are starting to get to me. I've never been the tabloid version of myself. I certainly don't want to be anything like that now I'm married with a child.

I'm a person who finds comfort in my own space. People think because of the way you play, because you adopt a persona in cricket, that you are like that in real life. I'm quite the opposite off the field: most of the time I just need myself and my family.

There is an image that the media flog of me, where I crave attention twenty-four hours a day, seven days a week. I don't. I accept the attention that comes with being famous. I wanted to be famous, and I benefit from it, so I accept a certain level of intrusion. And to be fair, I probably courted it for the first eighteen months or two years of my career. It was fun, seeing yourself in the paper. You've come to England and seen all the glossy magazines and you think, that's quite cool, he's on holiday getting photographed. And you think it might be quite cool to be in the public eye in that way. But then I've spent quite a lot of time trying to take myself out of that. Jess has helped me so much because she understands that world and how to deal with it. Big parts of my life are off limits now. After Jess and I married we closed the window on our life together. We are very private.

We now have legal letters lodged with the editors of all the papers: they're not allowed to print pictures of our child. We get invited to every premiere of kids' movies. Bring Dylan, they say. We never go.

I know the Twitter thing is a constant, but I have a moody relationship with it. Sometimes it is fun. Sometimes I hate it. I've deleted it off my phone so many times, then reloaded it and then taken it off again.

From the time of that long Australian tour I started to feel the isolation in the dressing room. I didn't get attacked for mistakes the way other batsmen did (unless you count Flower's sourness), but there were always sly jibes about the IPL and my lifestyle.

The mistakes I made when I was younger never really went away.

One thing that has always kept the media amused is to say, that poor Kevin Pietersen: all he ever wanted was to be loved.

Half right. There was a time when it was true. Again, it's like walking out and taking your stance for an innings. It's about body language. I'm not as cocky as my image suggests. I'm as insecure as the next bloke, and when I first played for England I was desperate to be accepted. I started speaking the right language, using the right words, thinking it would make me more English. I got three lions inked onto my arm.

I took a while to realise that people listened to me trying out my new vocabulary in my South African accent and just dismissed me.

You're not English. Please stop saying you're English.

I think the wanting to be loved thing started there. Wanting to be accepted, to be like everyone else.

Now I've had three months of sitting in dressing rooms,

listening to guys talking non-stop about themselves, their lifestyles, their clothes, their cars, their looks, while I'm worrying about Dylan and Jess, or looking forward to speaking with my brothers or my close friends later on.

Have I changed, or have the Big Cheese and the Baby Cheeses changed?

Either way, there's a bad moon rising.

We had four days at home before heading off to India for the World Cup. That's four days to shake the jet lag, unpack and pack again. We have been away for three months. Four days at home, then we are going away for a competition that will run for two months.

Even during the break there was a little media fire to put out: a couple of the papers revealed their insider shit that I was planning to quit ODIs when the World Cup was over.

Then, almost as soon as we'd arrived home we were off again. After we arrived in India I spoke to Andy Flower about the dynamic in the team. I hated the undermining behaviour that had crept in. We were going to be together for two months, and it needed to be stopped. In fairness, we did eventually have a team meeting.

The meeting was by the nets behind the stadium in Bangalore ahead of practice the day before the India game. Flower and Straussy both talked about the on-field abuse towards our own players. We'd just come close to losing to the Netherlands. I'd spoken about the abuse on the field that Prior, Broad, Jimmy and Swann were giving the fielders. Then it was brought up again in a team huddle before training and Swann and Broad both disagreed with what Flower and Strauss had been saying. They argued that fielders should apologise to the bowlers if they've made a mistake. They felt that bowlers were well within their rights to be angry and aggressive towards the fielders. I just stood there and realised that it was the closest I've ever come to thinking I could willingly slap two guys on my own team.

Your coach and your captain are telling you to stop humiliating your players on the field, yet you think you are so much in the right that you are actually going to argue it? Are you fucking joking?

And that's the way it was. So although we went through the good times, I hated the bullying behaviour on the field.

To add to this, in the one-day series in Australia my stomach had been an issue. We had some scans done and they showed that I clearly had a hernia. I tried to continue playing, but it was a shambles. I missed a couple of games, but played in the last few before we came home. I was struggling.

At the World Cup, I had to come home after we played South Africa. The problem had been getting worse. I spent time getting treatment during the South Africa game, but I was done.

I literally couldn't run, it was so painful. I had been playing through pain for a month, and I have quite a high pain threshold. It was decided to send me home. It hurt to be leaving, but I had scarcely had any real time at home since October. The six weeks' recovery I was going to need would give me time with Jess and Dylan, and the chance to catch up with friends.

I had hardly got home before I was screwed in the media. Flower was quoted in the *Daily Mail* as saying:

Early days in
Pietermaritzburg

Maritzburg College. The place that taught me respect has to be earned

A skinny kid who never missed a place kick. And who learned the value of practice along the way

School cricket – the sport I turned to after a broken arm put an end to my rugby ambitions

A wide-eyed little off-spinner
from Pietermaritzburg.
Playing school cricket

Getting familiar with
the bat, Michaelmas
week 1996

Mum, Dad and me
on North Beach in
Durban

Once a buddy . . . Ashley Giles and I were buddied up together on my first tour, to Zimbabwe in 2004, and here we are nearly a decade later. That first England team was full of friendships that have lasted

My greatest batting partner, Paul
Collingwood

With Rahul Dravid during the 2011
Oval Test. Not only a great friend, but
a great inspiration too

Mum, Dad and me with my best mate
Jon Cole-Edwardes at the golf day we had to
raise funds for the JCE Trust

Jess and me in Sydney at the end of the 2006/7 Ashes

We've learned to avoid the
limelight, so this is one of
the few red-carpet pictures
you'll see of us

My world

The timing is not ideal because we are in the middle of the World Cup. We had very clear medical advice that this hernia problem Kevin's got wouldn't get significantly worse and he was at no risk of damaging himself further.

He wasn't going to tear anything so we hoped he would get through the tournament OK, take painkillers when needed and bite the bullet.

Kevin says it has got worse, pain-wise, and he can't carry on playing like this. So it was a pretty simple decision to replace him.

In the *Telegraph*:

He's had this problem for weeks. We have been managing it for a number of weeks. The very clear medical advice was that he wasn't going to tear it or damage it permanently by playing on. After playing against South Africa, his feeling was it was too sore to play international cricket.

He came out and basically told the hacks that he was disappointed that I didn't play on through the pain. He implied that the medical staff felt that I should have continued. A couple of the more favoured hacks tweeted this, trying to imply that it was a widespread view among the staff.

I sat at home, saying to myself, hang on, Flower, the medical staff said no such thing. They didn't. We discussed this. *You* sent me home. You decided that I couldn't continue because I couldn't run and there was no point in me being there. Now I wake up and there are headlines on the back pages of the papers, quoting you implying that I should have continued on this tour. I couldn't continue because I couldn't run. That was your call.

Talking to myself was pointless, so I rang him and asked a couple of questions.

Like:

What the fuck do you think you're saying? Who the fuck do you think you are to hammer me like that?

He was the usual Flower.

Oh, I haven't seen the media. Look, don't get so aggressive on the phone. I haven't said anything. I haven't seen the media.

Well, call me back once you have seen the media.

He did ring back later and vaguely acknowledged that he was in the wrong. He said, I don't expect you to talk to me in that way, though.

Well, you've just nailed me in the media. I don't expect you to talk about me in that way.

I reminded him again that I had played with the hernia pain for a good month. That he knew that. That he had made the call.

We left it there.

Then, of course, I gave away the moral high ground.

I went for a night out with a load of my mates and yep, I should have known, my photograph was taken because I was out with some famous people.

I was with James Corden and one of his mates, my agent and friend Adam Wheatley and my brother Bryan. We'd gone to my bar in Marylebone and then on to a place called The Box. Nicklas Bendtner, the Arsenal footballer, was in there that night. Paparazzi dream.

I was having surgery two days later so it didn't really matter if

I went out for a night. I wasn't going to be playing until I was repaired and rehabbed. I was back home after a long winter and hadn't seen my mates in months, so we went out. I think I had the right to do that, but it looked bad.

When I came round after my operation two days later the surgeon told me that there had been two bad hernias, not one. He'd looked after both to make sure I wouldn't be back under his knife in twelve months' time.

Two. No wonder I couldn't run against South Africa in Chennai.

Flower made a good call in sending me home. It was a pity he couldn't follow through with a little loyalty.

13

Say Hello *Poes*, Say Goodbye
Poes – Hitting the Shots

Play resumed for me in the summer Tests against Sri Lanka. In
Cardiff, I was out for 3.

Then it was back to Lord's for the second Test, and I was
determined to show some form. I played a silly shot and was
caught at gully by Tillakaratne Dilshan. I had outside-edged it. In
the second innings I hit a 72. Not bad.

The Big Cheese was reprimanded after smashing a window.
He was run out for four, and after he returned to the dressing
room his bat fell against a window and shattered the glass. Strauss
said, 'He holds all his bats against the wall and he put it there and
it bounced off the other bat and hit the window ... we are always

annoyed when we get out, especially run out, but that wasn't why the window got broken.'

My 72 soon looked like a flash in the pan as my form didn't pick up through the one-day series with Sri Lanka.

But, because I don't make a song and dance about it, a lot of people think that bad runs are just water off a duck's back to me. They aren't.

There is nothing about batting that I don't take seriously.

The most nerve-racking part is just waiting to bat. I've always hated the wait. In the dressing room, I watch every ball before I bat. I'm watching what the wicket is doing, I'm watching what the bowler is doing and, if I'm on the subcontinent, I'm watching how much the ball is spinning. I'll be talking to the lads, trying to be calm, but the nerves will have me hitting the toilet every five minutes.

Same every day: just knowing that it's time. But as soon as the wicket has gone and it's my turn the fear falls away. I'm released. I'm a free spirit. Now it's up to me.

I pick up my helmet and put my gloves on, then I'll test my grip on my bat on the way to the field. Then I'll know if I'm holding the bat in a good position or a not so good position. That's when I can be overcome by nerves again. I go to the crease and take my stance, and at that moment I usually know if I'm in for a good one.

Some days I'm in my stance and I know that I'm in full control. Other days I go out there and, oh shit, today is going to be a lottery. That can happen a few times in a Test series. It can even happen in an innings. I can feel good and then feel bad again. I don't know if it's fatigue or what.

The one mental weakness I've always had is focusing too much on how someone is going to get me out instead of just believing in myself and knowing where my strengths are. As Rahul Dravid said in the email he sent me: KP, you're good enough. Trust yourself.

I've struggled with that on numerous occasions, especially where the wicket is low and the first ball that bounces off the wicket isn't true. We're not winning. I'm hoping to set the tone and the wicket is low. I'm thinking of Fordy's words: get your head to the ball, lower your stance and play straight up the wicket.

I've fought more with myself in my head then I have fought with any bowler. I can destroy myself far more easily than any bowler. I can be destroyed before I hit a single ball.

Fast-forward to the summer of 2012, when we were playing South Africa. Forget about all the other stuff that went on: I was playing beautifully in the first innings, then Jacques Kallis got me out – he just bounced me out. He got some spring on a pitch; it bounced up at the body. I tried a hook but I gloved it and de Villiers caught me

I was mad. As soon as he gets me out Kallis starts slagging me because he is one of my mates. He has this way of dismissing me when he gets me out: he just says, goodbye *poes*. It's funny the way he says it, but in my head I'm thinking, I can't really be going out to this *doos* again.

Forty-two runs and then it's goodbye *poes*.

When I go out to bat in the second innings, it's a situation where we need to save the Test match. We're not batting well. Morné Morkel is bowling. I come in. Go through the same steps that I go through every time.

I ask the umpire for leg stump. I take my guard. I check where the field is. Just a normal habit. I'll look and then I'll put my head down and go into my stance, and when I do there's just something wrong with either my pick-up or the way I'm standing. It feels horrendous. I look up at Morkel and wonder, how am I going to score a run here? He's bowling fast. I'm feeling all at sea as I pick my bat up. I'm going to do terribly. I'm dog meat. I get dropped by Kallis in the slips on the second or third ball.

Lucky me. Kallis holds back on his farewell.

A few balls later Morné knocks my stumps out of the ground. *Poes* makes his goodbye walk.

I walk over to the pavilion thinking that just two days ago I walked out here and felt amazing. Now I walk off the field not knowing which end of the bat I'm meant to hold. It is scary how much a part of my career that kind of mental conflict has been.

Everybody has the same version of me. I'm so confident, I'm so arrogant. I'm so in control. But throughout my batting career I have been fighting epic battles in my head.

Conveying arrogance at the wicket has always been about using my body language as a defence mechanism. Never let them see a weakness. Never let them know there is a war going on in your head.

I've always tried to simplify things by just batting straight lines, and I'll get to ten runs before I try to do anything expansive. You're out there thinking, shit, how am I going to get to ten? The answer is always to keep it simple. In that first period you have the weight of expectation, you have the verbal abuse from the opposition, you have the crowd on your back. It's a big deal.

I will talk to anybody who might have the key to unlocking this. I love talking cricket on that level. I love it if I can pass something on to a young player, and if I can learn from somebody I respect, same thing. I have worked with Mark Bawden, the former England cricket psychologist, quite a bit.

I was fascinated by Mark's line of thought about positivity and understanding what is happening in your brain; being conscious of how it works and how you can deal with pressure by knowing that the pressure is just one part of your brain trying to protect you. Mark is a fan of the Steve Peters model – the Chimp Paradox – and we have gone through that work together. The whole idea is that succeeding is basically a matter of keeping your inner chimp in check.

There is an emotional side and a logical side of your brain. The emotional side tries to protect you when you are vulnerable. Sometimes I'm batting and I am thinking, shit, he's bowling fast, how am I going to play this? How am I going to survive? That's the emotional side of my brain trying to look after things, trying to raise awareness to the point where I say, right, there's an issue here.

The logical part of the brain then needs to whirr into action. I've practised this for hundreds of hours. Can I go out and play? Of course I can. Can I defend? Of course I can. Have I practised this? Yes. Am I actually under that much pressure here? No, because I've practised this. I'm good.

So go out there and enjoy it.

When you start fighting with the emotional part, when you are giving it too much time and you start just believing what that side of your brain is telling you, that's when you unplug the logical part of your brain and the trouble starts. That's when you get into issues. I've done a lot of work on this with Mark and I've enjoyed it. I've also noticed a difference since we started working together. Small things.

I remember playing a county game with Surrey, and coming to the end of a long innings. I was fielding. The batsman hit the ball high, really whacked it, and I stood under it and had time to think for a second. I thought, you've caught these so many times before, thousands of them since you were a kid. Once I had that thought it was as if I had caught a million balls perfectly: I was never going to drop it. A few of the guys commented afterwards how relaxed I looked. Logic had won. If my brain had said, uh-oh, drop this and you'll look like a twat, things might have been different

That's just a simple example of the technique I've used and worked on. It has really helped me take so much pressure off, even in very stressful scenarios.

A regular criticism of me is giving my wicket away cheap. I can be playing well but then I'll take a shot that's too ambitious and I will come off. People will be saying, what was that? What were you thinking? They've got a man on the boundary and you still try to hit it for six? Why are you doing that in the second innings?

How can I explain? I think it's that I'm stuck with a see ball, hit ball mentality. If I see a ball, I'm going to hit it. I believe I can pick the spot where I want to hit it, and I can't break down the process of the bad shots any more than I can for the good ones. As often as people ask me why I played that dumb stroke to get out, they ask me, how did I think to play some beautiful stroke that they have remembered for years? Same answer: I don't know.

I see something in my head and the shot almost invents itself. The ball is coming and I'm thinking, can I hit this for six? All of a sudden it's over. I may be wrong sometimes. I may be right more times. I just can't control it. Instinct takes over. I'm a batter who's on the ball as soon as the bowler's at his mark. As soon as he turns, I'm on it. And this is what happens in the next three or four seconds while he's running up. What field has he set? Which side is he holding it? Is he holding it cross-seam? Is he holding it on the shiny side? What's he trying to do? Is he trying to swing it away? Is it starting to reverse? Then, this is where I think it's going to be. And if it goes right – *whack*. And away it goes.

People say, why the hell did you do that?, and I really can't explain why I did it. A spinner will come on. I will think, okay, I'm going to hit him out of the ground – I have to think that. And I know I can hit him out of the ground so I go for it. Next thing, I'm walking back to the pavilion listening to the silence. Just a voice in my head.

Why did I just do that?

I ask myself before the press or the coaches ask me. Why did you take that shot? Were you not playing for the team? Well, I was always playing for the team, but I'm a risk-taker by nature. Risk equals reward in my life. They say cricket is an individual sport, but it's a team sport played by a series of individuals. In cricket, there *is* an i in team because you have to contribute an individual performance for your team to win. I'm an individual who plays for a team. I'm not on my own. The guys are watching, my stats are brought up and everything is there for everybody to see. If I don't perform in my individual position I'm toast. What we do as individual performers decides how we do as a team.

Some days people tell me I'm a genius. Some days they tell me I'm a donkey. I just do what feels right at that moment. It's my personality: if I want something, I want it now. Ask Jess: she's always saying, stop, just wait, tomorrow we will make the decision. Jess always says to me, no, if you still want it tomorrow we will get it. Like I'm a kid. That's how she talks to me! To be fair, I need that. Jess not only has the ability to keep me grounded, to keep me humble: at the same time she can make me appreciate and be proud of what I've done, and encourage my more adventurous side.

The sense of adventure has never been coached out of me. To be honest, I'm not sure it could be coached out of me and I wouldn't really want it to be either

I like not knowing what is next.

Sri Lanka went home in June 2011. India arrived in July. We started at Lord's. The two thousandth Test in the history of cricket, and the hundredth between India and England. I hit 202 in the first innings: 202 not out as Straussy declared at that point. It took me past six thousand Test runs. Six thousand in six years.

As I say, I like not knowing what is next.

Suddenly I was playing beautifully. I started to think positively and really focus in. It gave me comfort to know that I was playing well, that this was my time to cash in and just enjoy it.

I really nailed it because I played positively, I played aggressively, and it is times like that that you really enjoy because you know that anything can happen the next day. Even when you're playing well, you know that you're only going to be playing well for a certain amount of time. Then, inevitably, there will be time when you are not playing well. That's the great thing about cricket: you can be king one day and mucker the next day.

And it was true of that Test at Lord's. I got 202 not out, then in the next innings I got 1. That happens, and you just have to accept it. Circle of life.

In the fourth Test against India I hit 175.

No more Test cricket was scheduled until we hit Dubai in January 2012 for the first Test against Pakistan. The touch, the mojo, the muse, the good luck . . . Whatever it was, it was back.

For now.

14

Yes, and the Answer is No

Sometimes when things are going well and you are happy it is easy to forget that trouble is out in the hallway, doing press-ups.

As spring 2012 rolled around we were in Sri Lanka. I was playing beautiful cricket.

In the first Test match I got 30 and knew there was better to come. We moved on to Colombo for the second Test.

What happened there is up with my greatest Test hundreds. Because of the heat – I sweat easily and can't handle myself when hot weather comes with suffocating humidity – Sri Lanka can be an incredibly tough place to play cricket. I'd never thought I'd get a hundred out there. I'd been on a couple of tours and figured that if I ever had to bat for the amount of time it takes to make a century I would be reduced to a pool of water in the grass. Throw in hitting the ball and running about as well? No way.

That week, Colombo was just ridiculous. They'd turned everything to max: 45° heat and 100 per cent humidity. Enough to liquidise me. And I scored 151.

I had practised brilliantly leading into that Test match: I was hitting the ball as well as I'd ever done. I knew that if I was going to score a hundred in Sri Lanka it would have to be quick; I couldn't grind it out.

I'd got the Sri Lankan net bowlers to bowl at me for half an hour the day before the match. Come on, you try to get me out: this is a challenge. Come on! These amazing, really competitive guys will let you know when they've got you out because they're high-fiving their mates at the mark. High-fiving because they've got KP out. But they couldn't do it that day. It was one of the cleanest half-hours of cricket I've ever had. I was hitting every ball. A slog sweep coming down the wicket – hitting it for six. Reverse sweeping. Hitting it over extra cover. All the positive moves I wanted to take into the next match were working. I normally go to sleep every night after training thinking, have I done everything that I want to, so I know I'll be successful the next day. That night, I had the best sleep.

In the session and a half in which I scored 151 I went through nine pairs of gloves and changed my top three times. It was crazy how hot it was. But I got them quickly. I was positive from ball one. A spinner came on and I just whacked it. A blistering pace, because I had to. It was so hot and so flat

I knew I could dominate the seamers. And although I was more circumspect against their best bowler, Rangana Herath, I still went after him. And the others, after the previous day's practice: I just took them to the cleaners. It was my twentieth Test century. Mum and Dad were there too, so it was an incredibly special feeling. One of the best memories I have of my days in an England shirt.

But of course something was brewing.

I had a meeting with Andy Flower in Sri Lanka at the end of the Test series, just before I went to India for the IPL. I said that we needed to have a serious look at my schedule: I couldn't keep playing so much cricket. I was fraying at the edges.

The crowded schedule wasn't a new issue. I'd had a meeting with a psychologist as far back as 2010 when we were on tour. Just before I had been dropped for the one-day series against Pakistan. Remember, to show me that I could be dropped. No mention of rest or burnout. The psychologist's verdict was that the management had to ease up and take some of the weight off my shoulders.

So now I was putting the case to Flower again. He said, you understand that I am the one who makes these decisions and not you. I'll think about it.

I had by then been playing international cricket for eight years. It was a serious request. I had been making the point for months, yet I was always made to play every practice game, every warm-up game, and that was just frustrating and pointless.

I came away from the meeting feeling pretty much as I always did whenever Flower and I had contact. Depressed. Disappointed. Annoyed. Patronised.

Lots of you reading this will be thinking, don't play in the IPL, then. For me, the IPL has become a fact of life. I love playing in India. I cherish the friendships, the atmosphere, the colour and the drama of IPL cricket. I love the ambition of the whole thing, and I'll be brutally honest with you here: I don't think there's anyone on this earth who would turn down the opportunity to earn that sort of money in the space of six weeks.

I know, I know, tut-tut. We've strayed into mercenary territory again. A gentleman doesn't talk about money. I should be embarrassed about these things. But money is important. I am a sportsman with a very limited shelf life – I could hope to play until my late thirties at the very best, assuming I manage to stay injury-free. I have a family to support and I simply can't say no to the sort of money the IPL offers when I don't know what's around the corner. I could be injured tomorrow and never play another day's cricket in my life.

A professional sports career is a short thing. You make yourself the best player you can be and you make yourself and your family as much money as you can while your career is still burning bright. I might as well be frank about it.

The century in Colombo had given me huge confidence going into the IPL. I was looking forward to playing with the Delhi Daredevils, and the warm reception that always greets me in India.

Delhi had bought me from the Deccan Chargers, where I'd gone after Royal Challengers Bangalore, and I hit form in front of my new home crowds. I played eight games and got well over three hundred runs, and had a fantastic time in an atmosphere that was always electric. I didn't have any injuries leading into it and I continued to play really well.

For some of the guys in the England dressing room, even the ones who are the most sanctimonious about the IPL, I know deep down that's the life they want. They are competitors and professionals. Of course they want to be there. They see the way the game is going. They want the IPL and the Big Bash and the feel of the big time.

Of course they do. But what are they going to do? Walk around saying they wish they were doing what I am doing? No. They're going to complain about mercenaries right up to the moment that somebody makes them an offer. Then they won't be complaining. Not with their mouth full, having bitten off the hand of their new paymaster.

These guys know that and I think there is a lot of bitterness towards me because of the IPL. When there is bitterness and resentment I know I should just hold my peace and allow them their moans, but sometimes I think, screw you, why should I? Mistake.

When I was signed by Delhi I didn't pay much heed to the fact that I was the only member of the England World T20-winning team to secure an IPL contract. I probably should have sensed there was something stirring.

I had to finish early with Delhi Daredevils in 2012; I went back to England to play Test cricket, missing two or three round-robin games and the IPL semi-finals. From mid-May, we were playing three Test matches against the West Indies, and one afternoon, instead of watching the lads I decided to watch Delhi on the television instead. The time difference was perfect: Delhi is four and a half hours ahead, so the IPL's evening matches start in the afternoon, English time.

I went off into a different room to see how the Delhi lads were getting on. A piece of my heart was still with them, but it was a huge mistake. I should never have done it. It wasn't right. I am embarrassed to think of it now. I hold my hands up and admit I should never have done it.

It was bad manners. Bad for the England team. Bad politics on my part. I knew that some of the main gripes players had with me were to do with the IPL. That I spent too much time talking about it. That it was too important to my season. Now I was off in another room watching it while my England teammates were playing outside.

I watched Delhi because I had an emotional attachment to the team. I still have. When I was with England, my relationship with Flower was always a cloud that blocked the sun. But he hadn't the power to make me go out on the balcony and watch England play, so I didn't that day. Bad mistake on my part. I wasn't hurting Flower. I was hurting myself and my teammates.

Around that time, I launched a missile at Nick Knight, a member of the Sky Sports commentary team. Knight retired from cricket a year or two after I came to England. He played seventeen Tests and a hundred one-day internationals, and like most retired cricketers, the longer he has been retired the better he was. Though to be honest, I never thought he was a great player. After retirement, he worked his way into the commentary box and, continuing in an honest vein, I've never found him to be particularly great at that either. He shows a better sense of balance sitting on the fence all the time than he ever did on a cricket pitch.

The game moves at an incredible pace but Knight is one of these commentators who you actually mute because he's just so boring. When I first heard him commentating on the Test matches I was like, how on this earth . . .?

So one day I just tweeted a question:

Can somebody please tell me how Nick Knight has talked his way into the commentary box for home Tests. Ridiculous.

Blue flashing lights in my rear-view mirror straight away. The ECB pulled me over. They said they were going to have to fine me.

Fine me? Why?

For your tweet.

The whole dressing room was talking about Nick Knight. Even Flower found him dull, and if Andy Flower finds you dull . . .

I had misjudged the dynamics, though. Nick Knight came to me after I tweeted and said, 'If you get into trouble it's not because of me – I don't mind what you tweeted. But, just to let you know, something might happen.'

So I knew then that the something which might happen was that the head of Sky Sports was going to call the head of the ECB.

Sky and the ECB are tight. £260 million of Sky's money was

riding on a rights contract with the ECB. So Sky have power and they have money, and the ECB are hugely obliged to respect that. So if Sky told the ECB that one of their players couldn't say mean things about a Sky commentator, I imagine the reaction of the ECB would be to ask if Sky wanted me publicly executed or discreetly disappeared.

The ECB fined me three thousand pounds – for breaching the conditions of the player contract regarding public statements – and they held another five thousand back from my earnings, for any misdemeanours that might arise in the future. I felt like I had bought five grand's worth of tweets.

I asked them if they had done the same when Swanny had slaughtered me in the book he brought out the previous year, saying I was unfit to be captain. I don't mind what Swanny says, but technically that would have been a breach of the same thing.

No.

So explain to me where the ECB stand. A current player can criticise another current player in his book and it's okay. I can query something on Twitter about a Sky Sports commentator and I get fined three thousand pounds. How does this work?

They couldn't give a proper explanation. They said they would put a press release out.

Cool. Can we do that tomorrow so I can see what it says?

Certainly.

I awoke the next morning and it was already out. I hadn't seen a word of it. I got on to Hugh Morris right away. He replied that it had been an oversight as he had been rushing to get the statement out. He hoped it hadn't caused me too many problems.

Well, actually it has, mate. I wake up and there are people hammering me here, there and everywhere. And you guys have gone back on your word.

It's strange to think that the cricket career of pretty much everyone playing today began in the time before Twitter. Now it is a fact of everyday life. I experience a lot of scandals and controversies through the medium of Twitter.

Swings and roundabouts. For me, Twitter has brought good things: a chance to communicate without the filter of journalists; a means of killing untrue media stories about me; some fun. Lots of fun. It's a very engaging form of media.

Twitter is also very hard if you are playing matches in the public eye. You open yourself up for all kinds of abuse that you see as soon as you turn your phone on. You've had a bad game, you feel like crap and there it is. What several hundred people think of you.

Even in the middle of the good stuff, on the great days, you'll find someone who will abuse you. It's human nature to hold on to the bad stuff and mull over it instead of appreciating the good stuff. So you have to have really thick skin to be on Twitter day after day. I qualify on that basis, but still, during an Ashes series or something big, if I get out to a stupid shot I won't check my mentions for a few days, until it's calmed down. And when I do eventually re-engage with those who follow me, I ignore everything that has been said during the three previous days and start fresh.

The best value I get from Twitter, though, is being able to defend myself without things being twisted. I think for me it's been really good because it's been able to quash certain stories, like when John Etheridge published an 'exclusive' in the *Sun* about how I had given back a gift that the ECB had presented me with. I just tweeted a picture of me in the house with the gift and killed it straight away. John Etheridge apologised. A lot of journalists can give it out; Twitter is a way of handing it back to them. Mostly, they can't take it.

Sometimes, the power of the thing amazes me. I was sitting on an exercise bike a while ago, wondering about this drink they sell in the gym I go to. I tweeted a picture of it, asking if anybody knew where I could buy it in bulk. Two days later, three crates of the stuff turned up on my doorstep. Thank you, by the way!

If somebody abuses me, I try not to respond when I am angry. That usually ends up in the media. Instead, I'll sometimes have a look at their profile and stuff. If they've got a really bad profile picture, I might have a bit of a joke about that. A guy had a go at me a while ago – just the usual stuff: arrogant piece of shit why don't you fuck off back to South Africa. On his profile, he'd got a head-and-shoulders photo and a fringe that looked like a barcode. So I said, mate, I think you might want to go and check your fringe out #barcodefringe. People retweet it and laugh at the guy, and after an hour or so he decides he doesn't like this Twitter game after all. Then I block him anyway and move on.

In the lead-up to the summer international series in 2012 I had gone to the ECB and told them what they already knew: I was playing too much cricket. I was one of the only members of the team who was playing all three forms of cricket and consistently being asked to play in every warm-up game. There was no let-up. We needed some sort of agreement to look at my schedule going forward. Not just my schedule, but anyone's in a similar position. All the senior England players. First, because a player's rest needs to be managed and scheduled as much as his playing time. Second, because I believe senior players have earned the right to have opportunities. Not being available for the duration of events like the IPL hurts other England players not just financially but in terms of the experience they could be bringing to the side.

Look at the England schedule for the summer of 2012. I came back from India for the three-match series against the West Indies at home. That was followed by the three-match ODI series and one T20 game against the same opposition. Then Australia checked in for a five-match ODI series before South Africa turned up for three Tests. When that finished we were supposed to play a one-day game against Scotland, five one-day internationals against South Africa and, finally, three T20 games against South Africa. To me, that shows a lack of understanding of the needs of senior players.

I went to the ECB with a full-on presentation I had drawn up with a friend of mine on the issues involved for senior players. It was received with open arms. They understood it and we had a very positive meeting. The next day ...

I got 230 for Surrey v Lancashire at Guildford. I walked off the field and journalists wanted to talk. Give me ten minutes, I said. Then: okay, shoot. First question: what is this about your meeting with the ECB concerning your schedule?

Ah. Round up the usual suspects. Somebody in the ECB has leaked something. When there is no rational argument, someone leaks to undermine you. Then, as the guardians of the game, the ECB turn down your request.

Following the second Test against the West Indies I made an announcement:

After a great deal of thought and deliberation, I am today announcing my retirement from international one-day cricket.

With the intensity of the international schedule and the increasing demands on my body, approaching thirty-two, I think it is the right time to step aside and let the next generation of players come through to gain experience for the ICC World Cup in 2015.

I am immensely proud of my achievements in the one-day game, but still wish to be considered for selection for England in Test cricket. For the record, were the selection criteria not in place, I would have readily played for England in the upcoming ICC World Twenty20.

The background to this was that although I wanted to continue playing T20 games, the ECB had taken an all-or-nothing stance. I had to retire from both forms of the limited-overs game or retire from neither.

In all the media hoo-ha before the summer Test series there was an undercurrent that I could retire at the end of the South African Tests to pursue a freelance career with the IPL. I'd perhaps just play Test cricket and the IPL – that's what was written. Often.

It felt like I was being railroaded in that direction. I needed to make a decision in terms of my career. I had retired from limited-overs cricket. I had been playing far too much, and I wasn't enjoying being coached by Andy Flower. I hated playing for England under him. There was a clique in the dressing room that I could not stand because of the way they bullied players if they misfielded.

It seemed that I potentially had the opportunity to play for England and yet still be free to pursue the IPL and all the other tournaments around the world.

I thought about it. Either I could control my own destiny and become a freelance cricketer, or I could prove everybody wrong and just keep on existing under the rule of Andy Flower and the ECB. If I took one path I would be happy, but I would miss the satisfaction that playing for England still brought me. If I went the other way I was guaranteed to be unhappy.

I worried about it for a while, and talked to people close to me. Eventually, I attempted a compromise.

Two days before the South Africa series began I spoke again to the ECB and offered to rescind my retirement from the shorter forms of international cricket if I was allowed to play a full IPL season in 2013. That would mean missing two early-summer Tests against New Zealand.

The ECB and Flower issued a definitive no.

Of course, many dismissed my proposal as being purely mercenary.

Contrast this with the attitude in New Zealand. Back in 2010, New Zealand Cricket had the foresight to make an eight-year deal with their players, allowing a participation window of at least five weeks for the IPL. At the time I was asking to miss the early Tests – which, though nobody in the ECB will ever say it, attract very little attention – it was already known that the top guys like Brendon McCullum, Ross Taylor and Daniel Vettori would be arriving in England late if they were still playing in India. The 2013 IPL was down to start on 3 April and to run until the end of May. New Zealand's first Test match would start on 16 May, so the players would miss all the warm-up games and turn up a couple of days prior to the Tests starting. The top New Zealand cricketers make more than the All Blacks, but nobody throws stones at them and calls them mercenary.

Instead, New Zealand Cricket has a really great attitude that the players can get behind. Ross Taylor made a good point:

New Zealand Cricket has done a very good job (by keeping window open during IPL). We don't have the same depth of players like some of the other countries, so it is good that our players come and play in the IPL. Ultimately by playing in IPL, the players get to play for NZ for a longer time. The way it has gone, NZC knows that to keep the players playing for as long as possible, both the board and the players will have to give in a little bit.

Nobody in the England hierarchy was keen on 'giving in a little bit'.

People were now speculating that the third Test against South Africa, at Lord's, might be my last for England. I had never given that as an ultimatum. I had no desire whatsoever to retire from

Test cricket. Test cricket was and always will be the pinnacle of my career. But I started to wonder if maybe these people were right. Maybe it would be my last Test. Maybe that was what everybody wanted.

15

Good Knock, Shame about the Press Conference

S omewhere in India, spring 2012 . . .
    Morné Morkel and I are doing our routine. Looking forward to the summer when we will play against each other in the Test series in England.

Warm up early, KP, I'll be getting Straussy out pretty quick and in no time you'll be out there.

See you then, *boet*. I am coming for you, Morras. I am going to annihilate you. You will be dropped by the second Test. Plan your holidays.

KP, my friend, I'm going to knock you over.

Fast-forward to the Oval, July 2012. Morné bowls poor

Straussy out before he has even rubbed the sleep from his eyes, then goes right for me in the first innings. I get away with it, but he bowls me out in the second. Have a look at his celebration – my wicket meant a lot to him. It's the same for me: he's a guy I do not want to lose to. I am close to Kallis. I am close to Dale Steyn. I am close to Morné. That's the South African bowling attack. Maybe the best in Test cricket. And as close as those friendships are, they make me want to play harder against them on the field.

I love those guys. I hate losing to them.

Some people don't understand that.

Second Test, Headingley.

Unbelievable! I cannot tell you how good a bowler Steyn is and that is as dismissive, even more violently dismissive than the last shot he played to the boundary. I mean, he played him as if he is a little off-spinner and he has lobbed him out of the park . . .

Match commentary, second Test.

We had lost the first Test against South Africa at the Oval.

It was around then that I was made aware by another senior player that some of the guys were laughing about a parody Twitter account, KP Genius, and it looked as if it was coming from inside the dressing room. That put me in the blackest mood. Just totally down.

I'd seen the account a while back, and knew it was growing in popularity. I thought the humour was pretty hit-and-miss, but when it was funny I saw the joke as clearly as anybody and enjoyed it. People see me in a certain way: I often play on that, and the parody played on that too. Me texting Barack Obama: Dear Barack ...

So I'd laughed along, but then had recently started to notice that the tone of the tweets was getting more snide. Guys I played with and toured with were following the account. Other guys were gleefully retweeting stuff from it. It wasn't so much what was being said as the fact that it was being done behind my back. And by my teammates. Again, if you transfer this behaviour to a schoolyard or office, it would be called bullying.

I was left feeling isolated and bullied, but nobody seemed too bothered as long as I did my performing-seal routine when I went out to bat.

Jimmy Anderson's birthday was the day before we all met at Headingley for the second Test, and he threw a party at his house in Manchester. I didn't go – couldn't face it. I was the only one not there. At Headingley I was incredibly fragile and emotional. This could be my last Test match, I kept telling myself.

I trained badly. I got very insular. Didn't speak to anybody. We fielded first. I didn't say a word all day. Not a word. It was the worst day of Test cricket I have ever had. I knew I didn't want to be there. I would rather be anywhere else than in that team. I knew what was going on off the field. What they were saying about me behind my back.

To make things even worse, I was concerned about my career and my commitments, and what was being leaked about my concerns. I felt that I was being shunted out of the England set-up. This made me even more paranoid. It was incredibly bad timing, with so many strands coming together. I felt ridiculously emotional.

So, day one and not a word on the field. Everybody knew something was up. Even the South Africans. I finished the day's play and left the ground. I got back to the hotel, very unhappy, and ate on my own in my room.

I got to the ground next morning. Still not talking.

Some of the senior players – Anderson, Prior, Broad – pulled me into the back room of the dressing room and said tenderly, what the fuck is going on?

I said, guys, look, I am incredibly emotional. I think this could be my penultimate Test match and after that I might never play for England again. I am wrapped in emotion. I was nowhere yesterday.

They said, well, it isn't good enough. You know what a big player you are. We have a debutant in our team. You need to pull yourself together.

I held up my hands and said, I'm really sorry.

Did they ask where it was coming from? What was troubling me? Why would they say that when they knew the can of worms they would open?

To me, the Twitter business and all the behind-my-back smirking was a clear case of bullying. People couldn't say the same things face to face, but they felt they could do it through the sneakier ways of social media. Hunting in a pack.

Whenever I have criticised anybody on Twitter it has been under my own name. The same with any newspaper articles, or this book.

It rained that morning. Andy Flower then called me into the

back room before the delayed start. He said, what is going on? Why aren't you talking to me? I know you aren't talking to me – are you upset?

I told him.

I have no interest in being here. I don't want to be here. I know what is going on in this dressing room. The guys have this Twitter account about me. It's just all making me incredibly unhappy.

And I started crying in front of Andy Flower of all people.

Why should I want to play for this team? Why do I want to be here when this is going on? What have I done to deserve this? I don't want to play for you. I don't want to play for any of those guys in this dressing room. That is how this is making me feel.

His response was one of embarrassment.

Oh, I don't think they are doing that. I don't know how we can resolve this.

I just repeated to him that I didn't want to play with these guys or for him or the ECB.

I am sitting here right now in front of you, crying and saying that I do not want to play for you guys.

It was also during that meeting with Flower that I said to him – for what was the second time – that I didn't think James Taylor should be playing for England. That he was the wrong choice.

I have nothing against James, but the fact is, at five foot six he's one of the shortest men currently playing county cricket. His dad was a jockey and James is built for the same gig. We were facing the fiercest bowling attack in world cricket; I didn't think he was up to it.

On the drive up to Leeds I had called Flower on the phone. Ravi Bopara had pulled out for personal reasons and James Taylor had been selected in his place.

Next in line should have been Eoin Morgan. I rang and asked Andy Flower, in my usual sweet way, how on earth have you picked Taylor? Why is Morgan not playing?

I bet I know why. Because when you asked Eoin to come back from the IPL he told you to go and do one. He told you that he was in India earning money; why should he come back and play county cricket? That got him a black mark. You were never going to help him again, and that's why he isn't playing.

More silence. Then:

No, no, no.

Again, it was nothing personal against James. As a senior player you have these conversations about other players all the time. As a professional you have to get used to being evaluated by other professionals. We all know that often when we have been selected or dropped the decision has come after a discussion in which somebody we know has argued our case and somebody else whom we know has argued against us. It's very rarely personal. Going in against Steyn, Morkel and company, I didn't think Taylor was good enough. And I had a right after the eighty-seven Test matches I had played to offer an opinion about who I thought should be playing in the team.

There is private and there is public. When the South Africans were sledging Taylor at Headingley it was me who stood up and told them to wind their necks in.

Not long afterwards an article appeared in the *Telegraph*, saying that I had criticised Taylor on his Test debut, in the dressing room in front of the rest of the team. An absolute fantasy. Never happened.

But the poor guy has never been seen again. He played at Headingley and at Lord's, and Flower didn't even pick him for the tour to India later that year. So I was wrong about Taylor, was I?

Will James Taylor make it? I don't know, but good luck to him if he does. He wasn't ready then: that was my only argument. And I made it privately. To the coach.

The second Test should have been a happy event for me. I scored my twenty-first Test century and became the fastest batsman to seven thousand Test runs. I beat the record of South Africa's captain Graeme Smith. Beat him by . . . what was it? A year.

I also played what was probably the greatest shot of my life.

I'd hit Dale Steyn over his head for six. I'd hit him through extra cover for six. I'd pulled him for six. And I just knew what he was going to do. He was running up a little quicker, so I knew he wasn't going to bowl too full, just a great length. I knew I could wait for it and punch it through midwicket, where they'd left a gap. When I'm that confident, sometimes the ball just comes at me as if it's been bowled in slow motion, and this was one of those times. And I thought, my goodness, you're batting pretty well here. Slow hands, slow motion. And off it went. I remember looking up at the big screen after playing the shot and seeing Steyn's reaction magnified for the whole ground to see. He looked at whoever was at midwicket.

Fuck me, that's a hell of a shot.

I took four wickets, too. Not bad for an old off-spinner.

To this day I don't know how I scored that hundred. I was

deeply unhappy every moment I wasn't batting. There can be a comforting solitude about batting. I often find peace there. The simple act of hitting the ball with the bat and doing it well has been part of my life for so long that it offers reassurance when things are going badly elsewhere.

When I got out, it was early in the morning. We were all gone a quarter of an hour before lunch. I then had a long stint bowling and some time in the field as the match went to a draw on the fifth day. Emotionally, I was still totally gone. The buzz from scoring the century had quickly vanished.

I know that I should never let emotion get in the way of my job. I don't like it when people use their feelings as a cop-out or an excuse. That day, though, I was totally overcome by emotion. I didn't speak to anybody, just walked around the field like a zombie for ninety overs.

I was depressed and unhappy. And I was heading into the eye of the perfect storm.

In May, after the leak about our confidential meetings and I had announced my retirement from one-day international cricket, I was for a period only available for Test cricket. Then on 9 July, during the third Test against the West Indies, I announced that I might return to one-day cricket in the future. I still hoped to play T20 for England, and especially wanted to be involved in the World Twenty20 tournament that September.

All along there were leaks of confidential details of my talks with the ECB. Not just the details but, it seemed, providing guidelines for journalists: Here's what he wants. Why does he want it? Tired? Extraordinary schedule? Overused by us? No, no, no. What we think is that he just wants to be able to play a full series in the IPL. Shocking, isn't it? Talk soon. Hopefully your headlines will help this delicate situation.

So I wrong-footed them by announcing that I might just come back. More headlines.

By the time we were playing South Africa at Headingley a few weeks later, I had only half swallowed my scheduling issues and the troubles that the leaks had caused. I felt that the issue was still open and dialogue would be ongoing. During the Headingley Test, the ECB had announced the provisional World T20 squad. I wasn't in it.

I had been portrayed as the guy distracting the England dressing room from its work, but I had made an honest effort to find compromise and common ground. Now this. And every day I hated that England dressing room a little bit more.

The KP Genius business was eating away at me too. Through all the bullshit team talks, all the huddles and the times I would be told, c'mon KP, we need you big guy and so on, I would look around and wonder who was laughing about me behind my back. Who in this room was helping thousands of people to laugh at me? Why not say it straight out if it's being done in fun? That was one of mine, KP. Gotcha!

I trudged back to the dressing room that last evening in Headingley, feeling lower than a snake's belly. Normally at the end of a match when a player does well for the team somebody else will stand up and say a few positive words about that guy in the dressing room. We will raise a beer to him. I didn't want anybody to talk about me or talk to me or have a beer with me. I had got 149 runs and I just wanted to get out of there.

I can't remember who spoke. I said nothing. It all meant nothing.

I was so mentally fatigued that I was just lost. My body wasn't there. My head wasn't. Not in that room. Just nowhere. There is always joy if you score a Test hundred and somewhere inside I was incredibly happy with that, but I had no shared feeling. That day there was no team in I; the environment felt far too toxic. I am sure guys were happy with me in the moment and they said the right things, but I had absolutely no interest. Character is the stuff you do behind a guy's back.

If you are going to ridicule me in this snide way, if you are trying to grind me down, don't pretend to be my friend now.

That evening I gave a press conference. No choice there as I had been given the Man of the Match award. Rhian, the media manager, asked me something out of the blue before I went to the press conference.

Had I been texting the South African players?

I just said, texting the South African players?

She said, there is a rumour going around. So as you are Man of the Match and have to do the press conference, I'm just letting you know.

I just said, whatever. Not interested. Don't know.

I went straight to the South African dressing room. I had been messaging a couple of them, and I asked them, what the hell is this, guys? They said they had no idea. Blank.

We left it at that. No worries. I went and did the press conference. Not a single question about texts. All the questions were about how long I would play for England, about my innings.

Immediately after the game I had spoken to Jonathan Agnew for *Test Match Special*. He asked me about the rumours he'd heard that the third Test, at Lord's the following week, might be my last.

Rumours and leaks, same as ever, but if it was coming from Aggers I thought there was likely to be some truth in it. He has good sources. I was tired and I was down. I said how I was feeling:

'I can't give any assurances, no. I love playing Test cricket for England. But there are obstacles in the way.'

By the time I got to the press room the media were pulling those three short sentences apart like wolves at their dinner.

I tried to wave the issue away but it was too late. They had their teeth into the thing. I tried to tell them that there would be nothing said by me while the Test series was still on. Then I conceded a bit of ground: 'Maybe it will be my last. We will talk after the next Test. Anything is possible.'

After that it was a free-for-all. Is it the IPL? Is it being available for T20? Is it all about money? Is it about being with your family? Tell us, tell us, please tell us.

I ruled out money. It was 100 per cent not about money. I said there was a list of things that needed to be talked through. There were issues within the dressing room that needed to be resolved.

I said that it was tough being me in the England dressing room at that particular time. That line has haunted me ever since.

Looking back at the press conference, though, it was all quite low-key. It was just that the questions wouldn't stop. Nobody intervened to say, okay guys, just one more question . . . I tried to answer the questions without making the situation worse. But I could see where it was all going. Whatever I said, it would be written up the next day as a rant or an outburst or a threat. Kevin Pietersen, drama queen and diva, having a hissy fit. Same old, same old.

I called my agent, Adam, on the way out of Headingley and

told him I'd just done the press conference. I mentioned some of the stuff that I said. I could tell by the silence that this wasn't good. No surprise, then, when Adam simply said, oh fuck, and just went quiet again. I explained why I had said what I did. Adam wasn't convinced.

I know, mate, but this could create some serious shit.

Ah, we'll just see what they print and I'll talk to you in the morning.

He rang me first thing and said, this is not good. He was right. It did create some shit that was serious.

With the benefit of hindsight, the ECB and Andy Flower knew what my emotional state was during that Test match and they should not have made me do the press conference. I had said I didn't want to do it, but was told there was no choice. Andy Flower should have pulled me away from that press conference or somebody should have controlled the questions and saved me from myself.

I shouldn't have brought the team issues into it. Was it tough for me at that time? Yeah, but millions of people going to work every day weren't going to see it like that.

After the Headingley press conference Flower asked Matt Prior to call me – he thought that we were close – to go over the wreckage.

Why had I said what I did in the press conference?

I asked some questions in return. Can you, hand on heart, tell me that people are not slagging me off behind my back about the IPL and my career in India? All the jealousy and resentment towards me – I asked about that too.

I asked why anybody in the England dressing room would be following or retweeting a Twitter account that demeaned a colleague. Why would they allow themselves to be seen to be doing this?

I said that nobody had supported me over Swann's book. Nobody. Swann had said in print that I was unfit for the captaincy and you all kept your heads down. Nobody even came to me and said, sorry, that should never have happened, it's just offside. You don't do that.

It wasn't a useful phone call, but it was a taste of what was to come.

16

Doos and Don'ts of Textgate

Once Rhian had mentioned the rumour about texting I knew that the guts of the story would soon come spilling out. That's the beast you deal with when you are contracted to the ECB. Night follows day and a lot of English cricket people have their favourite journalists on speed dial.

Sure enough, the next week the papers had it that I had been texting the South Africans. Raining shit again.

I then had a meeting with Andy Flower, Hugh Morris and Andrew Strauss before the Lord's Test. They called me to a hotel in Beaconsfield. I can't recall the name even though I've driven past it so many times since. That's the sort of hotel it is. Somewhere to put you in your place.

In Beaconsfield they wanted to know my intentions. I

reiterated that I wanted to go back on my previous resignation from one-day cricket and commit to all forms of the game. I missed it. I knew I had a lot to offer.

They picked through all the rubble again. Why did you resign? Why did you do it?

I was happy to explain again, though I didn't feel that I was being listened to. My main gripe was that in every single game I played the level of interest in whatever I did on the field caused huge pressure. If I did well, great. If I did badly it was all gloom. There was no middle ground.

I feel that. I read it. I hear what's going on. I see it all. I absorb it. It grinds me down. All I wanted from Andys Flower and Strauss was to pull me back and look after my schedule. By using me a little less they would get more from me.

At the time, I was one of the three busiest players in the world in terms of the number of days' cricket I had played in the previous three years. MS Dhoni and Mike Hussey were the other two. I'd had enough. I was starting to get niggles. I said that I needed to be looked after better in terms of my schedule.

The meeting went okay. It's great that you want to come back. Brilliant, they said.

And then, as if they had just remembered something, they asked me about the text messages. Were you texting the South Africans?

I said no.

Why?

I was defensive and I didn't trust them, and I wanted to see where they would go with it before I came clean. I also suspected that anything that happened in that meeting would most likely be in the next day's papers.

So I said no.

They said, okay, well then, what we want you to do is sign a press release denying the claims that you have been texting the South Africans.

Okay.

I left the meeting and was driving back with Adam. He said, we could be in for a few problems here, mate.

I said that I thought the meeting had gone well. Adam wasn't happy.

They won't let that slip.

Aw fuck, it's fine. Let's see where it goes.

The ECB got on the phone to me later that day. They said they needed to do the press release. I said, no, I'm not doing it after all. They were insistent. They demanded that I come out in the media and say that I hadn't sent any texts. I refused.

Why won't you?

Well . . .

I didn't want to do a press release saying I didn't do it when I knew that I had. I was 99 per cent certain that they already knew that I had messaged my friends. I suspected they were playing a game – let him deny it and then expose him. My denial was just part of the game. Let's see where this goes, shall we?

They had their backs up now. Tetchy. Clearly, then, you have done it.

Here we go.

*

The next day Strauss called me on his own and we had a fine big dingdong. He accused me of having done it. I admitted that I had been in communication with the South Africans. Yes, but it was nothing bad. These guys are friends. You guys have been treating me like shit for three years. You've been acting like a dick to me. I went through example after example. The only thing I was guilty of was not defending my captain.

Then Straussy, the elder statesman, gave his view.

Banter in private messages = huge issue.

Bullying in the dressing room = princess-and-the-pea nonsense.

This is just bullshit, Straussy said.

Flower called me next and told me I needed to do the press release.

Actually, I don't think I do need to do it.

Oh no, you do.

No, I don't need to do anything. Plus I don't need you to tell me what I need to do.

I am suspicious about what the long game is: is he scheming so as not to select me for the upcoming India series? He'll drop me for the final South Africa Test first. Then let the story play out and cut me from the India Tests. So I say to Flower,

If I put this release out will you pick me for the Lord's Test match?

Well, I can't guarantee that.

Okay, I'm not putting the press release out there, then. You aren't going to pick me, so why should I? Good luck at Lord's.

And I put the phone down.

*

TEXTGATE! The inside story.

There were no text messages. I'd been using BlackBerry Messenger – BBM – to communicate with my friends. Who started it? I've no idea: it was just part of a rolling conversation I've been having with my friends for years.

When I scored the 149 against South Africa one of the players messaged me that night. The teams had been at war with each other out there, but he sent me a message to say well played, well done, outstanding, buddy – brilliant knock.

And he asked me, what was Andrew Strauss's problem? After the game we'd briefly been chatting together and Strauss walked past. He totally ignored the both of us. Made a point of it.

In his message, he used the Afrikaans word *doos* to describe how Straussy had behaved. I suppose the closest translation would be 'dick' or 'idiot'. To be absolutely clear, contrary to what some journalists have written a *doos* is not a cunt. It's nothing close to that. I say it in front of my mum and don't get into trouble. It's that kind of word, and any person who actually speaks Afrikaans will tell you that.

Anyway, I didn't disagree with the sentiment. It was a private message between mates letting off steam. Nobody writes a BBM expecting it to be analysed by millions of people. It was just chatter. He said that Strauss was carrying on like an idiot and that was it. It was nothing that I wouldn't actually say to Straussy myself, at the time or now.

It suited the ECB to use the messages as evidence of my open rebellion against Straussy. Strauss has written that he never entirely trusted me after that point. I find that disappointing as he seemed genuinely to accept my apology at the time.

Straussy wrote in his book that I had crossed the line when I mentioned the dressing room, implying that I was being treated badly in there by my teammates. He said that I seemed to be 'at best destabilising and at worst undermining the carefully cultivated team environment'.

It was an odd comment from a guy who had also said, 'Looking back I think it was wrong that some of our players were following that [spoof KP Genius] Twitter account. But I still don't think it's a justification for what Kevin did.'

If the player involvement with the parody account was wrong, what did that say about the 'carefully cultivated team environment'?

As for 'what Kevin did': I replied to a private message from a friend in which I didn't disagree with the statement that Straussy was being a *doos*. That was leaked to the media and blown up into a major betrayal. What does that say about the people who had done all the 'cultivating'? They cultivated a couple of trees and hung me off one of them to dry?

Was there never a time to say, this guy is having some difficulties here. How can we help?

And that was Textgate.

It was a bizarre situation.

I knew that, as much as they wanted to, they couldn't cut me unless the situation got a lot worse. I wasn't guilty of anything. We were in a phoney war (no pun intended). I knew there was nothing in the messages that would make it a big deal. I, however, thought that they wanted it to be a big deal.

I could understand what the reaction would be as the little

story was leaked, drop by poisonous drop. I could see that the little nugget of fact at the centre of the thing was becoming an avalanche of speculation and rumours and lies.

I was going to have a huge image problem to say the least. So it became a PR battle.

Not surprisingly, considering that I was born and reared in South Africa, I know some of the South African players. I had sent BBMs to some of those friends. No war crimes. Just friendly messages.

It was soon in the wires that I had texted the South Africans information about how to get Andrew Strauss out. In terms of useless information that would have been the equivalent of messaging them along the lines of: FYI the stumps are *behind* the batsman. Delete this message as soon as you have read it.

There were retired second-string club cricketers in Bradford who would have known how to get Andrew Strauss out. Bowl around the wicket.

The fact is, it never happened. I have never and would never give any tactical information about any of my England teammates to anyone on the opposing side. It goes right to the heart of me as a professional and me as a human being. I just wouldn't do it. Simple as that. As for bringing the news of Straussy's weakness to the best bowling attack on the planet? They wouldn't have known if I was being funny or just plain pathetic.

That was the crux. Did I provide them with information on the captain? No. Pure bullshit. It never happened. It was the second Test of the series and Morné Morkel had already got Andrew Strauss out bowling around the wicket. He had done it in the first Test at the Oval. With all this action-replay mumbo-jumbo and computer analysis he had somehow worked it out for himself.

Regardless of how far-fetched it was, the story was planted to make me look bad. So we had a stand-off.

I wasn't guilty of giving the South Africans information. I knew that. But can you prove something that you haven't done? No. Just denying it makes you look bad. Flower and the ECB knew that.

I said it again and again: these guys are my mates but there is no way in the world I was doing anything for them. How would I? Why would I? Look at how I played at Headingley. How can you even think that? I am playing for pure bragging rights if nothing else. You want to be better than your mates. It means more to beat them.

Yet in terms of wanting to get rid of me, just forcing me to come out and deny the Strauss thing might be enough. As I had thought, if they could get me to publicly deny first of all that there were any text messages and then discredit me on that, they could finish the job by pretending I had leaked information to the South Africans.

The stand-off continued. They announced they were dropping me for the third Test. South Africa won at Lord's and replaced England as the number-one team in world cricket.

The big thing I regret is getting Strauss involved at all, however inadvertently. We've had our problems but at heart he is a good guy. We were just going through a bad time in terms of our relationship.

They didn't want me to speak to the South Africans, to some of my closest friends. The Andys were very big on that. It was a

The one-dayers in South Africa, 2005. A huge test of my character and my first hundred, helped by brilliant captaincy from Vaughany. But I should never have kissed the badge . . .

One of the best shots of my career: the switch hit in evidence against Scott Styris at Durham in 2008

And a few weeks later against South Africa at Edgbaston

One of the best innings of my career: against Sri Lanka in Colombo
four years later

A highlight of my England career: the World Twenty20 in the Caribbean in 2010. Australia in the final

Me and Kieswetter whacking it everywhere

World champions!

A circus that I wanted to be part of: the IPL. Tens of thousands of fans in the stands. Millions more watching at home. Teammates and opponents drawn from the best players in the world

Playing for Royal
Challengers Bangalore
in 2010

Six thousand runs in six years has got to be worth celebrating – July 2011 versus India at Lord's

And on my way to 186 in Mumbai in 2012, en route to our first series victory against India since 1985

typical Andy Flower tick-box exercise: no fraternising. Straussy, the enforcer, pulled me away from South African friends on a couple of occasions, embarrassing me.

Strauss never liked what he called 'this KP and South Africa thing'. He was constantly telling me to distance myself.

I just said no. I have known these guys for longer than I have known most of you. They don't treat me the way you guys are treating me. I know what is going on with the Twitter account. I know it is from the dressing room. You guys don't want to believe it because it won't sit well with you for it to come out and for you to believe it. You can deny it as much as you want to deny it, but I know that it's going on.

The drama surrounding me definitely took away from Straussy's final Test match. I regret that and of course I take some of the blame. I've said before that even though I knuckled down and did my best when Straussy became captain, I was a little bit resentful of the success that he had after I was kicked out of the job.

My relationship with Straussy before the captaincy issue was certainly a lot better than it was afterwards.

He wasn't my captain back then: he was my buddy, my mate, my teammate. Then, a week into his captaincy, he told me in the Caribbean that I couldn't go home and see my family at a really tough time in my life. The way that he conducted himself, the distance he put between us straight away: I just didn't think that Straussy was my kind of guy any more.

And clearly I didn't have a relationship with Andy Flower at all. Flower and Straussy had become inseparable. I felt all alone in the dressing room.

When the Twitter stuff started Straussy didn't get it. Literally: he doesn't know anything about social media. For him, it's a different world. He has no interest. If somebody said to him that they had an account on Twitter he would just shrug and ask if the interest rate was better than at the high street building societies. If somebody said they were following a parody account on Twitter it would be meaningless to him.

Textgate was different.

I made mistakes. I am the first to admit that, but people definitely saw a chance to nail me for something that they knew to be just a bit of bad judgement. The media and the ECB closed ranks. On nothing but rumours I was convicted of the greatest betrayal since Judas.

Straussy chose to take it personally when he didn't need to.

The friendship I have with some of the South African guys goes way back. I've known Jacques Rudolph since he was sixteen, as we played against each other at school. He was at Affies, the Afrikaanse Hoër Seunskool in Pretoria, when I was at Maritzburg College. So we would play schools cricket against each other every summer. Then I played for Natal and he played for Northerns. Our relationship goes back ages.

Morné Morkel I've known for ten years. Again, a very good guy. We became close playing in the IPL together.

People looking on from the outside often ask how I can feel loyalty to guys who I play with for such a short period every year in the IPL. Well, what happens in the IPL is that the small number of foreigners on a team always end up staying on the same floor of the hotel. It's not like being on tour where there is a large number of people and you are always on the move. It's usually just four or five guys who end up doing everything together. Breakfast. Swim or go to the gym. Go training in the early afternoon. Back again, and then maybe out for a function in the evening. It creates bonds with players from around the world and I love that.

A lot of people in England don't get it. Some guys might play county cricket for a few games with an overseas player but they don't more or less live with the guy night and day. They're in and out of their county scene but they're not really in each other's pockets.

The next question people ask is about sledging. If you play with these players in the IPL and then go play against them in international cricket, what's the level of sledging like? I answer honestly: I think sledging is on its way out and that's a good thing.

It doesn't mean that we don't want to get one up on each other, though. Take Ross Taylor, for example, who I play alongside in Delhi Daredevils. I remember one day when Ross was playing for New Zealand and his innings wasn't getting off the mark. He hit one to me and I misfielded it. I was mad with myself; Ross ran down and laughed at me. Thanks, buddy, he said.

That's one of those scenarios. Other guys are looking at this thinking, what the fuck? But I've played with Ross for six years in the IPL. When he walks out to bat I've got this natural instinct that I want to win. I want to get him out.

That's the thing with the South Africans. In 2012 England were having meetings about Dale Steyn. It was all Dale Steyn this, Dale Steyn that.

We are out there (and I hit one of the best shots I have ever hit in that series. Against Dale) and Dale would run in to me and say something funny or I would laugh at him after he's bowled a ball and he'd laugh at me in turn. He knows I want to hit a boundary every time he bowls. And I know he wants me out for a duck. There's respect there, though. With the other batters, who he doesn't know, he won't have a laugh, so from their perspective he's Dale Steyn the enemy. And when Dale and I have a laugh it looks to them that I'm betraying England.

That creates huge friction between me and the other players. People choose to think that I'm less serious about England's cause. But deep down I want to nail these guys and they are truly desperate to get me out too. That's part of our friendship: they wouldn't respect me if they thought I wasn't a 100 per cent competitor against them, and the same goes for me too. It works both ways.

I have that competitiveness in my blood. So why on this earth should I pretend to be nasty towards my mate? It won't make me play better. I don't have it in me.

It's the same when an England player plays against another England player in a county game. If Prior played against Broad in a county game there's no way Prior would abuse Broad or that Broad would abuse Prior. They would laugh if they whacked each other. That's the sort of relationship I have got with the foreigners when I play against them, but people choose to see it differently.

In the first Test of the 2013 Ashes in Brisbane, the friction started up. We need you, KP. We need you as our big player in this Ashes series. We need you to be strong because when you're strong on the field we're strong as a team. The team wanted me to get at Michael Clarke verbally. The two of us had a bit of a spat in the fifth Test at the Oval that summer, and the team wanted me to try to dominate him, personality to personality. They saw me as a key figure that could overpower the opposition physically, verbally and in my batting.

This is cricket. This is the kind of thing they say in the team meetings. I'm saying, yeah, absolutely fine. I am strong. I do what I need to do.

I know what they are trying to say. They want to convince themselves that everybody on one team hates everybody on the other team. Whereas I like to have fun out there. When I am happy and confident that's when I play best. I like to enjoy what I do. Occasionally that will get frowned upon.

If you speak to guys like Eoin Morgan or Ravi Bopara they'll tell you exactly the same. They have played abroad and become really close friends with guys from other teams. They've had that experience. They like to go out and beat those guys, but sledging them to order doesn't sit well.

I made mistakes in the messages business. I see now how it looked. At the end of the day, though, it was just mates talking to mates.

In fact, the South Africans were friendlier to me than the England dressing room. They were messaging me, asking why the fuck are these guys retweeting stuff from this parody account? These guys are your teammates. The South Africans were acting like genuine friends and so I was talking to them more openly than I was to anybody in the England camp.

Nobody wanted to see that, of course.

17

Badgers Come Out
at Night

Now, compare and contrast the ECB behaviour in Tweetgate and Textgate, which happened within weeks of each other in that summer of 2012.

Some guy just walked up to Alec Stewart at the Oval one day and said:

Can you keep a secret?

Alec shrugged. The guy kept talking anyway.

You know that KP Genius Twitter account? I'm running it, and some of the guys in the dressing room are tweeting from the account – they have it on their phones.

He went on to name names.

Alec looked at this character and said:

Well, I can keep a secret, but I can't keep that secret. Who exactly are you?

The guy's name was Richard Bailey, otherwise known as @bailsthebadger. And a close friend of Stuart Broad.

A few days later Alec came to my house and told me what was going on. I'd known since a senior player mentioned it at the Oval that the account was coming from inside the dressing room. Now Alec had the nuts and bolts.

The account had been set up by Bailey, who had explained to Alec Stewart that he had access to the account along with the players. Bailey might tweet as @kevpietersen24 during a game, when all the guys were without their phones, but they would then access the account when they got their phones back and they'd tweet from it at night and in the days after the Test matches. Very funny.

Alec passed all this information to Hugh Morris. Hugh had assured me, when I had previously raised the issue of the spoof account, that he would investigate it and if there was any suggestion it was coming from within the dressing room he would make sure that it was dealt with properly. Yet now there did not seem to be any proper investigation, despite what had come straight from the horse's mouth.

So the guy running the account demeaning an England player turns out to be Stuart Broad's friend. Broad later said to me, during our reintegration talk in Mumbai, that he knew about the account during the Headingley Test match. Yet his statement, released the day before the Lord's Test – so Headingley had been and gone – suggests that he had no knowledge of it whatsoever.

His statement was worded in fluent ECBese:

Following last night's statement by Mr Richard Bailey that he was responsible for creating a parody Twitter account in Kevin Pietersen's name, I would like to confirm that I had no involvement in this whatsoever.

I met with the Managing Director, England Cricket, Hugh Morris this morning and assured him that I did not play any role in the creation of this account or provide Mr Bailey with any information regarding Kevin Pietersen or the England team.

As has been widely reported Mr Bailey is a friend of mine, but we had no conversations regarding this issue at all and I am pleased that he has now decided to close the parody account down.

And then Hugh Morris added a fatherly note:

Having discussed this matter with Stuart, I am fully satisfied that he acted in a professional manner at all times and did not breach any confidences regarding fellow England players.

ECB also accepts the apology Mr Bailey offered last night to the England team via his Twitter account and his reassurances that no professional cricketers were involved in the creation of this site.

Note the careful wording: Stuart Broad had no involvement in *creating* the account. Did he have any involvement in tweeting from it? The statement is silent. Did the ECB ask him?

Somebody then commented in the *Daily Mail* that 'On the day the account was created there are plenty of photos to prove he was with the creator.' They even referred to a tweet from Broad on 4 July, describing Bailey as 'a social network genius'. Curious word, genius. KP Genius? Did the ECB investigate this?

Stuart Broad's mate sets up the parody account, which Broad follows, but Broad never discusses this with his mate, the one who he thinks is such a 'social network genius'. Right. The ECB accept Mr Bailey's apology to the England team. Why not make him team mascot?

So the tweets business was just deemed a distraction. They made it go away.

The texts? Instead of shutting the issue down, the ECB made it into a major drama series.

Straussy chipped in his view at the time:

I'm a big believer in not airing dirty laundry in public. It's one of our core values in our team that what goes on in the dressing room stays in the dressing room. Any time anyone has fallen foul of that they have been disciplined – and rightly so. It's about mutual respect and trust, and that is a core issue that is central to resolving this.

So publicly humiliating a teammate via Twitter meets the criteria of mutual respect and trust. Private messages never intended to be seen by anybody except the two people exchanging them fail the mutual-respect test. Okay.

The ECB wanted to investigate. First they wanted my phone. They said they wanted to take it to a top forensic investigation firm that would download all the software off my phone and search keywords and try to find out if there was anything said since the start of the summer about any of the players and staff.

The Professional Cricketers' Association chief executive Angus Porter said, basically, forget about it, guys. You cannot have it. You will not have it. This is his private phone, and these were his private messages.

I just said, are you all mad?

Newsflash, chaps: pro sports people bitch to each other about everything. We bitch about the bloke we have just been bitching to. We bitch about each other. We bitch about the bitching in the dressing room.

I was living day to day in a toxic team environment. I wasn't in a good place. So when friends moaned to me I didn't disagree. Do you think that at the football World Cup clubmates and friends from different countries don't keep in touch? That some of the time they don't have a good whinge about what's going on around them?

I told the ECB that if they wanted my phone they should get everybody's phones and put everything out there. Can we have Andy Flower's phone to see the shit he has said about me over the last six months? Or Stuart Broad's phone? I'll give my phone if you take all the other guys' phones. We'll publish everything. Then we'll all go and get counselling.

Angus Porter tried to help as an honest broker in the business. Angus told me that Flower had rung him and said that he had a conflict of interest. He didn't want Angus involved. Angus said, well, no, I look after the players. You look after the team. The players can speak to me whenever they want.

Jimmy Anderson rang Angus Porter after all this texting and Twitter bullshit came out and said, we need to stop all this crap. We need KP on our side. If we want to win, we need him.

I suspected that Flower was trying his utmost to make this an issue that wouldn't go away. Even then, as far back as 2012, he must have realised he couldn't get rid of me for cricketing reasons, so he had to find another way.

To this day I don't know how the text-message story got out.

I've heard a story that someone was at the table at dinner while my friend and I were messaging. He might have laughed when he got my BBM and said, ah, KP doesn't deny that Straussy was being a *doos*. Harmless. Then this person just passed it on to somebody else as a funny story, a small bit of gossip. We all do that all the time.

In the story, the person receiving the story was an agent and it suited him to leak it to a newspaper – he'd know he'd probably need to call in a favour in return quite soon after. He called the *Daily Mail*, and the guy who answered the phone won an award.

For me, it doesn't quite ring true.

I know the South African guys were incredibly embarrassed about it. They still are. I heard that during the Lord's Test the PR woman who was working with the team told one of my buddies that the Sunday papers had got hold of the messages that had been exchanged between me and the South African players. And he couldn't sleep that night. First thing in the morning he went downstairs to check the newspapers and see what the hell was going on.

Some people – including David Collier, the then chief

executive of the ECB – bought into the theory that the South African guys had played me. It has been said and written that if I played the third Test we would probably have won if my form had continued. If you want to go down that road you could say that the South Africans therefore played it perfectly. Again, with respect, that's bullshit.

I don't believe it. I think David Collier's accusation that the South Africans had duped me and his subsequent embarrassing apology says just about enough.

From the start of my career I have made a bargain with cricket. I give the game everything. I work as hard as anybody at getting my technique right. I care about what I do. I take pride in it. In return, I want to enjoy myself. I'm an open book: what you see is what you get. I have always believed that if players are in the public eye that is good for cricket. The game needs big personalities and outsize characters.

I don't really care if the media paint me as being a big, brash mercenary. I don't really care that in certain newspapers and certain pavilions a South African with an earring and a big mouth will never really fit. I know some people have looked at me, seen tattoos or dyed hair or a flash car and decided that they know enough. The people close to me, the people I care about, know who I really am. Beyond that, the best connection I have made is with those people who come to watch cricket and like to see some slash–and–burn from a bloke with three lions on his shirt.

Anything beyond that is just an image, built on my personality and magnified by the media. The media only deal in black and white. Suits me: I give them black and white when I can.

The South African series of 2012 was a turning point, though. I realised that everybody else was playing a different game from the one I was playing. Things that I thought mattered didn't really matter at all.

During the South African series, between two of the one-day games in September, I held a golf day at Tring to raise funds for the JCE Trust, which had been set up by Jon Cole-Edwardes, my best friend since our childhood together in South Africa.

Jon was like another brother to me, but now he was slowly dying of a rare form of eye cancer. I invited some of the England players to come to the golf day.

Sky Sports News were there, and did a report to camera. Flower saw it. The players who had come to support the cause were there because they were my buddies. They knew what was going on in my life; they knew about my friendship with Jon. Flower tore a strip off each of them.

Phone calls. What the fuck do you think you are doing? You are not supposed to be there. You are not supposed to be supporting him.

They weren't supporting me. They were supporting Jon.

The guys rang me and said, you won't believe who has just been on the phone!

Who?

Flower.

All through that summer he left me twisting in the wind. He never once backed me in public. He never once tried to put the fires out.

I understood why when I heard about those calls.

It was one rule for one player and another rule for me. They wanted me to be aggressive, a maverick and a playmaker on the field, but they wanted an obedient little puppy off the field. A bloke who would bow to them and tip his cap to them. Yes sir, no sir, three bags full sir.

I'm not that guy.

With summer gone I was outside the circle in body as well as spirit. The team were going to India for a key autumn series.

The ECB, despite having no affection for me, wanted me on that plane. Flower, despite all his talk of leaving a dominant legacy, didn't.

I waited. Then the ECB came up with their own little piece of theatre. I would have to reintegrate myself. On my knees.

Time to get the old pads out again.

18

Showtime

So, 2012 in highlights and headlines. Retired from international limited-overs cricket in late May. Made 149 in the second Test against South Africa. Cyber-bullied by teammates. Break down crying in a meeting with Andy Flower. Hung out to dry over private messages to old friends. Commit to all forms of cricket again. Dropped for third Test against South Africa. Left out of squad for World Twenty20. New ECB central contract withheld in early September. Then, later on in September, left out of the England squad to tour India.

And how was 2012 for you?

When it came to the issue of the India tour, the ECB were between a rock and a dull place. I wanted to travel. Andy Flower didn't want me there. It was no longer any secret that Flower just wanted me gone.

The ECB were very conscious of the importance of the India Tests. I don't think Giles Clarke really wanted to dump me. Not then. He likes to win. The Tests in India were going to be big, big, big, and if England lost there would be a price to pay politically.

If I wasn't on the plane to India, it was going to have to look as if it was my choice.

When England flew to Sri Lanka for the World Twenty20 in September, I went out there to work as a television analyst. The ECB did their best to block this, but failed.

That annoyed and embarrassed the ECB. I had been Player of the Tournament when we won in 2010. Now I was fit and healthy, and sitting in front of the cameras in a studio. Sitting there while England collapsed to 80 all out against India. I was in my pundit's chair again when England lost by nineteen runs to Sri Lanka and were on their way home without having reached the knockout stages.

The ECB might have been annoyed and embarrassed by me being in a TV studio, but things could have been much worse. Microphones weren't just picking up ambient sound out on the field, they were picking up all sorts of stuff that amazed the producers and panellists. When Broad and Swann were bowling they were abusing the fielders, shouting at them if they misfielded. It was a big thing: everyone had noticed it.

There was an up side to being at the World Twenty20, though. In Sri Lanka, my talks with the ECB continued.

Things were tetchy, of course. I could have sued over being refused a central contract earlier in the month. That was one stinking pile of dirty laundry that the ECB wouldn't want to think about airing in public.

I could see that Giles Clarke wanted a solution but he needed some way to sell the solution to Andy Flower. Not so easy.

Things moved forward slowly, until in early October the ECB had a contract for me to sign.

Before signing, I asked Clarke a lot of questions about sorting my schedule out. Okay, okay it's sorted. He told me how lucky I was that he was signing my central contract. He hadn't signed anybody else's. I just started laughing. Well done, boss!

It was announced in the press that I had signed a four-month contract, which would take me to the end of the India tour, but in Sri Lanka I basically signed a one-year contract running through to September 2013, contingent on me getting through the proposed reintegration process.

The ECB also asked me to sign an affidavit that I hadn't sent any text messages giving away tactical information. I signed. I asked if they were getting the other guys to sign one for the Twitter account. Clarke was annoyed at my cheek. Look here, I am chair of the ECB. I decide what happens at the ECB. I just laughed and said, okay.

Flower's reward for going along with the contract was to allow him to come up with a new form of torture. He'd 'let' me re-integrate with the team if I went through a series of one-on-one meetings with the main players. Actually, hang on: I don't think meeting is the right word. Or what Flower intended. I would go in front of management and senior players one by one and beg for their forgiveness.

They would purge me of my sins. I would be grateful.

If I was truly the mercenary I am painted to be I would have replied with three short words, the second and third words being 'off' and 'Flower'. But I still wanted to play for England, so I agreed to the reintegration process.

I agreed even though the implication was that everything that had happened over the summer was my fault.

The leaking. The refusal to look after a senior player's schedule. The parody Twitter account. The blowing up of some messages between myself and an old friend into a major controversy. I would have to apologise for it all.

Funny, I still wanted to play for England. So I agreed.

It was so ridiculous. I had to fly in to England from South Africa, where I had been playing for Delhi Daredevils in the Champions League Twenty20.

The original flight was cancelled, so I had to go a day later. Then we had the meetings in a hotel in Oxford, and I flew back to play in Durban a day after. I was still wearing the sackcloth and ashes.

A classic Andy Flower tick-box exercise. And classic PR by the ECB. All game playing. They could say that Kevin Pietersen was travelling halfway across the world to apologise like a good little boy. Some of the journalists knew exactly where the meetings were taking place, even though the location was supposed to be secret! But then, why keep a secret when you are staging a bit of live theatre? You don't reel in the big fish and not have your photo taken holding up your catch on the dockside.

It was interesting on one level. I made my mind up to apologise, but to make a few things clear along the way. The first of the meetings was with the big kahuna himself, Andy Flower. That was the only true one-on-one. For the rest a moderator sat in, and so did Flower and Alastair Cook.

When I spoke to Flower I asked why he had been happy to see me hung out to dry in the media. Why did he bollock teammates if they supported me in public?

I asked very specifically about the James Taylor leak. I had spoken to him about James in private, in that back room in Headingley when I was upset. And I had spoken to him on the phone when I was driving to Headingley.

The only other time I had mentioned James Taylor to somebody else was when Matt Prior was coming out to bat after Taylor had been got out. Prior looked white-faced, and to calm him I said quietly, listen, batting is easy. Taylor was just making it look hard for the last while. The South Africans were laughing at him. Just relax.

I asked Flower if he had been responsible for a garbled version of our private conversation getting into the media.

Flower said that, yeah, well, it was just a tough, weird time and he had to tell people what was going on.

I said, so how can I trust you going forward?

No answer.

Flower initially accepted that it was him, but then suggested that if I had mentioned James Taylor to Prior, it must have been Prior too.

Right.

For the rest of the meetings we settled into a pattern. Flower would go and fetch a player from reception. Then, to each lucky recipient of my apologies I would say I was sorry for what I said blah blah blah. Anything you need to say? Okay. Next.

And Flower would go and fetch the next guy.

I assume he prepped them all in the couple of minutes it took for them to make their way up to the meeting room. When Flower went to fetch Prior he was gone for ten to fifteen minutes. Because I had asked about the James Taylor leak, I suspected Prior must have needed more prepping than the other guys did.

While we were sitting and waiting I commented on it to Cooky and Sid, the guy sitting in with us acting as the intermediary and conflict-resolution expert.

I know what they are up to, I said: they are trying to get their story right. When I confront Prior their story will be 100 per cent identical.

It would have looked very odd if Prior came in and denied ever saying a word.

The one-on-ones that day were with Prior, Swann and Cooky. Broad I would meet with the first week in India in the Test series. I looked forward to that. Also in Oxford I had sessions with Anderson, Bresnan, Trott and Bell. The last two don't really count. It was like, hi guys, good to see you. Love you guys. No issues. Two batsmen – not part of the circle. They were on my side. Still are.

It was bowlers v batsmen in the dressing room by that stage. Broad, Swann and Prior playing the big dudes. The in-crowd, as they would have defined themselves. Doing well with their careers. Telling people what was what. Putting people down.

I went through all this bullshit with them because it was the only option, the only way forward. I had hated playing for England for some time, but I didn't give up hope that things could improve. We had all made mistakes that summer. If I showed the will to do all this and make things better, perhaps somebody would see what was going on in terms of the bigger picture.

Anyway, there was more to life than worrying about this political bullshit. It was over. Done and dusted. Time to move on.

To get through those meetings I thought to myself, you know what: the only way I will enjoy playing for England again is if I forget about it and move on. And I think we did. Look at when Swanny retired: even he said that I had been amazing since the Textgate business, that I'd had a really good time with the lads.

But for now, in this hotel in Oxford, it was show trial time. I did it all thinking that it was just a way to demonstrate control. Get the players to come in and then humiliate Pietersen in front of them.

We'll put him in front of the players and make him say he's incredibly sorry for what he said at the press conference at Headingley. He's so sorry he brought the dressing room into the media. He's sorry for everything that we have ever been annoyed about.

If he doesn't do it, if he refuses, then we can say that he wouldn't engage with the reintegration process. He showed no desire to play for England. He wouldn't leave the Delhi Daredevils even for a couple of days. He's one bad egg.

If he does do it, it will be like *Cool Hand Luke*: we'll break him in front of everybody. Then he can stay if he still wants to.

We can spin the process as a great opportunity for KP to come in here and apologise. Then we will draw a line under it so we can move on. Nobody will ask if this is what is best for the player.

Nobody will ask why nobody else is taking responsibility for a breakdown in relations, for the major distractions, for the problems in the dressing room that Kevin spoke about. Nobody would think to ask if Andy Flower had been aware of the Twitter situation and the way that might have affected everybody in the dressing room.

If he was aware, did he condone those things? If he wasn't aware, why wasn't he?

Okay, it was inappropriate to mention 'issues in the dressing room' at a press conference. Sorry. But what were those issues? Yes, it was inappropriate to message my South African friends at that time. But why was a senior player more comfortable with players in the other dressing room?

Nobody asked.

Of course, some of the players loved the process. Swann's wife was about to give birth. He said, I fucking blame you for fucking having me here.

I just thought, Swanny, you sad, sad bastard. If you don't want to be here, don't come. You are a grown man; your wife is having a baby. But if Andy Flower calls you somewhere you just go? You know what, Swanny, I wouldn't have come here to do this to you even if my wife wasn't having a baby.

I had a lot of thoughts like that and just kept them to myself. The only way to get through all the shit was to play the role. Sit on the naughty step. Let them have their three minutes. I just said that I was incredibly sorry. Again and again.

Most of the questions the guys put to me were about the IPL. How much time I devoted to it, and how that made the guys think that I didn't love English cricket. They said that they felt I didn't care about them. You would rather be in India, wouldn't you?

I wanted to ask, well, why would that be? Any guesses, guys? Instead I apologised some more, especially for watching IPL cricket during the West Indies series. I will always regret that.

They wanted their pound of flesh. It wasn't a time to put things in context.

I wanted to tell them about how frazzled I was during the Headingley match. The emotion. I was so drained that on the fifth day I had gone into a back room and slept for ninety minutes. Pure exhaustion from stress. I was absolutely shredded. Emotionally. Physically. Spiritually.

Instead, I apologised for messaging with my friends.

I wanted to tell them about how I was having a barbecue at home with friends on a Saturday night when my phone rang. I was absolutely determined not to think of cricket that evening, but I answered – it was Adam, my manager. He said, just so you know, the *Sunday Times* have called me: they are running a story tomorrow on you giving tactical information to the South Africans.

It was so left-field, such crap, that all I said was, bullshit.

Bullshit, tell them to just fuck off.

I knew it was bullshit so I wasn't bothered. I woke the next morning and it had made the headlines. I got nailed! The story was written by Simon Wilde. I have no idea where he got it from: I have never spoken to him about it. I remember that morning, though, saying to myself that some bastard had stitched me up good and proper.

In Oxford, I could well have been speaking to that very bastard. I wanted to tell the guys that but instead I just said sorry, sorry, sorry.

I wanted to tell them how I hadn't wanted to do the Headingley press conference, how I sat there, obviously emotional and drained, and was left sitting there as the questions kept coming at me.

Instead I just apologised for bringing dressing-room issues into the public arena.

I apologised while wondering how many of the guys had ever leaked stuff to their pet journalists or to @bailsthebadger.

Every flavour of sorry imaginable – I served it up.

And I was sorry. For all the things I had done to make the relationship with my team break down, I was genuinely sorry. I thought the process we were going through was a farce, but I hoped that if I played my role people would go away and think about how things could get better in the future.

When I left the one-on-one meetings I shook Andy Flower's hand and we walked outside to the car park. He seemed visibly upset as he walked away from my car. I saw that. For me, that was a sign of him knowing he had lost. I had played the game the way I should have. I had come back and done their meetings and now I was going to tour India with England.

I don't think he expected that I would actually come back from South Africa and put myself through all this. I imagine he had wagered on me refusing and handing him a reason to drop me from England for good.

He had lost.

19

Drinking Coffee and Ticking Boxes

I flew back to South Africa. Job done. Hugh Morris announced to the media that 'all the England players and management are now keen to draw a line under this matter and fully focus on the cricketing challenge that lies ahead in India'.

They'd run some anti-virus software on me. I'd had my system cleaned. Nothing got deleted, though. It was all stored in the cloud for later use.

A few days after my 'all clear' England flew out to Dubai for a training camp. I would join the squad when my Champions League commitments were done. Around that time Andrew

Strauss gave an interview. Straussy was now retired, and wearing the elder statesman hat he was born to wear.

He mentioned how after his resignation he had sat down and hand-written letters to every member of the squad. It was part of what he called 'the grieving process'. If I said the same thing it would be just seen as more soap-opera melodrama. The way Straussy told it, you could picture him in his cabin late in the evening, sitting beside his oil lamp scratching his quill on piece after piece of parchment. A wise old man hoping that he would get all his wisdom written down before the lamp failed or his health went.

He wrote to everybody except me. He sent me a text. The reason: the letters could be delivered to the players who were playing at a one-day international. I wasn't, of course. Hmm, the post, perhaps?

He acknowledged 'that some of England's players have not been blameless in the breakdown of relationships with their star batsman'.

Talking about texts, he mentioned that 'Kevin has since come up to me and apologised for it and I respect that. He seemed contrite and I think he was sincere.'

It sounded as if I had staggered over to him in McDonald's and interrupted his reading while he was eating his Happy Meal.

As the summer of 2012 lurched from disaster to disaster I realised that I'd have to do the damage control on my own. Nobody was swinging in to help me.

I tried.

In August, I had put out a YouTube video committing myself fully to England. It didn't get great reviews or too much attention in the media, but that was no surprise: it went up on one of the most exciting nights of the London Olympics. All I was trying to do was bypass the ECB and their mouthpieces and say something directly to the people who pay to watch cricket on television and pay to watch us live. I didn't want any spin on it.

With the South Africa series dead, I had another duty to look after before things could progress.

Things had been bad between Straussy and me, so I went to his house a few weeks later. I called him and asked could I go over and speak to him. I drove out to his house. We had as calm and as pleasant a meeting as you could hope for.

I said I should have defended my captain. I said that I was sorry if I had done things which marred his final Test match. I took my share of the blame, and was genuinely apologetic. We had been good friends once and the respect for him still lingers. I meant it all. I apologised not just to him but to his wife: I know the wives and partners go through all the pain and stress alongside us. Ruth wasn't there that night, but I said, please can you tell Ruth that I am so sorry. I fucked up.

I told him again I had never spoken about his batting. Of course not. The messaging was a big mistake. I was sorry and he was fine with it. I felt he appreciated that I'd made the effort to come to his house to apologise. We shook hands.

I wanted to move on with Straussy. I wanted to move on with the other guys too.

I hadn't just come up to him hoping to seem sincere.

Alastair Cook was taking over as captain. Cooky and his family were 'very much the sort of people we want the England captain and his family to be', as Giles Clarke put it. And he had shown all the signs of leadership which the ECB look for. You have to be able to say the word yes. You have to be able to say it a lot.

Yes sir is better.

Yes sir, three bags full is best.

Cooky is so decent and earnest that he was ideal for the ECB at that point.

Flower says jump.

How high?

Giles Clarke says jump.

How much higher?

Cooky hates conflict. He's another Mr Nice Guy – like Ned Flanders from *The Simpsons*. He's too nice for the politics of English cricket.

Cooky refused to believe the Twitter stuff. That was his way of dealing with it. It was as if he still writes to Santa Claus and puts his tooth under his pillow for the tooth fairy. Even now, he will say that he does not believe it happened. I'll say, Cooky, I know it happened because the guy himself told Alec Stewart. My friend Piers Morgan linked up all the tweets. A guy starts a parody account but doesn't mention it to his friend Stuart Broad? What interest has Alec Stewart in making all that up?

When I say this he just looks at me blankly.

Straussy was cut from the same cloth, but he was more of his own man. He made some effort to balance Andy Flower, not letting him go overboard the way he did when was he was working with Cook: talking and stressing people out, being all emotional. The Mood Hoover. Strauss and Flower formed a very tight connection, but Straussy could say enough, Andy. Dial it down.

It didn't take long for me to realise that Straussy would be missed. Out in India, Flower was as anal as ever. He always had it in his head, for instance, that he wanted us to wear trainers with our England kit. Flip-flops look bad, he said.

We play in spikes for six hours a day. Surely at the end of the day's play guys can wear flip-flops back to the hotel. It's just good for their feet. No? Anyway, I adhered. I wore the trainers; I did everything I was asked.

I'm not a team meeting person. You've probably sussed that out already.

If it's relevant to my game or if it's relevant to somebody else's game and they've come to ask me for help, I love to talk about cricket. I enjoy that, but not the team meetings, please. Especially not the one where they talk about commitment. They talk about fielding. They talk about being positive. They talk about focus. They talk about understanding where you need to be. They talk about everybody knowing how important they are to this team because of their energy.

It's the same every time. Oh my gosh, make sure your energy is up, guys! You're playing for England, guys! You're wearing the three lions, guys! Oh fuck off. Tell me something I don't know. We've been in dressing rooms listening to this brand of crap since we were ten years old. Is it the best you can come up with? Telling us which team we are on?

I know team meetings have to be done from time to time, but I think you've got to figure things out for yourself. You have to know what works for you. If you need to find something out, you go and find it out. If you want to be good you'll do that. If you are playing for England you should be doing that all the time.

We all understand what we need to do in general terms. Tell me specifically how I can do it better and you have my interest.

So when Andy Flower decided to bring me the whole team-meeting experience in the form of meetings between himself and me, I wasn't optimistic.

Instead of making sure I became comfortable as just another member of the ranks, he wanted us to have a one-to-one chat once a week. We could make sure we kept our relationship in check and that everything was okay. If there were any problems, I could speak to him about them in our meeting. He'd always given me the cold shoulder and now we were pretending that I could cry on his other shoulder.

I expected that he wanted to sit and meet with me about as much as I wanted to sit and meet with him. I thought that he was ticking the boxes, humouring me. I was wondering how I would get through the fifteen minutes or so that we would be together. What would I talk to him about? How could I humour him in return?

It was like trying to make small talk with the headmaster. Not scary, just uncomfortable. Two rules: make sure the meeting lasts for one coffee; make sure I buy the coffee.

There was one good thing about the meetings: I was able to question him about certain things. I was certainly able to ask him about his retirement from coaching one-day cricket in the middle of that Indian tour.

So Andy, a few months ago I was told I couldn't retire from one-day cricket. Big hue and cry, remember?

Now it's okay for you to call a team meeting and announce that you're retiring from one-day cricket? How does that work, Andy?

I could see how it worked.

Hugh Morris explained it all to the media lapdogs:

We all know how busy the schedules are. Andy is 44, has three young kids and spends a hell of a lot of time away from home. We play as much as India and more than pretty much every other nation.

Andy has been on 15 overseas tours and has spent 60 per cent of his life in hotel rooms since he started this job. It's not sustainable for one person to be looking after all aspects of the game. I don't see it as an erosion of Andy's power. Ultimately, he is still accountable for playing strategy in all three formats.

Only 60 per cent? Try walking in my trainers, Andy.

In May 2012 I'd asked if I could retire from one-day internationals. I was told to play all forms of limited-overs cricket or none.

I had been keen to play in the World T20 in Sri Lanka that September, but when I made myself available Flower announced:

The situation is the same as it was when he first approached us. The ECB are determined to protect all three formats of the game and part of that is not setting a precedent of allowing players to retire from one-day cricket alone. The intent behind it is that we are serving English cricket in its entirety. We have to take personalities out of the equation.

I was happy to talk about technique with him any time, and some of the things he had to say were very, very useful. Occasionally he'd bring up the hundred I scored at Adelaide back in the 2006/7 Ashes. He'd say, look at the technique you were using then. You've changed. Do you want to get back to that?

This is what you were doing in Adelaide; this is where your hands were, but now they've moved. Can you bring your hands in a little bit? That sort of coaching would help me. I remember him doing it in New Zealand on the miserable 2008 tour. I went and had coffee with him at a time I was stuck getting thirties and forties. I remember sitting with him and we looked at the way I played, and I got a hundred a couple of games later playing a lot better. That quality got lost in the power struggle that followed.

Instead of him going through the motions with me I wanted to feel useful or to be doing something useful. Not tolerated. I wanted to feel like I was wanted and valued. In all the time since my 'reintegration' Flower only twice properly involved me by asking me to do practical things.

In India he said, I want you to look after the youngsters and help them to play spin. So I worked with guys like Joe Root and Jonny Bairstow, and loved it.

My playing of spin has gone up a number of levels since I've spent time at the IPL, and in particular since I've spoken to Rahul Dravid. Rahul gave me a great deal of information about how to play spin on the subcontinent. Invaluable stuff. And if I can pass this on to someone at the start of their career, and they can go on and be the best they can possibly be? That's all good.

In England, batsmen get taught to play with the spin against spin bowlers. In India, the best players of spin get taught to play against it. If an off-spinner's bowling to a right-hander who's only been taught to play with the spin, which side of the field can he score on? One side. But if you can play on the off side then you'll be able to score on two sides of the wicket. It's simple. So the bowler's under a lot more pressure. Thinking, if I get this wrong here . . .

I went through a lot of drills with Jonny and Rooty. Throwing balls to them and, every time, hitting it through the off side. Hit it through the off side. And watching them both now? Bairstow's certainly playing better, and look at how well Root's playing spin. That's the kind of stuff that makes me happy.

In Australia for the 2013/14 Ashes Flower asked me to help the bowlers play against the Aussie seamers after we'd started getting bombarded.

I got to the nets and our seamers were very receptive. More than that, in fact. One of their throwaway comments was: we just get told to score runs, we don't get told *how* to score runs. That absolutely bamboozled me.

The coaches haven't ever told you how to score runs? They've never given you a technique? Some of them said no, they hadn't.

So I coached them on trigger movements, which is something that Duncan Fletcher and Clive Rice had both spent time teaching me. Trigger movements are all about getting yourself into position to strike or defend just before the bowler bowls, rather than waiting for the delivery. Because by then, at that speed, it's too late. So when the bowler's in his load-up I've moved my leg already, and as soon as he releases the ball I'm ready to pounce, rather than thinking, oh, he's bowled. Fucking hell, now I've got to move.

Again, I loved it. Absolutely loved it.

(And by the way, I have messages on my phone to this day from young guys I worked with telling me how sorry they are about how my England career ended. How grateful they are for all the work I did with them. I was a problem in the dressing room? Come on.)

There was one key person who hadn't been at the one-on-one sessions in Oxford. Stuart Broad.

I'm not sure if Broad is the sharpest tool in the box. If I were in his position I would have thought that, having missed Oxford, it would be a good idea to come to me in India and just say, listen, KP, no problems. Water under the bridge. Let's just shake hands and move on.

It seems obvious. Back in Oxford, the mood was different and the stakes were different.

In Mumbai, though, Broad and I finally had our meeting.

Broad told me that he only found out in Headingley what was going on with the Twitter account. Imagine his shock! I had to laugh.

I said, mate, he's your friend. His face went bright red. He knew he was bang to rights.

Piers Morgan had linked up all the tweets, and they created a trail that Piers could follow. The great investigative minds of the ECB couldn't. Piers did a bit of investigating and unearthed the whole thing.

He had told me that the tweets suggested Richard Bailey had been in Broad's house watching a boxing match on TV when the Twitter account was set up and sent its first tweet.

So Broad was red-faced and uncomfortable. Yeah, he'd been in the house, but he's just an acquaintance. I hardly see him.

I said, your mate told Alec Stewart that you were involved.

He said, ah he's bullshitting. He's not really my mate.

So he's not really your mate, though he says he is and he was in your house when it started?

Yeah.

My attitude by then was that we all make mistakes, we all fuck up. The guys would deny that any of them had fucked up, and in the end that was fine.

I wanted to draw a line under all this. I screwed up. I was in a bad place at the time, and I did and said things that I shouldn't have. I knew I had messed up. If nobody else was going to come clean on their mistakes, well, we'd just have to leave it behind.

Bailey would come back to haunt Broad. The England team returned to the UK after the Twenty20 series in India and went back out in the new year for the one-day international series, after which we would travel on to New Zealand. While we were at home, as the calendar flipped over to January 2013, a picture was taken of Alex Hales, Stuart Broad and this Richard Bailey bloke together at a New Year's Eve party in London.

The picture did the rounds because everybody was taking the piss out of what Alex Hales was wearing. Funnily enough, Alex had been the very first person to follow KP Genius.

Early on, one thing that impressed me about Cooky as our new captain was that he straight up didn't want any bullying behaviour in the team. I was glad. At last, somebody else seemed to recognise that we had a problem.

Cooky was clear: no more shitting on each other. No abuse on the field.

It sort of stuck for a while, but then came out again in India. Prior started it up, shouting at the younger guys in the field.

We had been through all the earnest reintegration talks, and this was quite soon after. The first tour of reintegration. I had eaten so much humble pie I was exempted from the skinfold tests. My own biggest discussion point through that time was the fact that these guys liked to shout at people on the field, and that really needed to change. Cooky wanted it to change.

The bowling clique was more subdued because their behaviour was becoming an issue again and they had to stop it. It was hurting people and it was obvious to the opposition that we didn't gel as a team.

I had told Flower that I was going to speak to Prior about it. That was a tricky conversation, but I had learned that being transparent about everything left less opportunity for people to wash their hands in the aftermath of events.

Flower, in my view, had allowed the clique structure to exist and that gave them protection. These guys were his high performers and his stronghold in the dressing room. Flower and Prior were pretty tight. In terms of my issues with Prior, it was Flower who had told Prior to talk to me about what I had said in the Headingley press conference. He had asked Prior to see if I could be brought closer to the team, if we could resurrect our friendships and try to sort things out.

Now I had to tell Flower that I wanted a few words with Prior over what was happening out on the field. The kind of abuse the

TV microphones had picked up on the field out in Sri Lanka was happening here as well.

In the end I called Prior into my room in Nagpur on the tour and complained to him about his behaviour towards younger players on the field. I said, stop, you are back to doing this.

He just said, okay, right. Thanks for telling me. Maybe I do need to have a look at it.

He took it well. No aggro. But nothing changed.

Stuart Broad went back to England in the middle of December with an injury. Prior was handed the vice-captain role in his absence, and after that I liked Prior's demeanour even less. Being vice-captain seemed to go to his head. Sad, especially when he isn't really vice-captain material at all.

India was a success, and overall I felt that I was absolutely fine with my place in the world. I had my energy back and was really enjoying playing with the guys again.

We lost the first Test in Ahmedabad. Pragyan Ojha bowled me out on 17 in the first innings. A slow left-arm bowl. The second innings was worse: two runs from nine balls. Ojha got me clean again.

I was disappointed. I was trying too many things, just to force the issue. I was worried about my defence, too worried about making an impact. I fell back on the old habit of planting my foot instead of waiting for the ball to be delivered, and so spent a lot of time in the nets between the first and second Tests.

I needed a pay-off. In terms of reintegration, for me it would only be a natural ongoing process when I was playing as well as my improved mood told me I should be playing. I wanted to make a difference. Give people a reminder.

At least my form in that first Test suggested I was reintegrating. We were awful. Bowled out for 191 in the first innings.

We moved on to Mumbai for the second Test. India batted first. That was a big innings for our bowlers. Monty Panesar took Sachin Tendulkar for eight runs. Monty and Swanny took nine wickets between them. Good work by our spinners. India all out for 327. We just needed to do the business with the bat.

When I walked out to bat in the Wankhede Stadium Cooky, who had opened, was still in but Nick Compton and Trotty had fallen cheaply to the dreaded Ojha.

I felt good. The bat felt like an extension of my body. What happened next is something that people in India still come up and speak to me about. I found what I was looking for: 186 from just 233 balls. Twenty fours and four sixes. It was a good knock, but what pleased me most was my discipline. In Ahmedabad I'd made myself look like a clown, trying the sweep shot at the wrong time. If you use the sweep shot right it messes around with the length the spinners bowl; it messes around with their fields. If a spinner bowls straight to you it can create a little leg gully that gives you problems. Using the sweep at the right time negates that.

I didn't gamble. I hit the big shots at the right time and held my peace in between. I didn't leap any invisible hurdles when I reached the hundred, even though I got there with a nice reverse sweep that I enjoyed. In India, against India, the satisfaction comes from silencing the crowd, not the fist pumps. The atmosphere in the grounds is always buzzing, the crowds absolutely deafening, when the Indian batsmen are performing, so if I'm batting, and whacking their bowlers everywhere, and you can hear a pin drop, that's the sign that things are going well.

I knew that the further I got past the hundred, the more the screw would be turned. In the end I was caught off a ball from – naturally – Pragyan Ojha. By then I'd had the pleasure of hitting a six to extra cover right over his head, though. It was one of the top three shots of my career. The ball landed at off stump, my hands went through it and it just flew. And that's a pretty hard shot, to get a left-arm spinner over extra cover from over the wicket, with the ball spinning miles. I can't tell you how good it felt. But I looked over at Dhoni in the field just after I'd hit it, and his jaw had actually dropped. Nooooo . . .

Coming off, the Mumbai crowd gave me a standing ovation. I thanked them later in a tweet in Hindi. A standing ovation in Mumbai for a batting performance against India, for a team that goes on to win the Test, is like getting flowers thrown at you for singing opera at La Scala in Milan. It doesn't happen much for blokes from Pietermaritzburg.

Swanny and Monty cleaned up again with their bowling and we levelled the series. We had the old feeling back now. I had a 54 in the first innings of the third Test in Kolkata, but Cooky rustled up an incredible 190 to set us up nicely. 2–1 in the series.

We went to Nagpur for the fourth and final Test. In the first innings I had a 73, as did young Joe Root, who was learning fast. India forced a draw but we had beaten them in their own backyard for the first time since 1985. It was an achievement up there with winning the Ashes. You couldn't help but be happy for Cooky. The captaincy was something I always thought he had promised himself since childhood. Being captain is just the start of something, though, not an end in itself. He had played brilliantly and led the team to a huge win.

We were all in a good place when we came home in triumph for our Christmas break. After the Mumbai Test Prior had tweeted a picture of me with the caption 'Reintegration complete. Well played.'

Now Prior explained to the *Daily Mail* that the phone call Flower told him to make to me after the Headingley press conference had paved the road to reintegration. He went on to say:

> Kevin was absolutely sensational . . . He was fantastic talking to the young players and passing on his experience. Because he'd been to India more than anybody else, he also knew where to go and what restaurants to eat at. Little things like that are incredibly important on a tour to somewhere like India.
>
> It wasn't just Kev who had to make changes, everyone had to. We did that well and proved we're again a tight unit and can move forward without having to talk about it any more.

The storm. Even during the calm before it, you just know it's coming.

20

Le Grand Fromage

By the time we got home from India, reintegration was perhaps going well enough to convince the cricket public that all the water was under the bridge. But there was another problem. The Big Cheese had matured and grown too large for his little box.

To get back into the squad for India I had sat in a chair for all those one-on-one meetings. I listened to Matt Prior in particular telling me that I was too wrapped up in the IPL, that in his view I thought too much about it and tweeted too much about it. It had all made Cheese feel that I didn't care too much about Cheese. The Cheese who was at the time following a Twitter account deliberately set up to make fun of me.

In India, the bullying problem had started to appear again.

What was it like? Small enough things, but relentless. Grinding guys down. Or rather, certain guys. If one of them were to drop a catch in the field all hell would break loose. Prior would be spewing rage all over them. If it was one of the Baby Cheeses? Not a whisper. Protected species.

I remember an instance in Kolkata. Sachin Tendulkar was under a hell of a lot of pressure; he'd been having a really bad run. Tendulkar hit one to mid-on with Finn bowling and Jimmy Anderson misfielded. Silence. I braced myself, but not a word. I'm wondering, what the fuck is going on? I mean, Jimmy has let Sachin get off the mark and taken a lot of pressure off him. I'm waiting. There'll be shit in the air now. Surely? Nothing was said. Now, if that was Panesar or Samit Patel or Trotty, oh, it would have been carnage out there.

Don't think that those guys didn't notice, either.

This was what I was reintegrating into. I was supposed to sit down and shut up in the corner of a dysfunctional dressing room.

Then the Big Cheese got a Big Bash contract in Australia. The Big Cheese down under – exactly what the world wanted. For the last week at the end of the Test series in India he's talking exclusively about the Big Bash in the dressing room. Cheese is talking about how Cheese's sponsor is going to change the colour of Cheese's equipment to match Cheese's Big Bash team colours. He says Cheese will be flying to Australia on Christmas Day to go and play in the Big Bash.

Am I actually hearing these things?

At our next meeting I asked Flower about it. Were you catching this stuff, Flower? This is stuff that I've now got to put up with. I'm listening to your vice-captain talk non-stop about the Big Bash, which he has never even played in. You know, because it was your idea, just how hard I got criticised by the players in those one-on-one meetings. They were so hurt about my love for the IPL and how it made them think I wasn't committed to England, no matter how well I played.

But this guy, who has not played a single game for his Australian franchise, is shouting across the dressing room for updates of scores in Australia. He needs to be told all breaking cricket news about what's going on there. This is at the end of a day's play in a Test, across the dressing room, talking openly about the Big Bash. What he will be wearing.

Is it one rule for me and a different rule for the rest?

Flower nodded. He seemed to see where I was coming from.

He had a lot to think about. Cheese had already been to him to have a quiet word. One of the younger guys, who thought he was under Cheese's wing (or gold foil), had been drinking. Cheese thought he should mention it. A whine and cheese evening?

Was Flower wondering if he had created a monster?

In India, Cheese had been temporary vice-captain in Stuart Broad's absence. By the time we got to New Zealand in spring 2013 the Cheese had been made permanent vice-captain. It made the Big Cheese puff out a bit.

Flower asked me at one stage who I would have chosen for vice-captain.

I would have picked Ian Bell, I said, because he was in the batting group and it would have taken power away from the other side of the dressing room, away from the clique, who would then have to deal with the rest of the team in a much more professional manner.

Flower said, well, Bell doesn't speak much.

I didn't agree. People don't give Bell the credit that he deserves. They've never really let him speak. I mean, he's a very quiet guy; he's not going to force that space for himself. The fact that he's not overconfident doesn't mean he couldn't be a good vice-captain. It probably means the dressing room should change in order to allow quiet, thoughtful guys like Ian Bell the space to make a contribution. Look at Cook: he's the captain and he's an introvert. He doesn't exactly talk up a storm, but he is sincere.

Hmm, said Flower. But he sounded as though he was just humouring me and amusing himself.

The Big Cheese made himself unpopular by insisting on bringing his bicycle out to New Zealand. Here's a thing about playing cricket at the other end of the world: you don't need to take your bike with you. They have bikes in New Zealand.

Who the hell takes their bike? You rent a bike like any normal person. We all rented bikes in Queenstown when we were down there.

Cheese had started taking his cycling quite seriously. He'd spent some time with the Team Sky guys and was telling everybody about it. If Cheese wasn't a top genius cricketer Cheese would have been a world-class cyclist. Obviously.

You'd see guys with their eyes glazed over, as they'd have had ten minutes of the Big Cheese dripping on about Team Sky.

At first, he'd get into his full-on Team Sky uniform like Clark Kent turning into Superman and go out on his bicycle, looking like a prat. Le Grand Fromage getting ready for Le Tour de

France. He went for a few rides early on in the trip, then nobody saw his bike again. Maybe he thought the rest of us should have been a bit star struck, and the locals might at least have started chalking his name on the blacktop roads.

I got 0 in the first Test match in Dunedin. Out first ball, lbw. Second innings first ball, I was looking at a king pair. I got off the mark with that first ball, though, and got two runs. Phew.

At that very moment the Big Cheese had a snigger and a snort to one of the players in the dressing room. Huh. If it were the Ashes KP would have run that two a bit quicker. You see, there in Dunedin I simply couldn't be arsed. At least that's what Cheese felt entitled to imply while I was out there batting.

If it was just any old KP-thinks-he's-a-big-shot jibe I wouldn't have minded. It was more toxic than that, though.

At fielding practice a few days earlier I had dived for the ball and felt two bones in my knee collide. I got a sudden shock of unbearable pain. Shit. I've done something bad here. A little shot of freeze spray ain't going to make this better.

After that I could hardly sleep, the pain was so persistent. I was on the strongest painkillers for about two or three weeks. Not being able to sleep wasn't the worst of it, though. When I was being bowled at I couldn't duck a bouncer. I couldn't squat. I could hardly run.

Cheese knew that my knee was busted. He knew I'd had scans. He'd seen me wearing a knee brace in training. Now when I'd hit a ball through square leg and sort of jogged the two runs because I was in pain, he started stirring the pot, cooking up the notion that I had ulterior motives. Another bit of schoolyard bitching.

Flower turned a blind eye and a deaf ear to that sort of thing.

He didn't appear to take notice of what went on in the dressing room.

Rules were made up as they went along. The Big Cheese, who had been up to Flower's room grassing on a younger player for having a few drinks in India, got a few drinks into himself before the final day's play of the second Test in Wellington. That's just Cheese: moral compass of the dressing room. Somebody in the management team made Flower aware of the drinking. Nothing done. If it had been me I would have been bundled on a plane back to Heathrow before you could speed-dial the media. Extraordinary rendition.

And now in Dunedin the Big Cheese is bad-mouthing me to players. He just didn't want to trust me; he didn't want to believe that I had an injury. He assumed I was doing it for my own good. Things people said got twisted to suit the agenda of the detractors.

I remember having a night out with some of the boys in Queenstown. We had toured India for the whole of that winter and now we were in New Zealand. After that, I would be going on to the IPL. It was a long slog and we were all having a little moan. I remember actually saying that, man, I could do with a break. I know somebody took that and used it as ammunition when I did my knee a couple of days later.

The Big Cheese put two and two together and got five: he said he wants a break from cricket; he's got his IPL money covered by insurance. Aha, this all works perfectly. We don't believe him. We don't trust him. We can hang him again. When the injury was hurting me and taking me from the game, the Big Cheese was happy to spread word of the new formula: two and two equals five.

It was a sad time. I had been friends with Cheese. Now he was slowly losing any sense of himself as he turned up the volume and made himself the main man in the dressing room, an endless foghorn booming about his perfect life and the tragic imperfections of those lads he didn't rate.

I'd had my turn out there under the stage lights and didn't like the heat after a while. I'd wound my neck in when I realised the only interest the media had was in using me. I'd married and started a family. I'd come to realise that, at the end of the day, you just have yourself, your family and those close to you. Some people don't care about anything other than running with the big dogs. Or rolling with the Big Cheese.

Our Cheese was out there, growing runny in the heat. A Dairylea triangle thinking he was Brie.

Eventually, after the second Test it became inevitable that I would have to leave the tour. The scans had showed up a bone injury and bad oedemas, or bruising on the bone. Plus a possibility of cartilage trouble.

I had thought that the thing would take just a couple of weeks' rest to heal up. When I got back to England it became clear that it would take at least six weeks, and that was just the start. It turned out to be a career-threatening injury.

Meanwhile, back in New Zealand . . .

After I'd gone home Flower was chatting to one of my buddies and my name came up.

Oh, we all know why he's gone home with his 'knee'.

Well, no, I don't.

So he can claim his IPL insurance.

This is the head coach to one of the players. He's so damn stupid he thinks I won't get to hear of stuff like that. Flower had sat in my room two days before that and said, look, we've seen the scans: you can't play the way you're playing. You're just in too much pain.

I said, I know, I can't sleep at night.

What makes me sick about the whole thing is that I got the injury, got the brace, took the painkillers and Flower was happy to throw me in for two Tests instead of resting me. Then when he sends me home he tells a player that I went because it would look good for my insurance claim for the IPL wages I was going to lose.

I never wanted to miss Test matches for England. We had a double Ashes period coming up. I wanted cricket. I wanted time in the middle. I wanted to be ready. I never wanted to miss the IPL. I love playing in the IPL – it's a mental break, a cricket holiday. Lastly, if you are making a claim for lost wages the insurers require the same medical scans that Flower and his team looked at. Nothing else. Not a note from your mum or a ticket stub for the flight from New Zealand to England.

Then a sly tweet from a tabloid journalist. At a meeting in New Zealand a member of the management team questioned my injury: exactly what's wrong with him?

The medical team were saying that, actually, he has a chronic knee injury. Nick Peirce, the team doctor, was there and he knew what sort of pain I was in. Scans don't lie and Nick thought that going home was the right thing for me to do.

There was never any trust from Flower. I didn't trust him and he didn't trust me. He was happy with my results on the field

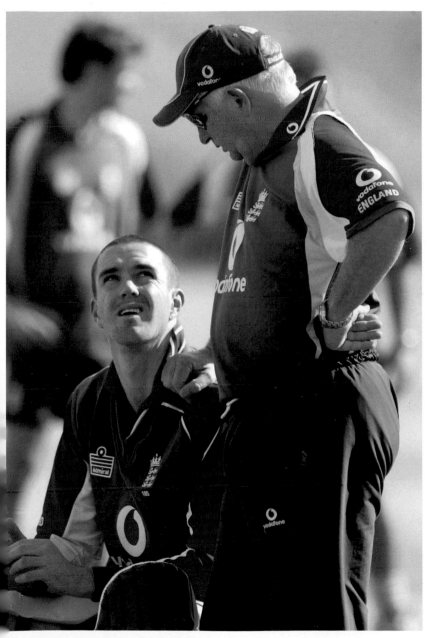

The kind of guy who makes you happy just to see him: Duncan Fletcher,
the quiet facilitator

It's fair to say that there are certain coaching styles I don't find inspiring: Andy Flower and Peter Moores – two of my less successful working relationships

The ups and downs of the ECB. Being unveiled as captain, reintegrating in Colombo and Whitaker and Downton chewing the fat shortly before the end of my time in the ECB set-up

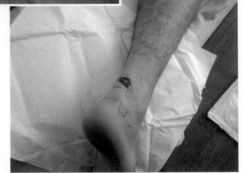

Recovering from surgery in 2009. No wonder I looked unhappy, given the state of my Achilles injury

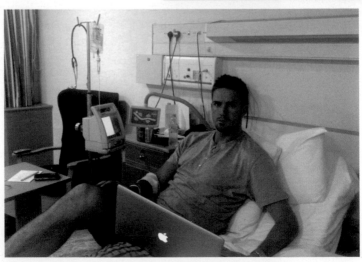

Recovering after my double hernia operation in 2011

Not quite the only one marching out of step. Training in Adelaide before the second Test of the 2010 Ashes series

Inspecting the two broken window panes at Lord's in 2011. They were smashed by the Big Cheese's bat falling against them

And the Big Cheese himself, in full Team Sky regalia on the 2013 New Zealand tour. I opted for slightly more casual gear

I love training. Full stop. Eighteen-year-old Sri Lankan bowler Adarsh Hosahalli Shivalingaiah advises me on my technique at the 2011 World Cup

In the nets ahead of the second Test against Pakistan in Abu Dhabi in 2012 (and opposite)

I love passing on whatever advice I can to younger players too,
even match mascots

Having fun at the Lord's Bicentenary match, July 2014. A day full of good things that helped me see the incredible journey I've been on for what it was

Pietersen or Pieterson? My hundredth cap, finally corrected and proudly on display at home

when I got them. Those days were good for his reputation as a coach. In terms of our relationship, there was nothing there. I became convinced it all stemmed from me wanting to get rid of him when he was second in command.

So the whole thing was toxic again. Vice-captain Cheese bad-mouthing me. The management bad-mouthing me to journalists, to players and to other management. Media tweeting about my injury.

Finally, in April, I rang Flower. The New Zealand series was done and dusted, but I was still hearing versions of the story being put about to the effect that my injury was my ticket to a paid holiday.

I gave Flower the update on my knee. I had been told that if I had surgery it would take at least nine months out of my career. The alternative was to manage the injury through permanent rehab and painkillers. I didn't much fancy that, but with two Ashes series approaching it was the better scenario. Flower agreed.

I started talking about the backbiting and all the shit that I heard about my knee; I was talking about the Big Cheese in particular, and how he was bad-mouthing me to the players, especially to the younger ones. I said, Flower, you know what's up with my knee. My knee's fucked – you've seen the scans. What are you going to do?

Flower arranged a one-on-one between Cheese and me before the return Tests with New Zealand in the summer. He must have read about one-on-ones in a management book he'd got out of the library. He loved them. This one-on-one was facilitated by Mark Bawden, the team psychologist. The idea was that we had to throw everything on the table. Get it all out of our systems.

I saw it as yet another tick-box exercise devised by Flower. So did Cheese, I imagine. My first thought as we sat down was that I was wasting my time because Cheese clearly doesn't listen. He'll turn this one-on-one into a funny story.

Flower told me that Cheese had been spoken to in New Zealand about the way he was carrying on in the field, getting at less senior players, in particular Monty Panesar. So I opened the bidding by telling Matt Prior that he was a classroom bully.

I spoke about his on-field as well as his off-field antics. I said he wasn't captaincy material, or even vice-captaincy material. I didn't like the way he spoke about people behind their backs. How he belittled younger players. How he was always complaining about Duncan Fletcher, who was and is a friend of mine. The easy knock on me is that I don't get on with coaches, but the fact is, I've got on great with any decent coach I have ever had.

The idea was that Cheese would then have his say. He did. KP doesn't care. IPL. Too individual. IPL. Careless shots. IPL. Texts. IPL.

After that we would have fifteen minutes of thought and reflection before Mark opened his laptop and showed us a montage of pictures and words from the good times. Then we would embrace with tears in our eyes.

We did it all except the embrace and the tears. It was a tick-box exercise for us too. All shipshape, Flower. Many thanks. Another triumph for your patented one-on-one system. You'll be ECB Employee of the Month, what with all those ticked boxes.

Nothing changed. In the dressing room, if I had to pinpoint the epicentre of resentment towards me I would say it lay within Matt Prior. I'm sure we had both changed as people since our days at the academy. I'd rocketed into a world of madness after 2005, while Prior had plodded along, steadily progressing up the ranks and, I expect, picking up some resentment along the way. When Prior finally made it through the doors of the England dressing room and found his feet, I think that he brought all those resentments with him.

Off the field, I'm a much quieter, more solitary person than people imagine. I will go out occasionally on tour, but some of the lads regularly enjoy good nights out, either with one another or with the Barmy Army. My relationship with our supporters is great when I am on the pitch, and their presence throughout my Test career has made the experience really special – and often hilarious – but on tour I feel the need to escape cricket rather than talk about the game the entire time. So I'll read or watch DVDs, or just talk to Jess and friends at home. I like to sleep about ten hours a night too, which makes me even less likely to go out.

When you isolate yourself like that you get talked about. That's the price. When people talk about you through a mouthful of resentments and jealousies you'll get painted not as somebody who likes their own space but as somebody who is stand-offish, who sees themselves as above the group.

That creates an environment in which people on your own team don't see anything wrong in following parody Twitter accounts and bitching about you out of earshot. It creates a scenario where the noise and the laughter stop for a second when you walk into the dressing room. Then somebody quickly, obviously, changes the subject.

I don't know what Andy Flower saw in Matt Prior when he

made him vice-captain. He was playing well, fantastically well, and he is a good speaker, but too often he is, to me, an empty vessel making a lot of noise. It cost everybody in the end.

I could see through his bullshit because I had known Prior a long time. I knew the Cheese when he was just milk. The younger guys on the team were very timid around him. He had his close followers and he had those who cocked an ear every time he opened his mouth. And he had a lot of other guys in the dressing room and in the management who couldn't stand him.

If he is still playing Test cricket when you read these words then everybody will deny that was the case. Players love the official version. It's a safety blanket. If he is out in the wilderness with me, then who knows.

I don't care, really. I know the truth of that England dressing room. It was a bad place to be, and the proof would come with the bad times. We were on the verge of a huge collective failure, for which just one person was going to take all the blame.

The knee never healed. I missed the Champions Trophy in England. I missed the New Zealand home Test series and it was a race to get fit for the Ashes. I had a number of cortisone jabs, and the scans and medical reports were common knowledge. Nobody ever said, sorry mate, that injury was much worse than we thought.

21

Gabbattoir

I love the Ashes. I don't enjoy all the build-up to an Ashes series. In 2013 the home Ashes series seemed to be the start of the longest-ever drumroll for the trip down under at the end of the year. We won the home series, but it was low-key. None of the fuss of 2005. We were only at the halfway point, and knew we would really be judged on how we performed in Australia. If we left the Ashes behind, there would be no point in arguing that we had been pretty good in the summer.

It was a double Ashes series in name, but all the pressure was loaded on the five Tests in Australia. There, in 2013/14, we would be pulled right out of our comfort zones. The pressure of having to beat the Aussies in Australia is always intense, but Andy Flower had got it into his head that this tour would be about legacy. We weren't just playing to win: we were playing to write our own gushing obituaries; we were playing to be remembered and immortalised.

We had spent the summer playing Australia and we were going to spend the winter doing the same – a process in which we'd end up playing the same team virtually non-stop for six months. My knee held together in England but it needed a lot of managing. I had a cortisone injection between the fourth and the fifth Tests, just to kep the pain at bay as it was inhibiting my batting. I got out twice in the Durham Test to the spinner Nathan Lyon because I couldn't play him off the back foot. Playing spin off the back foot helps to decrease the size of the area in which the spinner feels comfortable to bowl. Therefore, it opens up a lot of scoring options and allows me to score through the off side. But because of my knee I was unable to score that freely and had to change my game, which twice cost me my wicket.

If anybody had given that any serious thought they would have written us off even before we left for Australia. The pressure is always immense down there. England's media love to gang up on England. The Aussie media – and the Aussie public – love to gang up on England too. No matter how the home series went, Australia were going to be cock-a-hoop if they could chop us up and throw us on the barbie in their own backyard.

A month after winning the home series we were on the plane to Australia. Or rather, the rest of the team were on the plane. I had to go to South Africa first, for the sad duty of giving the eulogy at the funeral of my departed friend Jon Cole-Edwardes.

*

When I arrived in Australia I was made aware that the players wanted the freedoms that the players had on previous Ashes tours. And they weren't getting them. They needed a night or two to socialise, to get to know each other and become a team, but that simple tradition became a PR battle. It was about appearances: if we were going to be in the papers it was going to be for cricket, or helping little old ladies across the street, rather than enjoying ourselves.

Flower and Giles Clarke wanted the England team to look like a sweet bunch of eager boy scouts who never did anything wrong on or off the field. Keen young gentlemen. Always prepared. They wanted us to win in a certain way. Individuality reflected badly on Flower's reputation as a leader. He was forced to pick a few guys who could go either way on the individuality thing, and he decided he would have to come down hard on them. Keep them under the thumb and retain some sort of power.

I believe in a positive team environment: that is where you build your friendships and where you build your team. You don't build your team on a stupid army-camp exercise just before the tour leaves. Yes, sounds good. Bonding exercise? Yep, got it out of the way before we got on the bloody plane. Excellent.

The pre-Ashes camp was the biggest shambles, and gave us a hint about what our winter was going to be like. We were sent to a remote location in the Midlands, to take part in a mock surveillance exercise that would apparently make our team stronger. To achieve this new level of bonding, some guys were stationed in fields with only horses for company for hours on end, while others of us were sitting in cars, tailing 'dangerous drug traffickers' or whatever, and being encouraged to communicate over the radio in this ridiculous foxtrot-oscar lingo.

Bonding? No. Boredom? Absolutely. It was one of the most frustrating experiences of my life, purely because I knew I wouldn't see my lad for however long when we were on tour, and we were here doing this nonsense.

No one really got anything out of the camp. The only surveillance we were going to be experiencing in Australia was while we were being treated like schoolchildren for a few months. Everyone was tired and bored, and had been taken away from their precious days at home with their families for this. We wouldn't be allowed to see our families until the third Test match, and we were playing silly buggers around the countryside. One of the guys got so fed up he took off early and headed home. Respect to him, but imagine if I'd done that. Tabloids for a week.

Then the guys hit Australia and went on lockdown.

On the 2010 Ashes tour, we went out in Perth one night. With permission: it was three or four weeks from a Test match. We were all out together till four or five o'clock in the morning, getting hammered in a place called the Llama Bar, and then had to go training a few hours later. The boys ran around and some of them were spewing when nobody was looking. The fitness coach was getting guys who couldn't stand properly to do hamstring stretches, and assumed they were still jet-lagged, still tired – not still pissed. People were still talking about that night before the 2013/14 tour. Everybody was saying we had to have a night in Perth like we had back then. That will be the real bonding exercise.

Flower got wind of all this before we arrived in Australia. Then, when they got to Perth, he told some of the younger players that they weren't allowed to go out with the rest of the team that night. This was the night they arrived. Three weeks before the first Test. He was basically putting a stop on all the good stuff that brings young players into the group.

Take Ben Stokes, who'd joined the team for the Ashes tour. He'd had a couple of run-ins with the management, and been sent home from the England Lions tour of Australia earlier in the year, but he's young and very talented. Ben was one of the players Flower wouldn't allow out in Perth. Give him a break. I totally get that drinking is not the way forward on an Ashes tour: no Ashes tour is ever going to be one long party, but you don't have to turn it into one long funeral either. On previous Australia tours we'd had some incredible times together off the field.

I made this point to Flower. I asked him why the hell he wasn't letting youngsters go out with the team on the night they got to Australia. When there are three weeks before the first Test match? What are you trying to achieve?

Flower didn't go out with the team, but still managed to suck the good mood out of the night. Those guys who were permitted to go out in Perth said it was one of the worst nights they ever had: they weren't allowed to do anything. Everyone had been absolutely buzzing for it, but it turned into another shambles. There was still also a lot of resentment about the days at home being stolen for the stupid bonding exercise. We were starting off on the wrong foot.

What was Flower afraid of? Not being in control? A night out wouldn't be hard to supervise. We had three security guys with us at all times, and guys look out for each other on nights like that anyway.

*

My form going into the Ashes was poor. By the time of the first Test I hadn't made a decent score in two months. The warm-ups were typical Harvey Norman zero-interest jobs. I was out for just 8 against Australia A in Hobart. I did manage to get a bit more into it when we played the Cricket Australia Invitational XI in Sydney, with 57 runs in the first innings. I could now smell the battlefield.

The knee wasn't co-operating. While the team moved to Sydney after the game against Australia A in Tasmania, I went to Melbourne for more scans and another cortisone injection. Sometimes the injections work. Other times, not so much. Either way, long days in the bent-knee postures of either batting or fielding aren't among the recommendations the doctors give you when they discharge you.

The first Test, at the Gabba – or as the Aussies like to call it, the Gabbattoir – was my hundredth cap. A pretty intimidating venue for such an important personal landmark.

After we'd warmed up on the pitch, Giles Clarke walked out and presented me with a beautiful silver cap to mark the occasion. Everyone's happy. I'm feeling special. I give the cap to the manager to look after, and some of the lads say,

Did you see your name? They've spelled your name wrong.

Fuck off.

But they were correct. Pieterson.

So I asked them, politely, to send it back to the ECB and get it corrected. They presented the cap right back to me at the end of the Test, and they'd just engraved a line through the O. So halfway between an O and an E. That just typified my relationship with the ECB by that point: they didn't have the courtesy to do it properly. They thought it was okay to do something like that for someone's hundredth cap. The lads in the dressing room were actually pretty horrified.

Meanwhile, on the field we soon realised there was bad news about Mitchell Johnson.

When Mitchell Johnson had been bowling really badly in the 2011 Ashes the Barmy Army made up a song for him: 'He bowls to the left, he bowls to the right, that Mitchell Johnson, his bowling is shite.' I remember standing at mid-on in the Melbourne Test and they started singing it as Johnson walked out to bat. We were just about to win, and I just started singing along. It was one of those moments when the pressure is about to go and you just get carried away. Sometimes you feel so good and relaxed that you forget you aren't one of the crowd.

Mitchell Johnson noticed I was singing, and in fairness to him he saw the funny side of it. However, the Mitchell Johnson who turned up in Brisbane for the first Test in November 2013 was a different bloke entirely.

The Aussies had set 295 in the first innings. Not impossible, but it was hard to remember when we had last hit over 400 in an innings. Still, we had hope.

Cooky was looking more worried than a captain should and got out cheaply to Harris. Michael Carberry was still in, and coping. We'd get a real idea of where we were when Jonathan Trott faced the first ball from Johnson.

Trotty had hit an early four off Harris's bowling. We hoped it would steady him like a shot of brandy.

Boom: first ball from Johnson hits Trotty on the glove as he jumps back and tries to shield his face. It was a violent bumper that jumped up at him like a startled rat. Everybody watching says, whoa, shit. WTF?

A shudder ran through the dressing room.

Trotty had been anxious when he went in to bat. Johnson had tortured him a bit during the summer and had been living in Trotty's head ever since. Shortly afterwards, Johnson had Trotty out with the last ball before lunch.

I was going to face the first ball after lunch. The way that Trotty had played and the hype leading into the series was one thing. The way that Mitchell Johnson was bowling was another.

Lunch? No thanks. I was sitting there, thinking: I could die here in the fucking Gabbattoir.

How could Trotty, this calm, collected buddy of mine, play like that? Get hit like that? Get out like that?

I was really worried. I'd been spending a huge amount of time on my own in the nets, but suddenly it didn't seem enough. So I asked our spin-bowling coach Mushtaq Ahmed to come with me to the nets. I took a tennis ball, wet it and said, Mushy, for the next ten minutes just try to take my head off.

I needed him to try to destroy me. I said, what we just saw Trotty face looked ridiculously fast. Mushy looked at me as if I was mad, but he saw the method in it. He said, let's do what you need to do.

For ten minutes those balls came at me hard and fast in the indoor school under the stand at the Gabba. Mushy isn't very tall, so from half length they were hopping up just at head height. I found the zone.

Then I walked out for my first ball. I had been petrified: if

Trotty can get played like that there is no hope for me, because Trotty is normally so calm and cool. That walk out with my gloves and bat always takes my nerves away, though. I said to myself, this is my game. This is not impossible, why am I so scared? I've played this guy before. I've just spent lunch coping with what he's going to throw at me. This is your hundredth Test, kid. Play the cricket that got you here.

It started okay. He bowled a short ball to me; I got out of the way with a bit of a jump. The second or third ball I played, I got off a single – just pushed it into the off-side. Up and running. There's an old joke about me drinking a Red Bull before I come out to bat and being all jumpy and edgy for the first over or so, until I get a run to settle me. There was no Red Bull run today: settled already.

The next over, and I hooked Johnson to deep square leg for four. Pleased. I just threaded it through the gap between deep square and long leg from a short ball on leg stump. Ha.

Then I got another one which I helped around the corner, and as I ran past Mitchell Johnson I said to him, it's me or you, buddy, and believe me, I'm less scared of getting out than you are scared of giving me a lot of runs.

He looked at me, just stared at me, he didn't say anything back. He kept staring and walked past. Shit. Shit. Shit. On so many occasions in the past Johnson has always bit back: shut up, KP, fuck off, shut up, big shot. This time he didn't say anything, and immediately I knew he was different. I would have preferred him to have said something, to engage with me, but he didn't, and that's when I knew the series could be tough. It proved to be extremely tough.

This new Mitchell Johnson was nasty and very aggressive. He had found himself, he had found an inner peace, and he knew that he had control. He knew the power of his aggression. He knew we feared him being nasty. He knew not to switch it off.

He knew where the ball was going and he knew that he just needed to continue with his process because what his process was doing was shaking me. He was bowling hostile, bowling fast and aggressively, and he was bowling in really good areas. In previous Ashes he wasn't doing that: he was always giving you a release ball where you could score. That gave me confidence and took his away.

Johnson gave us nothing to score from. He was aggressive from the first ball. Michael Clarke captained him brilliantly by using him in three-over bursts to keep him fresh throughout the day. He always took wickets in those three overs, so his confidence built and built and built. It was just brilliant bowling. And because he was never tired, the threat of him hung over us like a sword all day long.

Part of Johnson's deal this time was that he was in our heads even when he wasn't bowling. I got out cheap in that first innings, after just eighteen runs. Harris bowled me and I clipped it straight to midwicket and into George Bailey's hands. I was all wound up about dealing with Johnson and made a dumb move against Harris. I hated that.

The second innings didn't go any better. Trotty was gone just before lunch again. I was up after lunch and got to twenty-six. Then Johnson bowls short and I take it on with a pull. Why? Because I thought I could. Got a top edge on it and hit it to long leg. Caught handily by Chris Sabburg.

My one hundredth Test done with. Not one for the scrapbook. I thought to myself, I'm probably going to have to get rid of that pull shot for this series. It's too risky for the way Johnson's playing.

After the game, I was presented with another gift, from the team this time. I made a little speech, saying how much it meant to me that the team could give me this. I also told the team that while we had lost this game I truly believed we could improve. I also said that, for all the troubles of the past, I was enjoying playing with them. I really felt we had moved on from everything and were forging a good relationship.

That was Brisbane.

Johnson was brilliant and he was used brilliantly. He was their match winner, he would be their series winner and he was sensational. By the time the Ashes finished our two top bowlers, Broad and Stokes, had taken thirty-six wickets between them. Johnson had thirty-seven on his own.

You very seldom hear people in your own team saying that they are physically scared, but our tail-end batsmen were scared. I heard Broad, Anderson and Swann say they were scared. When you've got that, you know that a bloke in the other team is doing damage.

We were done, then, until the next time. My knee was hurting. My pride was dented. Trotty was in shreds. The tail-enders were scared. Cooky was dithering. It was clear that Johnson was already a weapon that we had no answer to.

22

Watching the Nightwatchmen

Jonathan Trott went home after the first Test.

When Trotty had gone, Andy Flower said to me, I want to shake your hand. I should have listened to you.

I couldn't believe what I was hearing.

I should have listened to you?

I am a buddy of Trotty's. We are different personalities from the same background. We look out for each other. I like to watch Trotty. He is so earnest and intelligent and serious about what he does. It fascinates me.

As the summer of 2013 went on I could see he was suffering a bit with his stresses and anxieties. The wonder of it is that more cricketers manage to keep it hidden. When Trotty went home from Brisbane in November, Stuart Broad explained something about cricket to the media. He said, 'it's a stressful environment when things are not going well. We spend 270 nights a year in hotel rooms and, although I'm maybe not the right man to answer the question, it is harder for those with families and kids.'

In hotels for 270 nights. Andy Flower knew this. Trotty is devoted to his wife Abi and their daughter Lily. Andy Flower knew this. Stressful environment? Australia is always stressful. Andy Flower knew this. Mitchell Johnson had given Trotty a hard time in the one-day series. Andy Flower knew this.

I saw the signs in Trotty. I went to Andy Flower and said that he had to look after my friend. The anxiety was weighing him down and, whatever the rules were for the rest of us, Trotty should have his family around him from the start in Australia. He needed a good, positive, relaxed work environment and he needed to be able to get away from that entirely and just be himself.

No. It can't happen.

Our families were not due to come out until the third Test, in Perth.

Trotty is number three in the batting order. I'm batting after him. I told Flower in terms he might understand better that it would affect the whole batting order if he didn't look after Trotty.

Then we lost Trotty after the first Test because no allowances were made.

Should have listened?

I guess so.

We had one really good day in Australia. Almost.

The warm-up match in Hobart against Australia A. We got to

250 without loss: Carberry on a century, Cook on a century, and a few overs left before the end of the day. For five or six years, the plan had always been to play warm-up games the same way as we play Test matches. In this case, it would mean putting in a nightwatchman if either Carberry or Cook got bowled out before close of play.

The day has been long. Trotty, batting number three, is on edge, waiting and waiting for his turn to go in. Now it's evening and energy levels are low. The wicket has been cut up a bit. You don't send Trotty in now, you send in a bowler whose wicket isn't too valuable. We've done it all over the world.

So we are in the dressing room, and we are one happy team, when Flower approaches Trotty.

Do you want a nightwatchman?

Yeah, of course I want a nightwatchman.

Flower winces. Trotty has personally disappointed him. Flower comes to me. Same question. Same answer. Flower is exasperated now, and the good vibes have left in a taxi.

Flower turns to young Gary Ballance. Now, Ballance is a batsman on his first Ashes tour. He's hoping to impress – put in a good performance and maybe get a chance to bat in a Test. Flower lets him know he is expendable.

You want to bat?

No, it's not my turn.

Ballance went up in my estimation about ten times over. Big balls on the young guy.

Flower turns to young Joe Root. Same story: a young batsman.

How about you?

Oh, okay.

Poor guy. The pressure was on and everybody in the room felt sorry for him. The logical nightwatchman was either Jimmy Anderson or Steven Finn. Bowlers. Poor Joe Root had been told that he was more expendable than a tail-ender who specialised in bowling.

I was upset. Trotty was upset. What had been a good day had turned into major tension.

I went to Flower.

Can I ask you what you think you are doing? We have just had a great day and now the mood is gone.

I want you to do it the tough way.

We are 250 without loss. Where's the tough way?

I'm in this job to get the best out of you.

Well, Flower, don't ever tell anybody that I never said everything to your face. The other guys won't. I will.

That was a small but typical event. As it happened, we got to close of play without loss. But the Mood Hoover had done his work.

Trotty was back in the dark place again.

By the time Trotty left I was 100 per cent sure that the way the tour was unfolding was being made worse by bad management. The pressure put on players from the whole environment outside the camp is huge when you are in Australia. To have the coach ratcheting up that pressure turns it into madness.

Flower thought we were devaluing the legacy, and didn't take it well. He went into himself. You can't have that when your players are out there, getting hammered by the Aussies every single day. You can't have a coach putting extra pressure on the players by the way he conducts himself.

I knew Trotty was in trouble. I always suspected Australia was going to be tough on him. I certainly realised after we'd arrived that it was going to get even rougher when the Tests started, because in the one-day series Mitchell Johnson had bowled really fast and aggressively at our early order. The team was also fatigued. Mentally, playing ten Test matches against Australia is hard. Then throw in all the other limited-overs games. And you always know that the Australian media will turn up the heat big time.

I spoke to Trotty a lot, about how he was feeling, about what was going on. I wanted Trotty to do well. There is no fear in the man. He was just a guy who, in Australia, got to a point where he was all shot through. Cricket. Exercise. Being in a team. Those are things that should have helped. Those are escapes from the pressures in a bloke's head. But our environment was just making things worse. Trotty didn't need to escape to cricket. He needed to get away from it.

Time to state the bloody obvious: being a batsman high in the order is very different from specialising in bowling. When you are bowling, it is eleven against one. You are all out there, crowding around the poor sap with the bat. When you are batting, when somebody is about to chuck a ball at you with all the energy they have, in front of an Ashes crowd who are baying to see you get out, when you desperately need to stay in, you are as on your own as it is possible to be in a packed place. That is pressure.

In the lead-up to the first Test, the pressure was being wound up. That's how it is in Australia – the culture is very macho. In interviews, Mitchell Johnson was telling people to look at the one-day series and how he had deliberately gone hard at the England players. Especially Trotty. And Johnson had no intention of letting up in Brisbane. He told the press that 'I think he's come out and said he's not worried about the short ball, but we saw what he was like in the one-day series, he definitely didn't like it.' In the one-day series, Johnson had hit Trott on the head with a bouncer, and had no problem with fast, physical bowling: 'If I can get a few of those rearing balls towards the ribs or those throat balls, and if he gets in the way of it, that's his own fault.'

When the Aussies think they can see a weakness in you, they are like sharks. They didn't, of course, know about Trotty's problems.

The proof is in your innings. You are a long way from home and there is no escape.

You would never know for sure with Trotty until he went out to bat. He fought the mental battle and won it so many times, I reckon, but in Brisbane he was totally gone. You could see it in his eyes: he just wasn't there. I wasn't cross with Trotty, but I was mad with the system. When you are stressed, burnt out, depressed, whatever, you don't see things the way you normally do, and your team's support is supposed to protect you. But ours didn't.

I remember the last one-day international in Southampton, in September 2013. We were warming up, and Trotty was in the outfield, visibly upset.

I had gone to Ashley Giles earlier in the day, before we went to the ground, and asked him to please let Trotty go home. Don't make him play. Let him go and chill. Let him go to his family. Tell the media he was being rested or he had tweaked something in his back.

The answer was, no, he wants to play.

Of course Trotty says he wants to play. He'll put himself through this for the team, but I don't care if he wants to play. He needs a break.

I asked Giles to go and speak to Trotty, to have a look at him. He did, and then Trotty just disappeared; Luke Wright was there in his place.

It should never have been left so late in the day. It just needed a short announcement: we're going to rest Trotty for the last one-day international. The point is, Ashley Giles knew that Trotty was having a hard time before we left for Australia. If Giles knew, Flower had to know too. Trotty was key to our order, so needed looking after for a while. The system should have wrapped him in bubble wrap. Instead, it let him down.

I would argue that, to have achieved what I've achieved, my defensive play must have been reasonably good. In fact, playing in England where batting is very difficult with the ball swinging, the ball seaming and so on, you can't play without a defence. So I do play defence, but then I go for the occasional reckless-seeming shot and that rubs people up the wrong way.

After Brisbane, a lot of people were rubbed up the wrong way. Even when things go bad I'm still somehow expected to pull runs out of a hat. When I don't, it's usually because I'm irresponsible.

I think it actually has very little to do with cricket. People formed their opinions of me a long time ago, and everything I have done since then is used to confirm that opinion. I do well and the people who like me say that is why they watch me. The people who hate me say, yeah, just wait. I do badly and the people who like me say, he takes risks: that's just what comes with the territory. The people who hate me say, told you so.

I think that as a South African kid who came to live in England I had some tough battles, but I also gave as good as I got. I was abrasive, and made no secret of the fact that I had come to England to have a Test career, not to tug my forelock and thank everybody for having me.

So I came across as arrogant. Then 2005 happened. A few years earlier, the ECB had said that they hoped to generate stars on the same level as football players. After 2005 the ECB had Freddie Flintoff and me on their hands and they shit themselves. It wasn't what they wanted after all. They couldn't handle either of us and neither could they help either of us handle it all. Soon I wasn't just arrogant, I was out for myself. I was a big shot. The flip side of being confident and adventurous – which I was on the good days – was being arrogant and irresponsible on the bad days. You can't afford too many bad days if you are a big shot.

Irresponsible isn't quite the right word when it comes to shots I regret. It's instinct, and sometimes it can be controlled. There have been times when, say, I have played the most expansive drive shot to backward point and I am the first to ask myself, what the hell did you do that for? It's instinct. I'm just down there in the moment.

It's so easy, sitting on the balcony or above the sidelines, to make judgements. But I'm the one standing down there on the grass. I'm thinking, what are my hands like right now in my gloves? Am I feeling okay mentally? What's the bowler going to do here? What is my weakness now and what is my strength? That's what is going through my head. There's a lot, and it's very personal.

If you are watching from the outside you probably have a very holistic view. You can see anything that is going on, and have the time to examine all the permutations and contexts of the game. As a result, most of the time you can make better decisions than the bloke out in the middle. The sun is on me, it's sweltering, I'm thinking that anything can happen. You just see the batsman tapping the surface with his bat. So what? I'm the batsman, though. I'm thinking, what the hell? Look at that crack in the earth right there. If the ball hits that it's curtains. I'm tapping that crack, then looking at the field and thinking, okay, where is he going to try to bowl this one? These are split-second decisions and adjustments that every batter has to make. And sometimes batsmen don't make the decisions that commentators or the general public think they should make.

That's what makes cricket fascinating. The guy down there in the helmet and gloves can't access the big picture.

He can only sweat the small stuff.

The way he's standing, his foot positions, what the wicket is going to do, what he is seeing in front of him on that surface, glancing up to try to read the bowler. You get one chance as a batter, so sometimes you can't control the instincts. When I'm in good form and not worried about what's actually in front of me in terms of the wicket, I have two aims: see ball, hit ball. If I see the ball I'm going to hit it.

See ball. Hit ball. Those instincts have brought me more good moments than bad. I find it very hard to say, I don't care what's bowled to me here, I'm just going to play it safe and knock it down in front of me.

No. I'm going to hit whatever I see if it's in my area.

When I am not playing well, I will always refer back to twelve, thirteen, fourteen years ago and say to myself, you're an off-spinner, how the hell have you actually ended up batting for England? What got you here?

That's frustrating. Sometimes I've stood at the wicket and felt nothing but anxiety. My head tells me I'm a free spirit, that I'm not really technique-based. I play on feel; my game is touch and instinct. What am I doing here?

We had a team meeting before going to Australia, and Flower gave us all his talk about legacy. What legacy can we secure by the end of this Ashes campaign? What is going to be *our* legacy?

Everybody was wondering what he was really saying. Is he telling us he's finished after this series? What is all this legacy stuff? What's this *our* stuff? Do you mean *your* legacy?

We win and the legacy looks after itself. Simple.

He asked me what legacy could we get from this and I just started laughing.

Why are you laughing?

I said, you don't want my answer. Let's just win the Test series. Let's not worry about anything except winning, not how many bottles we pick up in training or how we appear in the media.

The public adore their national teams when they win. They aren't interested in bullshit in the tabloids. They want us to win.

That's what we are doing here.

When I walk out to the middle, find my stance and lift my bat, something is transmitted inside my head by the way that I lift that bat up. In that moment, I know if I'm in good form or not.

I've done quite a bit of work with the psychologist to try to figure out what my neutral position is. If I think that I am nowhere, how do I change that into making myself believe that I am somewhere? That's the hardest thing I have dealt with throughout my career. On most days I feel fantastic, but sometimes I have walked out there and thought, uh–oh, this must be how Monty Panesar feels when he's having a bad one.

I was like that in that second Test in Adelaide. My knee was hassling me, so I wasn't able to get into correct positions when I was defending. I just didn't know what I was doing with the bat in my hands. It was horrendous, because there's such big pressure on my wicket. I'm the one the Aussies most enjoy getting out.

What I played in Adelaide was a terrible shot in anyone's book, but when I was batting, as Peter Siddle was running up, I was lost, mentally and technically.

Siddle has always been a tricky customer for me. He is patient, and gives nothing away. The Australians could send in a big gun and we'd butt heads like stags in the glen, but Siddle digs in. It's a long haul and I get nothing but scraps. Then finally I decide enough is enough. This is it. I hit to mid–wicket. George Bailey catches it. I'm gone for four runs.

Then the same old criticisms start coming down. Irresponsible. Wasteful. When will he grow up?

It's very difficult when you get bowled out like that. I don't do anything or say anything, I just take my pads off and I go straight off to the balcony to sit and watch the team.

The Big Cheese, Swanny and Cooky also gave it away cheaply in Adelaide. In the second innings, Broad did something I would be crucified for: he hit Siddle for six, then tried to do exactly the same with his very next shot. He was caught at deep square leg.

Flower has burdened us with all his bullshit talk about legacy, and has kept us buttoned down and on edge. There was no enjoyment, and our families would not be with us until the third Test. But what is pathetic is that we can see that the Aussie pressure is getting to him more than anybody.

For years, when we have won we have done it ugly. We have done it the Flower way, slugging it out. Since the summer, the Australians have gone away and learned what will work for them, how they can win the war of attrition.

Now, in Australia, Flower risked losing it as the press needled and ridiculed us at every opportunity. In Brisbane, the *Courier-Mail* had it in for us. One day they ran a picture of me on the front page. I had my shades on and my earphones in. I don't really care how that looks. It was sunny – shades keep the sun out of my eyes. I wanted to get into the zone – earphones keep the Aussies calling me a wanker out of my ears. Splashed across the photo were the words 'He's so arrogant not even his own team likes him'.

Big deal. It wasn't even that smart, but the journalist tweeted in triumph:

Loving C-Mail front page today. Hits the nail on the head! #KP pic.twitter.com/x2zj8LJ7pE

I saw the tweet and replied:

Kevin Pietersen ✓

Follow.

@bendorries so do I mate. Putting me on the front page does wonders for my ego! You've done me proud. Thank you x

It came up at a press conference, where I said that I hoped I'd added a few followers to the journalist's Twitter account. It got a few laughs.

The same paper ran a team picture of us on the front page with the headline 'Team of Nobodies', and they also had a go at Stuart Broad.

During the first Test of the summer series there had been a fuss about Broad not walking after he had edged an Ashton Agar delivery. In retaliation, the *Courier-Mail* decided not to use Broady's name while he was in Australia. Instead, they referred to him only as 'the 27-year-old English medium-pace bowler'. Broady got the joke. Even when crowds sang 'the 27-year-old English medium-pace bowler is a wanker' he got the joke.

Meanwhile I looked at the Aussie set-up and I almost envied them. They had brought in Darren Lehmann.

Two quick points on Lehmann.

First, Michael Vaughan, writing in the *Telegraph*, described him as 'a fun character who laughs all the time, likes a beer and just loves to talk cricket . . . also one of the hardest cricketers I have ever met', and went on to say: 'His ability to make people view cricket as just a game is his strength. He makes a player, even during pressurised situations, feel as if he is playing for his club side on a Saturday afternoon. He knows it is more important than that but he makes the player feel relaxed. It is a refreshing mentality to have.'

Wow.

Second, Lehmann actively encourages aggressive batting against spinners on the principle that 'There are no fielders in the car park.'

Wow again. Are you reading this stuff, Flower?

Lehmann was big and very Australian, and he kept his players chilled. He was also out-thinking us the whole time.

He had been appointed in June 2013, just before the summer Ashes, and while they were losing the series three–nil Lehmann and his captain Michael Clarke were learning fast. They knew that whoever won in Australia would come away with not just the Ashes but the bragging rights. The Aussie batting order was rejigged again and again. They moved David Warner around, then put him back at the top. Chris Rogers joined him there. Shane Watson went to number three, Steve Smith to five. Clarke became four, while George Bailey settled at number six. A few guys like Ed Cowan, Phillip Hughes and Usman Khawaja drifted out of the order altogether. The Australians settled on a line-up that saw every ball bowled by Swanny as a chance for a six. No fielders in the car park.

Among the bowlers, Ryan Harris, Peter Siddle and Nathan Lyon earned their places in England, but Mitchell Johnson was used carefully and cleverly in the summer series. He didn't play the Tests, but they let him loose in the more aggressive settings of the one-day games. There, he gave a glimpse of the shock and awe to come before going back under wraps. Then, in the meantime, the Australians got lads to bowl gently at us in the warm-up games and let us worry about Johnson until Brisbane. It worked.

The Aussies had worked out what they were best at, and had a coach who saw the merits of his players and established a system that played to their strengths. We were all at sea. We were a mix of fear and fake cockiness, pretending to be up for a fight that we hadn't the weapons for.

We had a dressing room in which the bowlers were allowed to cow the batters. Flower was like a deer in the headlights. He hated the Aussie aggression. He had produced an ugly team who ground out wins by playing within our limits. Now guys who would normally be conservative were swiping at things madly. We didn't have any new ideas, and had also forgotten how to do the old things we were good at. My role had always been to bring a bit of adventure to the batting order, but now we were just a series of individuals trying to survive out on the field. Then we would go in and devour each other in the dressing room afterwards.

23

The Fremantle Doctor
Will See You Now

At the wicket in Adelaide, I might as well have been holding a hockey stick.

I just didn't feel right at all, standing there saying to myself, fucking hell, what is happening? Only negative thoughts were running through my head.

I hit a ball that should have been business as usual. But I walk, knowing I am going to be crucified.

When the adrenalin stops, I think to myself that, even after all these years, the game is still a mystery. I batted beautifully in Brisbane last week. I didn't get the numbers, but my action was good. The two outs were silly, but for the second one I literally felt a hot flush and snatched at it. I felt great, though. Now, in Adelaide, this happens. Where is the logic? I know I've got to take one of the coaches aside and ask him to help me. I've got to find my rhythm, or else I won't be able to sleep tonight.

At the end of the day's play, five minutes after the last ball had been bowled, I went straight out to the nets with Richard Halsall, our fielding coach, and batted for about forty-five minutes. At the Adelaide Oval, the public can get up right next to the nets, so there were hundreds of people watching, booing and hissing – I'm the pantomime villain in Australia, after all.

I had Australian guys abusing me from a metre away: you're fucking shit, mate . . . what a fucking shit shot . . . you can't score runs in the nets, mate . . . great shot today, I'm sure your teammates are proud . . . you've let your country down . . . why don't you fuck off back to South Africa . . . hey KP, you're a wanker . . .

It's a lot harder to zone into my game with people around than if there is nobody there, so it's a mental exercise as much as a physical one. I've done it in South Africa too, going out to train when I know people will be around to heckle me. I'm in the nets, being abused, knowing I'm not batting well and that I have to solve it. I have less than an hour to cure myself.

So, for forty-five minutes that day in Adelaide I had to block out what was being said a couple of metres away from me and focus in on how my hands felt. It was amazing. Suddenly, after about ten minutes I just clicked and started feeling really good again.

I suppose the question is, why didn't I go out early in the morning before my innings and do all of this? Was that not the time to find my rhythm?

Well, my knee had been a huge issue for the past year. Some

mornings I would wake up and wonder if I'd be able to make it down to breakfast, my knee felt so sore. I'd been playing on the strongest painkillers. I've been using paracetamol, ibuprofen, diclofenac, celecoxib – if it promised to kill pain, I was all over it.

As a sportsman, managing that chronic pain really interferes with your mental state and affects how you play. When I bat, I normally crouch down and get quite low. (Ian Bell mimics me to an absolute T. It's very funny how he has it down.) It's a case of finding my stance and then bending my knees a couple of times to find my balance. After injuring my knee, though, I wasn't able to do that and so immediately knew that I was only 75 per cent of the player I could have been. Some days I felt okay, but most of the days I was nowhere. Well, not nowhere, but 75 per cent, and it was incredibly frustrating.

Sometimes, I've stood at the wicket and felt nothing but anxiety. Before my second innings in Adelaide I knew that everybody wanted me to play defensive cricket. They wanted me to grind out a long innings. I'm not that player, but I will try. I know that's what Australia want too: put me on the chain gang and make me grind. They know I am dangerous when the adrenalin is going: I try to dig in to be defensive, but I'm in trouble. I don't have the technical game or the mind for it.

I did better in the second innings: 53 runs off 99 balls. A couple of fours and three sixes, the rest all singles or bait that I didn't take. There was no joy, though. I hated it. Australia were quite happy to give me 53 and then say goodbye. Alastair Cook went for a single run. Monty Panesar was out for a duck. Ian Bell and Swanny each made six. Yes, I was definitely the problem child in the class of high achievers.

After the series had ended, and I had been England's top scorer, somebody quipped that it was 'like being the best player on Snow White's basketball team'. Nailed it.

If I had been alone in my struggles in Adelaide, it would have been a sideshow, but we were collapsing all over the place. I was a symptom of something bigger, something that was destroying us.

The Aussies pummelled us with aggressive, hostile cricket. We had a bad game plan and we were executing it badly. When your legacy is going down the drain in Australia, does it swirl clockwise or anticlockwise?

There would be no heroic last stand in Perth.

The WACA was barely half full when Australia took the Ashes back. They had only needed fourteen days of cricket to do it. All over with two Tests left to play.

Anderson and Broad had been at the crease when it ended, and had to shake hands with our conquerors. I was glad to be away from it all, behind a pair of sunglasses up on the balcony. I was very much on my own.

I couldn't be happy with any of my dismissals in the series. They were bad, and mostly they were inexplicable. It was head stuff: I was deeply unhappy, and I knew that was never a good way for me to play. I was hurting: literally, physically hurting and hurting in every other way too.

The team was out of ideas and falling apart bit by bit. We had a coach who was withdrawing in a sulk about his legacy, a coach who had got it all wrong.

He had taken the three–nil win in the summer as proof of his superiority. Truth was, we had slices of luck all summer.

In England, in the summer of 2013, the Aussies had come and they had seen. They had figured out how to conquer. Now, on home turf, they were ripping us apart. Our batsmen were demoralised. Our fielders were dropping as much as they were catching. Our bowlers weren't hurting them. Swanny was playing too much, while Mitchell Johnson was almost playing too little. They were just using him as a hit-man.

I was standing behind Andy Flower and Alastair Cook during the first innings of the third Test. My innings had just taken me past eight thousand runs. A landmark, but not in the happiest circumstances. Still, we always celebrate people's success in the dressing room.

Personally, I was having a shit time of it: by then, my average in the series was 24. My career average was more than double that. I needed some encouragement, so Alastair Cook, good man that he is, decent at heart, told Flower we were going to have a beer to celebrate my eight thousand runs.

And Flower said, what for?

I wasn't in a mood to celebrate either. It was a bad out, to Siddle again. The stats hurt me. Siddle had now bowled me 390 balls, I had scored 174 runs and he'd got me out ten times. This time, I'd slugged a half-tracker straight up in the air and down to Mitchell Johnson, standing at mid-on with his hands stretched gratefully up to the skies.

I needed an arm around me, rather than the usual cold shoulder. By then everybody was in their own little hell, though. Especially the experienced guys. Nobody was happy with how they had played, but the great micro-manager left us to our torments. Flower was the only person not in the room when we had a drink at the end of the day. He'd told Cook that he had to be somewhere else.

You try to take a lift out of anything while there is still hope, and it was the first innings – there was still a slender chance that we could save the series if we found something within ourselves.

Was it a big deal? The players always share a drink in the dressing room if there is an achievement to celebrate. If somebody gets a hundred or a bowler takes five wickets, then at the end of the day's play we all, team and management, stay in the dressing room, have a bottle of beer and one of the blokes will stand up and talk about how great it was. It's just a little way to acknowledge the team's happiness and joy in one another's successes.

Flower was so pissed off with the way I'd got out and so pissed off at me, at the whole situation, that he didn't want to acknowledge my eight thousandth run. He couldn't stand to do what was good for the team. Any good coach would have seen it as a chance to give a guy some encouragement, and make him feel good and enthusiastic again. You don't need to be a sports psychologist to know that most players perform better when they are happy and confident.

Even if he didn't want to give me that lift, Flower should have been there for the team. He wasn't, and it was noticed.

He made us feel bad about almost everything he couldn't control. For example, the occasional night out was always an issue. I don't mean the sort of benders that get splashed across the tabloids, just the letting-the-hair-down kind of night out that brings people together. The things that all teams do once in a while. The things that take the pressure off when a team is struggling away from home. Loosen the grip, let them breathe.

A night out with the team builds close bonds because people come out of themselves. They bring their personalities and not their cricket game. When they've had a beer or two the difference between the junior player and the senior player is forgotten.

Take a young guy like Gary Ballance, for instance. On the 2013/14 Ashes tour he was very quiet and reserved at first. Tiptoeing about, walking on eggshells around the senior players. But then we had a couple of nights out and he became a brilliant, boisterous, lovely guy. You could wake up the next morning and say to yourself, what a great night: Ballance is bloody funny. Before that it was like, shit, how am I going to build a relationship with this lad? He's very quiet.

We needed more of that. More time to build our friendships, to find what we liked about each other again. We needed to work as a team. Not a crew hired to nail down some legacy.

After the Perth Test I had to fly to Melbourne to get another cortisone shot in my knee. I hadn't even been going to play in Perth because my knee was so bad, but we were two–zip down and we needed to be at full strength on the field. I was in a lot of pain, but I dearly wanted to play so I loaded myself up with painkillers. Off the field, I tried to manage my knee with injections and rehab.

I'd tried my hardest to fight off the prospect of surgery for nearly a year. I needed microscopic surgery, which would mean down time of about nine months. I had decided to grin and take the pain, and see how far I could go.

24

Night of the Long-Winded

What next?

Well, after three Tests we lost Graeme Swann. A few days after the Perth Test he announced his retirement with immediate effect, packed his gear and went home. He had been struggling with an elbow injury, leaking almost four runs an over and had taken only seven wickets. He had seen the sixes fly away in large numbers.

There was more to come. At the start of the limited-overs series Steven Finn, having not bowled a ball during the five Tests, was deemed 'not selectable at the moment'. He went home too. I thought it was very encouraging for a talented young player to be told he was 'not selectable'.

Tell me this, Andy Flower: how does a good coach bring a

team to the Ashes and things just get worse and worse? How does a decent coach have a player so beaten down in the first Test that he goes home? How do you have someone else retiring from the sport after the third Test? Finally, how can you have a kid who, six months before that, was among the world's top bowlers suddenly be told in public that he is 'not selectable'?

Talk to me about managing. Talk to me about coaching. I am telling you, I know you are a dreadful coach not by how you won but by how you lost. Bad times are when coaches prove themselves. In bad times you were the problem, not the solution. Your methods created an environment where people became terrified of failing. Every time we came off the field you behaved as if one of us had run over your dog. Your legacy had become roadkill. You tell me what good came from that.

You were applying too much pressure and we were suffocating in your hands.

We were whitewashed by a team that, before the series started, hadn't won in nine Tests. We took seventeen players out to Australia but ended up needing eighteen. We used eighteen players, but Australia used the same eleven all the way through. Australia hit us for ten centuries. We managed one. Our highest first-innings total was 255 over five Tests. Six times we were out for under 200.

My hand is in the air: I did not have a good tour. I know why, and so do you. Where are all the other hands? Where are the rest of the people taking responsibility?

A while back, a guy called Crispin Andrews wrote the following in the *Bucks Herald*. Somebody sent it to me.

Cliques create certain cultures within sports teams. These cultures might seem to have the team's best interests at heart, but they're actually more often about an influential group maintaining a way of doing things that maximises their own role, influence or enjoyment. Whether a player buys into this culture or not, determines whether they are perceived as a maverick or a team player [. . .]

Unfortunately, when mavericks come up against cliques and entrenched cultures, there's more back biting, rumour mongering and politicking than there is open and honest communication.

All too often, when the maverick has gone, the clique remains. And while it's there, the team will continue to suffer. But without the clique's biggest critic, the team will suffer quietly and undemonstratively.

I don't know Crispin Andrews, but he answered my question about where all the hands that were supposed to be up in the air had gone. I just thought, bang on, mate. Nail on head.

England has chosen to suffer quietly and undemonstratively. That's the legacy.

I got to the end of the first day in Melbourne on 67. Next morning, I opened with a four and was feeling good. Then Mitchell Johnson bowled Tim Bresnan out at the other end. For some reason, seeing Brezzie go made me want to punish Johnson. I swung for the fences at a ball that had some inswing. The fences were never troubled. The ball hopped in and took leg stump. Shit happens.

Afterwards, the media asked Jimmy Anderson what he thought of my dismissal: 'I'm not sure. You would have to ask Kev about it. He obviously felt that it was the right way for him to go.'

Now, back in Perth Jimmy's bowling had conceded a world-record-equalling twenty-eight runs to George Bailey in the space of one over. But you'd have to ask Jimmy about it.

Sometimes, I can read the situation I am in and play accordingly. In that sense, I think I have matured more throughout my career than I am given credit for. Brisbane and Perth would not be the best examples, I know, but I stand by that fourth Test in Melbourne. I batted for a hell of a long time in that first innings and got an ugly 71, and I was one of the last men out. I batted with real patience because I knew I'd let myself and the team down with the shot I'd played in Perth the previous week.

Everybody had their own problems in Australia. Four games gone and the whitewash was coming at us like a tsunami. We each had to find our own way of staying afloat.

In Melbourne, Alastair Cook called a players' meeting.

I didn't see how it would help when we were four–nil down. Nothing but a time machine was going to rescue the situation now. Still . . .

We were in the dressing room, about an hour after we lost the fourth Test. It was just the players, no back-room staff, no coaches.

As usual, Cooky started it off and then Matt Prior took over.

This had been a problem for the whole tour. If Cooky said something clunky – if he mumbled or mispronounced a word – Swanny would give a little snort. He wasn't being malicious – I don't think he even realised he was doing it – but you could see it was making Cooky less and less confident, so he had Prior speak for him.

By Melbourne Swanny had gone home, but by then the Big Cheese was used to chairing the meetings.

He might have been vice-captain, but he had been dropped for the Melbourne Test and nobody was very interested in him just then. He'd been walking around like the poster boy for sulking and bending everybody's ear, saying that maybe he should just go home. He was talking to people as if he had been given a few weeks to live.

Look, Cheese, between my thumb and forefinger. Can you see it? It's the world's tiniest violin, playing a sad tune for you. Now go away.

He'd been wearing a face that was half grief and half thunder, and then all of a sudden he was making a whole lot of noise in this players' meeting.

I had a problem with that. The Big Cheese had a lot to do with the atmosphere in the team before he was dropped. He'd had no complaints when he was rolling with his posse of Baby Cheeses and ruling the dressing room, but now Cheese had been dropped he was out of the game. All of a sudden, he had a lot to say about the state of the nation.

Ian Bell was vice-captain now. If Cook had got injured in Melbourne Bell would have led the team for the final Test in Sydney. So give Ian Bell some responsibility here. Let him talk.

I said this to Cooky and he said, oh you know Belly, he doesn't talk.

I pointed out that if you're going to continue that way of thinking through Bell's whole career he's got no chance, absolutely no chance.

One of the things that finished off my relationship with Alastair was me taking on Prior. Prior was a sidekick for Cooky and he was also a crutch. I had said quite openly that I thought he should not be vice-captain, that he shouldn't have any sort of power in the dressing room. I don't think Cooky took too fondly to that.

I didn't know exactly why we were having this players' meeting. We'd been having a beer in the dressing room. I imagine Flower and Cook said they needed to get everyone together to see if we could resolve any of the situation. The players needed to be open and honest, and perhaps they would be more likely to do that without their coach being present.

Stable door. Horse bolted. But anyway . . .

All the boys had been getting on reasonably okay away from the cricket. I was keeping my head down, doing some coaching work with the younger players and really enjoying it. That, and my practice time alone, were what was getting me through the days.

It's Flower who was the problem. Walking around with that 'somebody stole our legacy' face. The environment was horrendous. The whole series was horrendous. And now the Big Cheese was telling us what's what.

We were all sitting in a circle, having pulled up our chairs when the meeting was called. The Big Cheese told us we needed to sort things out. The environment was shit, he said.

No shit, Sherlock. When did you become such a blast of clean air?

Then Prior said, fuck Flower, this is not his team.

This was coming from a player who, to most people's way of thinking, had been the worst player in the tour, and certainly the least constructive. He'd been dropped. We didn't really want to hear from the Big Cheese right now. We knew where he was coming from. An empty vessel spouting what we already knew.

That's one of the facts of life in sport. You have standing when you are playing well. Unless you are something really remarkable or somebody really dumb, you just shut up when you are playing badly. I have seen remarkable. Cheese ain't remarkable.

He said, you know all this. It's not just our fault but the management's too. They are creating an awful work environment. They treat us like schoolboys.

He said, we've got to sort this out. We're the ones who score the runs, we're the ones who take the wickets, we're the ones who go out there to do the business.

Then he opened the debate to the floor.

At that point I looked up and said, that's fucking strange, Cheese, because this is something I've been saying for a while. The environment is shit. Flower's created a shit environment. I've been saying this for the last two years.

Why did I make this point?

Well, I had been in the same place two years earlier and I'd had the balls to say it to Andy Flower's face. I've always been up front about what I am feeling.

Prior is not the brightest. He turned and said to me, well, not all of us have played a hundred Test matches.

As if that made any difference.

I said, two years ago, Cheese, I'd only played sixty or so.

It doesn't matter how many matches you've played: you could see Flower was coaching the players by fear. Now, in a private meeting, some people were agreeing. I just wanted to remind them that what we were talking about was nothing new. I asked people in the room if they were scared of Flower. It was ironic that, although the Big Cheese and I weren't getting on, we were coming from the same place.

I remember Monty Panesar saying, actually, I don't think this is right at all. I think Mitchell Johnson is the reason we're losing every game.

Prior shot him down straight away. He said, fuck off, Monty, it's not Mitchell Johnson. This environment is shit and we are going to have to change it.

Did I misjudge the mood at that meeting? People like to say so.

The spin ever since that day has been that I judged the atmosphere wrong. I went on a run and found myself over a cliff like a cartoon rabbit, still running but with only fresh air beneath me.

I don't think I misread anything about the mood in that room.

I heard what was being said by players in a meeting at which the coach was not present. I said my piece, nothing anyone hadn't heard before – including Andy Flower.

At the end of the day, every player who was there in Melbourne knows exactly what went on.

The meeting probably lasted for about half an hour. I spoke. Some others spoke. Monty Panesar had tried to speak but he was shut down very quickly. Cook didn't talk much.

I am sure that Prior and Cook would have had to feed back a version of events to the management after that meeting. If you edit out what Prior had said, it's easy to make it look like Kevin Pietersen was the one who was out of step with everybody else. By now, I know how this all works.

A lot of the players probably left the dressing room in Melbourne wondering what version of events would get back to Flower. I wasn't bothered at all, though I knew for sure there was going to be a falling-out. I have said nothing and written nothing that I wouldn't say to his face.

I think I did the right thing. I stand by it.

I had seen how Andy Flower did business and I spoke up. Another player who is a close buddy once told me that he felt like a racehorse. If he was doing well, Flower wanted to speak to him. He was the best little horse in the yard. If he wasn't doing well, Flower didn't want to know.

As a former show pony myself, I knew that was a typical story.

What I said needed to be said. I'm quite proud that I stood up to him and said what I did. Flower stopped speaking to me, but I had other things to be worrying about so paid no heed.

In the last couple of Test matches the Australian media had their guns trained on Cook's captaincy. There was a lot of chat about how Cook was having a very bad tour, and was called Captain Cock-Up and stuff like that. It was also being said that Prior was a poor vice-captain. I disagreed about Cooky. After Prior had gone he was transformed. He led the team, made his decisions and we had okayish days. We were shot by then and didn't have a strong enough team, but at least our captain was back in control of the dressing room.

By the time the Melbourne Test had been lost people such as Shane Warne and Michael Vaughan had said in the media that I should be Alastair Cook's number two, since Prior had been dropped after Perth. This idea seemed to be gathering a bit of momentum, so Prior confronted Vaughan on the first morning of the Sydney Test and said, what would you want him as vice-captain for?

Vaughan said, fuck off, mate, you're not even in the team. Now do one.

After Vaughan had hammered him I heard a rumour that the Big Cheese went to our media liaison officer and said that the situation was unacceptable, and that there needed to be a campaign in the media to make sure I didn't get the vice-captaincy. Did he really do that?

I think Cooky felt a hell of a lot of pressure at that time. It wasn't going to happen, but he would have thought, fucking hell, KP as vice-captain? KP wants Prior gone? Where would that leave me if everyone's saying that I should go too? I think that process probably made it quite easy for him when he was given the option of getting rid of me.

I think the thought of me becoming vice-captain probably scared him, and I certainly know that Prior felt that I was backstabbing him because I've still got the texts on my phone from when I messaged him about his proposed media campaign.

I said:

> I've heard from several different sources in the last twenty-four hours that you tried to start a media campaign to stop me taking your vice-captaincy, wow what a team man. Please don't respond, your deny, deny, deny won't wash on this occasion, I'm on the other side of the fence now.

The Big Cheese replied:

> Bore off mate you're talking shit as always, you're the bloke doing the media campaign and spreading shit as you always have, I know what you did and what you said to Flower and everyone knows about how you stabbed me in the back. You obviously never have and never will care about the England team which is a shame because you should have been the best, how you can go at me and use your mate Piers Morgan to try and create problems is just unbelievable.

I said:

> No denial, goodbye.

The Big Cheese said:

I don't have to deny anything.

So that was that from him. Radio silence ever since.

25

Now, Live from the Sydney (Soap) Opera House

On the plane from Melbourne I sat with Stuart Broad. We are both tall so we bagged a couple of emergency-exit seats and chatted on the short hop to Sydney. We talked about the players' meeting we'd had back in Melbourne. Broad said, that was interesting, where did it come from?

I said that I didn't know, but I was certain that it was something we had needed. I said I'd been trying to tell Flower for years that his scare tactics weren't working. Then I asked Broad a question about Flower.

You know, how are you getting on with him?

He laughed, and said, fuck knows. He hasn't spoken to me for three weeks.

This guy, Broady, is actually beating the system: he's one of the few of us who's having a very decent Ashes series. And Supercoach isn't speaking to him

Bad behaviour thrived in a bad atmosphere, so Australia was perfect. We were conquered and divided. It was too easy for the guys who came in later to be drawn into the loudest group. Easiest and safest. For example, Prior had connected with Broad on a very friendly level, but I know things about Prior bothered Broad. The more he saw, the more he thought, and especially in Australia he would talk openly with other players about Prior's unending negativity. He was always talking about retiring. Finishing. Getting out. He wasn't playing well and he dragged everybody down.

But the dressing room had been awful for years. Flower didn't grow players by nurturing individual talents, he created a regime. Success papered over a lot of problems. There were wins and star players, but the dressing room was sick all along.

The Ashes in Australia was the first series we had lost since I was dropped in August 2012. I had reintegrated. I made the effort. I ate the humble pie. Before the ECB got their ducks in a row people admitted the truth. Even Graeme Swann said so, in February 2014 between announcing his retirement and being reminded that he needed to get back on message with the ECB. Writing in his column in the *Sun*, he said '[Kevin] made a huge effort to improve his attitude around the dressing room. I saw or heard no issues with him in Australia this winter, his approach was exceptional.'

It was. I was quiet. Boring. Reprogrammed. Reintegrated. As soon as the powers that be needed somebody to blame, though, all the old resentments came out.

I spoke to a coach as soon as I got back to the UK, after the final Test in Sydney. He quietly told me that there were undertones he was picking up on. He didn't like them, and he suggested I watch my back. He didn't want to say more than that.

I knew then that knives were being sharpened.

In Sydney, the day before the final Test, poor Alastair stood up like a kid whose mum is making him ask his friends to tidy up at the end of his birthday party. He gives a little speech about how we are not fit enough, how we need to really, really work on our fitness. It's the last training session before the final Test of a disastrous tour. Alastair is telling a beaten battalion, four Tests and two men down, that their uniforms need to be ironed.

I stood there, thinking it was insane. We're playing tomorrow. When are we going to do all this training? How, in under twenty-four hours, are we going to get fitter than the Aussies?

It was a move right out of the Flower playbook. Don't just stand there, tick boxes.

I totally understood Cooky's right to talk about fitness. I just didn't understand the timing. It wasn't the thing to say for his inspirational speech before the match. By then, gallows humour had settled in with the boys. They were starting to take the piss, making little jokes out loud: 'Who's going to the gym in the morning? If I'm not there at half six don't wait for me.'

Was this not the perfect time to say, look, guys, we're four–nil down, let's go out there and enjoy ourselves. Bowl as fast as you can, we'll catch whatever we can. Let's see ball, hit ball whenever we can. Express ourselves again. Feel good about playing for England.

We needed to be reminded that, somewhere lost in the middle of all the shit, we were a decent team with some decent cricketers. We needed to relax, then go out and find that team again.

Cooky needed to say, you know all our families are here now, so let's make this good. Let's finish with something successful on a personal level, and then go out and enjoy Sydney with our families.

Instead, we got a fitness chat. He spoke for about two minutes and then the guys went back to whatever they had been doing. I thought to myself, what was that? Why are we getting this? We are four–nil down.

So, me being me, I took Cooky aside after training to a private area outside the dressing room and said, Cooky, I think you got that totally wrong, mate. I don't think you should have talked about fitness. The key to this week is to encourage the lads to get the best out of it. We have one week left in one of the greatest cities, let's enjoy ourselves.

He said, no, no, we're not as fit as we should be.

I just said, Cooky, with the greatest respect, this is one of the fittest English teams I've played on. I don't think fitness is the issue. Skills and management structure are the issues here. We talked about it in Melbourne, when your vice-captain stood up and said they were the problem. We talked about Flower walking around being a Mood Hoover.

Cooky sort of agreed. He said he didn't know what Flower was going to do when the tour finished, but we needed changes. He agreed that the environment was shot to pieces.

I said, I hope you don't mind my having said this, but I've played a hundred Test matches and I think I've got the right to say this. Cooky said, no, no, it's absolutely fine.

After that, we returned to the hotel and I received a message from Flower, saying he wanted to see me in his room when he got back.

Shit. On a list of things I don't need, number one would be another meeting with Andy Flower.

Flower got back to the hotel, but the security system meant that I couldn't access his floor with my room key. I had to wait for him down in the lobby.

Honestly, I had never seen a face like it when he came to get me. He looked like somebody had pissed in his pocket. It took the tension away as, inside, I was just laughing to myself. Are we really going to do this?

We got into the lift and then Paul Downton, the new ECB chief executive who had just arrived in Oz, stepped in too and we made small talk until he reached his floor. Once Flower and I were in his room I asked, what's up?

He said, you really disappoint me.

I sat down on the opposite side of the table from him, and then he spoke again.

I've spoken to Cooky and I know everything that's been said. Yes? Do you?

Yes, I do. And you really disappoint me. Who else have you been speaking to?

Nobody. Cook is the captain, I spoke to him.

Then we got into a huge argument.

He said that he was at the end of his tether. From a man who had put most of us on the express train to the end of our own tethers weeks ago, this was kind of funny.

He said he didn't know if he was going to continue as head coach. He didn't know if I was trying to instigate another push against him to get him out.

This was the guy who had been busy gathering us around him a few weeks earlier, talking so much about legacy that some of the players were sure he was going to retire after Australia. It had been a constant topic of conversation. But the obsessive micro-manager had read it wrong. He had thought that by hinting that he was finished his team would say, oh no. Then: well, if he has to go let's win one last big one for the old man.

Instead guys just thought, hey, this fucker is bailing out and he needs us to make him look good.

Flower loves to talk about how once he met Sir Alex Ferguson, and he makes it sound like Fergie passed on all his wisdom on tablets of stone. If he did, Fergie should have reminded Flower what happened the first time he announced he would be retiring at the end of the coming campaign. Things fell apart. Fergie scrapped the retirement plan that Christmas, with United in ninth position. When he announced he was staying, results improved right away. That's the story with feared generals.

We got going hot and heavy now, Fergie-style.

I said to Flower that, if we were talking about being disappointed, it really disappointed me that while he of all people knew how much I went through off the field and how hard I worked just to make it onto the field, he still wouldn't give me any responsibility. He had supposedly reintegrated me but always kept me at arm's length, always made it clear that I wasn't his cup of tea. He would never speak to me in an honest and open way, as coach to senior player, about how I thought the team should be run. Instead, he always wanted to go to people who gave him the comforting answers he wanted to hear.

I said the funny thing was that he, Andy Flower, knew full well the lengths I went to in preparation. I work: I'll get the early bus to training with the coaches who are going to set up the sessions and I'll work alone. I prepare hard for whatever bowling I am going to face. Flower knows because I remember him once hitting me on the head with a ball in Cape Town. I'd asked him to help me prepare for bouncers.

I trained harder than most people played. I'd do rapid-fire short ball training: I'd get a guy to bowl at me fast from five metres away, six cricket balls *bang-bang-bang*. I'd say, try to hurt me – just bounce them and try to take my head off. I've built the confidence to know that if I can get through that, then when somebody is bowling at 90 mph from 22 yards I'll be able to defend myself. I've done that for years and years and years. I'll get hit in the head, hit in the neck and shoulder, but it's fine. You learn to deal with it. Muhammad Ali talked about practising harder than you play, and I've always been a great believer in that.

Flower professes to share this philosophy, but he never gave me credit for the work I put in. He spoke with a forked tongue when he talked about my knee injury. He'd done the same with my double hernia.

He knew all about the painkillers and the injections I was having in my knee. He knew the choice I'd been given. Any surgery would have to deal with a micro-fracture because the bone had softened. The surgeon would need to harden that bone and put pins in it, then he'd have to deal with the oedemas and get the bone to heal and compress. It would be a nine-month job.

Yes, surgery was so medically necessary that my insurance would take care of my loss of income, but I wanted to play in the double Ashes series. I didn't want to give up those particular nine months of my career. So I settled for long-term pain and rehab.

I didn't expect Flower to gush with gratitude, but I'd hoped he would start treating me as a serious and integrated part of the team. That was never the case.

I put it to him: if I'm the big player you always say I am when people ask you, if I'm as important as everybody else continues to say I am, why do you treat me like I've played one Test match? You continue to treat me as if I've only played one Test match. You don't listen to me but you expect me to give performances on the field because it's for your credit. I perform and you get held up as this great coach. If I win a Man of the Match award you are very happy to go and have a glass of wine with whoever you go and have it with in your room. You are happy to take credit for stuff I've done but you treat me like a bloody kid. Why?

In that meeting in his room in Sydney, I told Flower that all I had said to Cooky was that I thought he got his fitness speech wrong. I reiterated the sentiments of the players' meeting in Melbourne, saying that this is not Flower's team, this is our team.

And the quote 'Fuck Flower' was not from me, it was from Prior. Prior, his own creation.

I said the environment stank. I wasn't asking players to go against him, but the man's paranoia was just something else.

Why were we even having this talk? I assumed Flower must have seen Cooky and me talking and his senses went on high alert. Then he summoned Cooky and demanded to know what I had said. I was a little pissed off with Cook for telling him, but then again he is the captain. He could hardly have known that Flower was going to haul me up to his room.

In his defence, Flower said that he had asked me to help the youngsters play spin in India, and to help the seam bowlers with their batting in Australia. He had, and I'd loved those things. He also said that he'd asked my opinions on teams in Australia, and I had to put my hand up. I said, Andy, if you do that, you're doing it for the sake of doing it. You come to me with these questions but you have absolutely no interest in what I have to say. I humour you when you ask me. You humour me by asking.

I reminded him that he had called me outside the hotel to ask me if I thought he should drop Swann for the third Test. I said no, because I knew they were never going to drop him. My trust was in such a place that I felt that if I said yes, do drop Swanny, well, Swanny would be hearing about it sixty seconds later.

Of course I would have dropped Swann. He was a complete waste of space at the time due to his elbow injury.

Flower had asked me before we left for Australia if I had anything to contribute on team selection. I suggested bringing in someone like Ravi Bopara, because I thought we needed something a bit different. Bopara had been through a tough enough time with the bat, but he had come back into the England team for the Champions Trophy in 2013, batting in the number six spot, and made an unbeaten 46 against Australia to help England win. He had done well in the second game too and held his place through to the final. In the final against India Bopara bowled 3 for 20 and made 30 runs during a good partnership with Eoin Morgan. He kept his place in the England squad for the one-day series against New Zealand. I thought he had enough of everything to be worth thinking of, but it fell on deaf ears. He said, don't you manage him?

I said, my company manages him, but what has that got to do with it? Are you going to punish him because of the company that manages him?

But Flower always thinks there is an ulterior motive. He had switched off long before I finished talking.

We laid it all out that evening in Sydney. I told Flower everything for one last time. I said, you have this team that you think loves each other; you pretend that we take happiness from each other's success. I am telling you that is bullshit, and I tell you because I am man enough to do so. The others won't because they are scared of you. You have tried to create a situation in the dressing room where everybody is scared of you, but I'm not. I looked right into his face. He hated that.

As I was leaving the room after our discussion Flower said to me, I hope you score some runs in this Test match.

That lodged in my head. Interesting. Okay, Andy.

Actually, I get what you are saying. I get the veiled threat, so why don't you just fuck off, Flower?

That was the night before the Sydney Test began. You know

what is funny? One of the last things I said to him was that I'd seen glimpses of him when he forgot himself and smiled and tried to be encouraging. During that Sydney Test match I walked past him on several occasions and never said a word to him. I didn't even look at him, but I watched him and he was trying to be that person I'd told him to be. He was encouraging guys and giving pats on the back; he was being everything he hadn't been.

On my life, I was watching all this and I was laughing and just thinking to myself, you probably should have tried this six weeks ago, or four years ago, buddy. Then you'd have a legacy. You know the last thing the players need from their captain and their coach is more pressure. They put enough on themselves, so don't give them more restrictions. In the end, people only care about what happens on the field.

I think Flower realised that in the end.

On the last night in Sydney most of the players, along with their wives and partners, went to the Star City casino. Everybody was drinking, just drowning our sorrows. We all stuck together and had a good night – exactly the sort of thing we had needed to do before the series started.

We stayed up until two in the morning, and when I got up the next day the skies were blue, the war was over and I decided to go to Bondi with the family. Jess had been such a support throughout the series, and my family had been amazing, so I wanted to spend some time with them. It was great until it turned into a media scrum. Suddenly journalists and paparazzi invaded the beach and made the day a bit of a shambles. Within hours it was breaking news around the world that I was having fun after being humiliated in the Ashes.

I found that incredibly funny. On a beautiful day in Sydney, what should I do? Stay in my room and cry while the people I loved waited outside the door?

After the final Test we all got texts telling us that we needed to get our skinfolds measured before we left Australia. Why? In case we were smuggling koala bears out in our great flappy skinfolds? Does anybody think that smacks of a good management structure? We've been whacked five–nil. We are demoralised. The dressing room stinks. And we get texts about having our skinfolds checked. The last boxes have to be ticked.

The skinfolds message came from the team manager Phil Neale, and it worried me slightly. They got Al Capone on tax evasion. Maybe they were finally going to do me in on skinfolds. My knee trouble had meant I wasn't able to run, and running is my thing. I love it – it's brilliant for my head. Running is when I do all my thinking. But since New Zealand in early February 2013 I hadn't run because of the knee. I just couldn't.

Generally, when I had previously done skinfold tests my fitness levels were fine because I was doing other things like cycling to keep them up. Immediately after the Ashes, I was wondering how the test was going to go.

The test result comes out as a sum of numbers. They take a pair of callipers and measure the fat on about seven spots on your body: calf, thigh and on up. A number under 80 is perfect. I've never really gone above 80, but in Sydney I was worried that the number might be up and that they would use it as ammunition.

I don't drink a lot. I socialise, but I don't drink much. Maybe every few months I'll go out and go hard for a night, but then I won't touch alcohol again for months. Jess gets annoyed with me, because if she feels like a glass of wine in the evening she's on her own. I won't put those five hundred calories into my body when I know it takes half an hour of hard training to run them off again.

It turned out I was ten points down in the skinfold test. I was probably the happiest I'd been on the whole trip. They can't get me for my fats! Yippee. I left Australia with a smile on my face.

Nobody in the media seemed at all interested in my skinfold number being down ten points, though. It must have been about the only story concerning me that wasn't leaked.

From the moment I left Flower's room in Sydney I had a sense that the inner circle were telling each other that they had to find some way to get rid of me. Giles Clarke and David Collier listened to Flower, and he worked well with Hugh Morris. Really well. Flower had a remarkable talent for getting on with the people who had the power. Everything underneath, he just controls. Managing upwards – Flower is world class at it.

He was able to convince them that I was a huge problem in the dressing room. That I was a huge problem around the younger players. That I wasn't committed to helping other players grow as cricketers. He convinced them that they had to try to find a way to get rid of me. Paul Downton would later say, 'I have never seen anyone so disengaged from what was going on.' The slyness of the ECB still sickens me: they knew why I was on the boundary – did no one tell Downton? Their medical people have the scans, and they knew my knee problems had been eating away at me for the past year. There was a clear message from my surgeon to the doctor to Flower to the fielding coach: while his knee is the way it is, Kevin Pietersen cannot crouch in an attacking position to catch the ball. He just can't do it. I wanted to be closer in. To have more input in the field. To talk to Cooky. They knew this, but my fielding out on the boundary was just used as a way to take a swipe at me.

I'd been on the physio bed a hell of a lot during the Ashes in Australia. I was rattling about the place I had so many painkillers in me. I was getting a lot of treatment. I was getting a lot of jabs in my knee.

Oh, but he looked disinterested in the field, hanging out on the boundary all the time.

The phones on sports desks at the *Mail*, the *Telegraph* and the *Sun* started ringing.

My relationship with the media had been non-existent since the texting scandal in summer 2012. I turned down all interview requests from cricket journalists and also refused to do a press conference unless I was contractually obliged by the ECB. I just didn't want to speak to them. Things were so bad it took a lot of persuasion for me to even agree to do a press conference the day before my hundredth Test, which should have been one of the easiest press conferences ever. I'd been burnt enough; I was done with cricket journos. I know this will have had a bearing on how they responded to the information they were now being given.

The media started hammering away: rumours, whispers, an imaginary dossier. However, my agent got calls from more sympathetic senior media figures, telling him they were being briefed to a ridiculous degree by the ECB, and that we should be aware of it.

People like Swanny changed their story about everything they had experienced in Australia.

I was accused of everything from causing global warming by the sheer force of my ego to booking flights home while we were still playing, to whistling at a bad time. The felony of whistling allegedly occurred after I got out in Sydney. He whistled when he got out. He whistled in the dressing room. He whistled the team ethic right out the window, according to one shocked teammate.

Even journalists have credited me for one thing over the years: when I get out, whatever the circumstances, I walk to my place and take my pads off. It's the same if I get zero or a double century. I don't throw my bat and I don't throw my gloves. I don't throw a fit. I don't create an atmosphere. I don't sulk. I'm silent. It's not me, me, me. I'm out, and there is nothing I can do to change that. What I can do is affect the dressing room, and it's my choice whether that's positive or negative. By coming back in a calm manner I try to be positive. I internalise the whole thing. I always have a post-mortem in my head, but you have to support whoever is going in to bat after you.

But often when I am annoyed I channel the anger through whistling. It's something my dad would do when I was growing up: when he got really angry he would whistle. It's a mechanism that I picked up. Did I whistle in Sydney? I don't know. I do it a lot when I'm trying to contain myself so maybe I did, but genuinely I don't think so. If it happened it was conveying nothing but the anger I was trying to hold in.

It's a good story, though. It just adds to the wonderful perception that I really didn't give a shit about playing for England. It's all bullshit: I love playing cricket. Getting out for the last time on a disastrous Ashes tour hit me hard.

But seriously, guys? No takers for an exclusive on Pietersen's Sydney skinfold shocker sensation?

26

Nuclear Winter

There were some tricky knots left to tie when my contract was terminated. But in the end, we all got what we wanted and it didn't take long.

Am I bitter?

I have Surrey, the IPL, the Caribbean Premier League, the Big Bash. I have more time with my family, so I'm okay, really I am. There are people out there with real problems; I'm not worrying about the rest of my life. I am happy where I am. If the opportunity to play some more came around, I would jump at it. But I don't lie awake at night worrying about it.

Fourteen years ago I came to England to see if I could play first-class cricket. I left everything I knew and had a punt. I ended up playing in 104 Tests and scoring more runs than anybody has ever scored for England so far.

Am I grateful? Of course I am. And because of that I've always given 100 per cent to playing for England, truly. I've given 100 per cent to practising; 100 per cent to analysing my game to figure out how I can do better. During a home Test I'll wake up at seven o'clock and head straight out for an hour's run along the Thames, to give myself the space to think about the match: how I can improve, where I can improve. So I hope I've given my role the respect and dedication it deserves.

Should I still be playing? Probably, but I feel lucky to have achieved any of it.

People may think that dressing rooms are places of milk and honey and soothing music, but they're not. I had dinner in India one night not long ago with some great players from a few different countries, guys who are stars in their dressing rooms. The stories that were swapped would make your hair stand on end. I have rugby friends, football friends, and the stories are the same.

Come on: it's a grown-up world in there. When you get somebody who tries to dictate like Flower did, you run into problems. When you hit those problems during a whitewash in Australia, you have disintegration.

CHEESEGATE!! READ ALL ABOUT IT!!!

Matt Prior blasts back at claims from Piers Morgan!!!
Morgan tweeted what Prior said in a 'team meeting'!!!

Adds that Prior 'slaughtered' Andy Flower in a statement!!!
Morgan accuses Prior of being a hypocrite
over Kevin Pietersen!!!
TV personality says wicketkeeper 'stabbed KP in the back'!!!
Prior tweets that he 'doesn't know where those
words have come from'!!!!
Morgan urges Prior to take legal action if claims are untrue!!!!

A day after I was sacked the great Twitter war started.
Piers Morgan tweeted:

> I'm about to tweet what @MattPrior13 told England
> players in team meeting after Melbourne Test.

Then,

> Flower's behaving like a headmaster, this is a schoolboy
> environment. F**k Flower! This is OUR team! —
> @MattPrior13 to England team.

Piers then added:

> You stabbed @KP24 in the back @MattPrior13 – yet you
> agreed with him re Flower's dictator style. Makes you a
> flaming hypocrite.

> For the record, @MattPrior13 led the England team
> meeting after Melbourne Test. And slaughtered Flower.

If you didn't say it @MattPrior13 – then sue me. That
should clear things up.

Phew. Say what you like about Piers (and people usually do),
he doesn't pull his punches.

Prior arrived on Main Street, Twittertown, soon afterwards. I
thought he was a bit lame for a gunslinger.

I don't do this PR, spinning media rubbish but I refuse to
be attacked by a bloke that knows very little about what
goes on in the England setup apart from rumour, gossip
and hearsay from certain individuals (most of whom I'd
take with a pinch of salt).

Maybe I was recorded or 'hacked' but if not I'd like to see
where these words I apparently said have come from?
I'm not the kind of person to divelge [*sic*] what is said in
team meetings but all I will say is that Flower, Cook and
the rest of my team mates know exactly what I said & the
way in which it was meant!

I loved that last one from the Big Cheese. So now we know,
if he did say 'Fuck Flower' he meant it in a good way.

You know what? It won't be hard for the ECB to work out
where the rot set in once they stop their politicking. The cricket
writer Scyld Berry spelt it out in the *Telegraph* sports pages as long
ago as March 2013.

He noted that, for a long time, if England scored 400 in the first innings they would almost always go on to win. Following this rule of thumb, we won twenty Tests, drew seven and lost none between spring 2009 and the end of March 2013. The key was, clearly, to rack up a big score in the first innings – specifically, according to Berry's analysis, a score of 386 or better.

The first West Indies Test in 2009, the first under the two Andys, after I had been dumped as captain, proved this rule. In Kingston, we scored only 318 in our first innings. Then, having fallen short of Berry's magic number, we lost by an innings. Strauss and Flower were left scratching their heads.

(That was when I went for a six on 97 and was christened Dumbslog Millionaire. To be fair, I was looking for my third six on the trot – having gone from 85 to 91 and 91 to 97 – and I'd just gone for $1.5 million in the IPL the night before, so whoever made up the nickname got it just right.)

Berry pointed out that after the Kingston Test we ascended to the top of the world rankings, but then by spring 2013,

England's batsmen have lost the knack – notably abroad and especially in the first innings of a series. Thus they were reduced to hanging on by the skin of their teeth in Dunedin and Auckland, instead of bossing New Zealand.

Again the maths are simple. Every time in the last four years that England have scored fewer than 200 in their first innings, they have invariably gone on to lose. Only twice have they scored fewer than 330 yet gone on to win – both times in England, when the ball was swinging, and they dismissed India and Pakistan even more cheaply.

England's decline began in the UAE when they were

dismissed for 192 in the first innings of their series against Pakistan. Since then they have opened their bidding with 193 in Sri Lanka, 191 in India and 204 in New Zealand. No wonder South Africa have overtaken England at No. 1 and raced ahead.

This failure by England's batsmen has been collective – with the exception of Pietersen. Indeed he has become a specialist in making first-innings runs. He has not scored a 50 in the second innings of a Test since July 2011.

This was true right up until I injured my knee in New Zealand. Since then, if you draw a graph of my scores there are fewer high points. In the thirteen Tests I played after my injury – three against New Zealand and ten against Australia – there was just one century, against the Aussies at Old Trafford, and a few fifties. My better totals were, for some reason, coming more often in the second innings: I wasn't getting the big scores, the 'daddy hundreds' as Graham Gooch called them, when we needed them in the first innings. My career average has dipped just slightly, though, and the graph of my performance doesn't dip nearly as drastically as the team's.

After being a team that regularly scored the 386 first innings total which would virtually guarantee a win, we imploded. We scored 465 in the first innings of the second Test in New Zealand, but then did not reach 386 in a first innings during the other twelve Tests. In Australia in 2013/14, we never got above 255 runs in a first innings.

In other words, my injury and my unhappiness eventually dragged me down to the rate of decline that the team had been showing for some time. Being the outsider in a clique-driven dressing room, I carried the can.

They say the trust broke down. I was winning games, doing everything I could. Andrew Strauss has finally acknowledged that I never texted information about how to get him out to the South Africans. In this day and age, the South African bowlers and their coaches would have been analysing how we were playing and coming up with their own tactics, so they wouldn't have needed any hints anyway. At the time, though, Straussy milked it.

In the summer of 2014 the boot was suddenly on the other foot. I played for the Rest of the World against the MCC at the Lord's Bicentenary match in July. I played with a lot of heroes and friends, and afterwards we were all shaking hands in the Long Room when Brett Lee said to me,

Have you seen what Andrew Strauss has said about you?

No.

He's called you a C U Next Tuesday. Live on television.

What?

Yeah: 'an absolute C U Next Tuesday'.

Later on, I was sitting next to one of the greats of the game and he said that Straussy was pretty much all that anybody was talking about – it was all kicking off out in the real world.

What did I feel? Sad. That's all. We had been good mates, we'd been through stuff together. Out in Australia, during the Ashes tour, we'd had lunch with some of the other boys. It went well, I thought.

That afternoon at Lord's I was sad because we'd had a great day, but I knew what was coming. Some of the world's greatest players had gathered in London to celebrate two hundred years of the MCC, but all the headlines the next day would be negative stuff about Straussy and me.

To me, it was a storm in a teacup. Straussy had been caught bad-mouthing me, and I'm cool with that. I've stood in the field for England listening to people bad-mouth me for hours. I've stood and listened to teammates and opposition bad-mouth me. I've walked down the street and had people abuse me. Straussy said something stupid to impress the company he was in, but his timing was bad. I'm over it.

It was strange for me, being at Lord's with those people, that whole weekend, but I began to feel at peace with the world again.

For the MCC game, we players were together almost the entire time, regardless of which team we were on. I was looking around at the faces.

Rahul Dravid: a man who has been there, done that and got the T-shirt. And he's done it all in the most dignified and professional manner. A great friend, a great inspiration, who was always there when I needed him. He has nothing but sadness over all that has happened: he says that in India people ask about me. He tells them the man he knows is not the Kevin Pietersen of the newspapers.

Adam Gilchrist — what a superstar. Pure Aussie. A fierce competitor, in-your-face-tough when you're playing. A quality guy when you're not.

There's Sachin Tendulkar and Brian Lara over there. What can I say? Sachin set the benchmark. Such a special man: no ego, no arrogance. A genuinely nice guy. I look at Lara. The same to be said all over again.

Yuvraj Singh. I've had some great battles with that man. He

used to get me out a lot, so I started insulting him. I used to call him the Pie Chucker, but I couldn't rattle him. He loved it – he even started calling himself the Pie Chucker. That's the mark of the guy. He beat cancer a few years ago. I never thought I'd be friends with a left-arm spin bowler, but I can't help but love him. He's a great friend.

Shane Warne – I'm sitting next to my mate in the dressing room again. Smiling, laughing, joking most of the day. What a superstar. A true inspiration throughout my career. He helped me so much, and always supported me. It's just what friends do. Love him.

Over there, Virender Sehwag. I think everybody smiles when he walks into a room. An out-and-out superstar, but the most carefree joker in the world. He's just a joy to be around.

Brett Lee: fast and furious Brett Lee. Another star and a fine man. Bing, we call him. The Binger. As genuine, kind and good-hearted a guy as you could hope to meet.

On around the room. Every face reminds me of a story or a battle. My old buddy Paul Collingwood is here. My greatest batting partner. He's playing for the MCC today so we won't get to bat in partnership, but we tell each other how lovely it is just to play together again.

At the dinner to mark the MCC celebrations the players were introduced individually to the audience. As we waited off stage we could hear the sort of response each player was getting as he went out. Colly was behind me. Typical Colly: he leant forward just as my turn is coming.

Eh, you could get booed here, mate.

I just started shaking.

It went okay. In fact, it was amazing. A nice cheer. I felt warm and at home.

After all these years in England I understand who I am better than I ever have. I understand the mistakes I have made. I know what other people did too. What people are still trying to do.

Let me sidetrack for a minute, to give you an insight into the workings of the ECB. I had been invited to play for the Rest of the World XI at Lord's, in a letter from the MCC. Banished from England, I was very keen to play and I responded in writing, saying I'd love to take part. What an honour. A press release was put together and I agreed to it being used by the MCC as one of their announcements of the star-studded line-up that would be playing in the bicentenary match. There was little doubt that, with the players on show, the game would be a sell-out. Some time later Adam, my manager, had a call from Derek Brewer, the chief executive of the MCC, asking if he could come to Adam's office to discuss something; he insisted they met face to face. Adam knew something was wrong: Derek Brewer is a busy guy.

Derek was clearly very embarrassed and said that while my invitation had already been sent and accepted, the ECB had not at that point approved all of the names of the players on both sides. The MCC are an independent body, but they work closely with the ECB. It was suggested that it would be better for me not to play, but the MCC was sure that there would be opportunities for us to do something together in the future. Derek had clearly been put in an invidious position, one that he was not comfortable with. He was trying to do the honourable thing.

Adam pointed out that you wouldn't treat a dinner guest in this manner, let alone a guy who had played 104 Test matches for England. It was also pointed out that the media frenzy around this decision would be far worse a scenario than having me play in the game. Derek agreed, and asked for forty-eight hours to try to resolve matters. Then the ECB changed their mind. They apparently hadn't realised that an invitation had already been sent and accepted. I would ask the ECB the simple question: why did you not want me to play?

Thankfully I got to spend a wonderful weekend with some of my heroes.

At the time Straussy made his slip, I was thinking how lucky I was to have had a career and a life that gave me the opportunity to spend a weekend in the company of these guys.

They heard about Straussy and they shook their heads. A shame for you, KP. A shame on this weekend for the MCC. His halo has gone.

Sky didn't need to warn Straussy. What he had said brought its own punishment. Knowing that the world's best players were judging him that weekend would have killed him. I know the man: that was torture enough for him.

If there was a disappointment it was that I missed a call from Straussy that day, and never heard from him again.

We'll be okay. That weekend at Lord's was full of good things, and I could at last see the journey I had been on for what it was.

Best of all in that amazing weekend was Dad.

Dad, our strict disciplinarian. I have lots of respect for Dad. He always pushed us and there were times when we all thought he was too hard. He's so different with his grandchildren – a real puppy.

That weekend, Dad and I found ourselves sitting in the kitchen of my house. Just Dad and me in the kitchen, talking for a few minutes. He said, we feel really proud of you, Kevin.

I was taken aback. He never talks like that.

Why, Dad?

To see you taking the field with the greats this afternoon. Where you were, where you have been, how you have been brought up, where you were brought up. It has led you to here. To see you playing with all those men, walking out at Lord's, to see how you have handled it all. It's something that your mum and I are really proud of.

Old Afrikaners don't say stuff like that cheaply.

27

Not Down, Not Out

Since my contract was terminated, the ECB have been desperate to justify their actions. They insisted on a gagging order till October 2014. Then they broke it. Then they had to apologise for it. The speculation continued until people got bored.

If I have any regrets, they aren't to do with the ECB. They are to do with mates. The guys I was in the trenches with.

I know, for instance, that when the pressure came on Alastair Cook got nervous. When we went to Australia, besides wanting to win I had two objectives: to help Cooky with his captaincy, and to help the youngsters. I told him that again and again.

I know that when things between Matt Prior and me got bad, Cooky felt vulnerable. Matters weren't helped by my friend

Piers Morgan tweeting when things were going badly in Australia.

I met Piers at one of his book launches in 2005 and we ended up becoming good friends; he's been incredibly supportive. People who don't know him can't believe that, but let me tell you: he is a fascinating man. If you got to know him, you would like him.

Piers has been a huge fan of English cricket all his life. He would give anything to walk out to bat at Lord's. So his views are strong. England were losing and Piers, like every other English cricket fan, wasn't happy about it. He tweeted it as he saw it, but the fact that the Australian broadcaster put his tweets on air caused problems.

When Alastair got out to a careless hook shot in Adelaide, Piers tweeted something about how they should drop him from the captaincy; that wasn't a captain's innings. I was waiting to bat, waiting beside Flower, Prior, everybody. Piers's tweet came up on the TV screen in the dressing room and they read his words at the same time as me. I was muttering, oh Piers, no, no, no.

I talked to Piers about it when I saw him in person a few weeks later, and stressed that he should lay off Cooky. He was a decent guy under an extreme amount of pressure.

There was never any time, in Australia or at any other point after I'd been sacked as captain, when I wanted the vice-captaincy or anything else to do with the captaincy. Too many meetings, too much politicking. I had found a little niche for myself, helping the younger players, and I was perfectly content with it. In all the time I was on the England team, there was never a time at which I had a problem with Cooky.

When I came home from Australia in January 2014, Cooky was getting ready for the one-day series down under. He gave a press conference and was asked about me and my future in the team. He was as neutral as he could be: 'If I gave one player reassurance there could be seven, eight, nine, even ten players who want that ... it's unfair for us to do that. I can't talk about what happens in the dressing room at this precise moment in time. I refuse to do that.'

I was disappointed. I had gone out of my way to support him on the Ashes tour.

I texted Cooky straight away:

Hi mate, I've just seen your press conference. I completely understand that you can't guarantee anybody's selection but on a personal level I am pretty gutted that you couldn't say anything positive about me. You know what I have been like on this Tour, you know that the things the press are saying aren't true. I've always had your back. I've always supported you. I want nothing more than for you to be successful as England captain. Go well tomorrow.

He messaged me back five days later:

I'm sorry I have not got back to you. It's been a tough couple of weeks. Let's meet up when I am back home.

I replied:

Sure buddy. Stick to what you know. You know it will turn around. I'm backing you.

That was 16 January 2014. The next time I saw Cooky he was staring at his shoes while I was being told I would not be included in the England squads in the Caribbean or in the World T20.

I was disappointed in him then. I thought the way he behaved called into question his qualifications to be captain. But I know too that he is a decent guy and he was paralysed by how uncomfortable it all was.

One day we'll all be old guys playing a charity match somewhere, and we'll look around at the craggy faces in the dressing room and wonder how we let our friendships fall to pieces.

Again, am I bitter?

No, and no again.

There should be more cricket in these pages, but there was a story that had to be told.

My England career was cut short, taken away from me. My son will never get to see me in an England shirt and actually understand what it means.

I had a bad day recently. We were unpacking after moving house, and Jess discovered a box of cricketing mementoes. Framed pictures of some of my best times on the pitch. Centuries I've scored, partnerships I've treasured. I told her to put them in the garage. Perhaps keep the silver cap out, but don't worry about the rest of it. Put it in the garage and leave it there. As always, Jess managed to cheer me up. No, she said, I'm not doing that. You should be incredibly proud of what you've achieved. Who's scored more runs for England than you? Name me one other England player who's won Man of the Series in a World Cup. Or a player who's caused the MCC to have a meeting about a shot they've helped create? She reminded me of the good things.

For now, with Surrey, the IPL, the Caribbean, the Big Bash and everything else, there's still cricket in my future. Life is full of new adventures.

Jess and I, and our family, have to be prepared to lead a life outside cricket, of course, so we've got quite a few businesses. I've got a clothing company, a number of bars, a foundation, a cricket academy. Jess devotes a great deal of time and attention to property investments we've made. And I've been to meetings where I've had to sell something other than my cricketing ability, and I realise there's a bloody hard world out there. While you're in the bubble of professional sport it's easy. In cricket, you go and play in a match and as long as you're performing it's okay because there's another match soon, and another, and another. So we do real things. Jess works a lot in the evenings because she's been full-on with Dylan during the day. I'm more of a morning person so I'll be up with him at seven. But by nine o'clock in the evening the sandman pops into the living room and I'm a goner.

We try to maintain as normal a family life as possible. We do everything we can to ensure that when I finish playing I don't get the biggest shock of my life.

But if I was offered the opportunity to play Test cricket for England again I would jump at the chance. I dream of playing for England again. It was an honour and a privilege. That's not said for effect. Any player who has been to the top mourns the excitement when it ends. Nothing can replace that buzz.

I hope that it might not truly be over. As they always say, anything can happen in cricket. If all the things that happened to this off-spinner from Pietermaritzburg over the last fourteen years can happen, it just might come to pass that I can play for England again.

I've changed. People change. Someday my caps might go back into my travel bag and it will all start again.

Play it safe, play it safe ... ah, what the hell. Swing for the rooftops.

Acknowledgements

This book wouldn't have happened without the help and support of a great many people, not all of whom can be listed here. How can I thank all of the fans who've supported me during every innings? You're the reason I've been able to enjoy such an incredible journey, and I'll never forget that. And to the many players and coaches who've helped me and stuck by me through thick and thin – I'll always be grateful to you.

I'd like to thank Jess and my immediate family for their constant support throughout my career. You understand me, and you inspire me every day. Thanks, too, to David Walsh, whose expertise helped me say what needed to be said. At Mission Sports Management, Adam Wheatley has been with me every step of the way. My gratitude goes to the sponsors who have played such a vital role over the years. And finally, I would like to thank my publisher Adam Strange, as well as Maddie Mogford and Zoe Gullen at Little, Brown, and everyone else who has worked so hard to bring this story to these pages.

Index

Picture Credits

© Philip Brown: 1, 2, 3, 4, 5, 6, 7, 8, 13, 14 (*top left*), 18 (*bottom*), 20 (*bottom*), 21 (*top*), 24 (*bottom*), 25, 26, 27, 29 (*top and middle*), 30, 31, 32 (*top*)

Rex: 10 (*bottom*)

Getty Images: 14 (*top right*), 17, 18 (*top*), 19, 21 (*bottom*)

© xposurephotos.com: 15 (*bottom*)

© Emmanuel Durand/AFP/Getty Images: 20 (*top*)

Courtesy Board of Control for Cricket in India: 22 (*top*)

Hindustan Times/Getty Images: 22 (*bottom*)

IPL via Getty Images: 23

© Adrian Dennis/AFP/Getty Images: 24 (*top*)